A History of Wales
1485–1660

WELSH HISTORY TEXT BOOKS

General Editor

PROFESSOR A. H. DODD, M.A., D.LITT.

WELSH HISTORY TEXT BOOKS · VOLUME I

A History of Wales
1485–1660

HUGH THOMAS

UNIVERSITY OF WALES PRESS
CARDIFF
1972

© *University of Wales Press*, 1972

ISBN 0 7083 0466 4

First Printed 1972
Reprinted 1974
Reprinted, with Additions, 1976
Reprinted 1979

Printed by the
John Penry Press, Swansea

Preface

THIS book, the first in a series of three on the history of modern Wales, is designed for the use of sixth-form pupils and students at Colleges of Education. It is hoped that it will, in part and for a time at least, meet a need which has in recent years become increasingly apparent among teachers of Welsh history.

While the over-all plan of the book has been influenced by my own experience in the teaching of Welsh history, its contents have in very large measure been based upon the researches and writings of a host of scholars to whom we owe much of our understanding of the Welsh past. To all of them I acknowledge my debt. I must, however, record my special indebtedness, as must anyone who attempts to write anything on the history of Wales in the sixteenth and seventeenth centuries, to the works of the late Professor Glyn Roberts, of Professor William Rees, Professor A. H. Dodd, Professor David Williams, and of Professor Glanmor Williams. Professor William Rees has a further claim on my gratitude in that he allowed the maps that appear in the book to be based upon the relevant maps in his invaluable *An Historical Atlas of Wales*. I also wish to acknowledge the kindness of Mr. Peter Smith and the Cambridge University Press for permission to reprint the drawings of the houses (*a*), (*b*) and (*c*) from *The Agrarian History of England and Wales* (edited by Joan Thirsk), 1967, and to the Brecknock Society for permission to reprint the floor plans of Newton, St. David's Without, Brecon.

I should like to express my appreciation of the great kindness shown me by Professor A. H. Dodd, the general editor of the series, and by my former teacher, Professor Glanmor Williams. Both read the book in typescript, made many valuable comments and suggestions and guided my path away from a number of pitfalls. To them the book owes much of whatever value it possesses: I need hardly add that for the errors, of fact and interpretation, that remain I alone am responsible.

Finally, I must thank Dr. R. Brinley Jones, Director of the University of Wales Press, for the interest which he has shown in, as well as encouragement which he has given to, the production of this book.

HUGH THOMAS

July 1971

Contents

Maps

Introduction

THE years covered by this book saw the final stage in the political absorption of Wales by its more powerful neighbour. This, with all that it entailed, found acceptance among the leaders of the Welsh people, many of whom exploited the situation thus created for their own ends. Out of it all there emerged a new Wales different from the old whose future was bound indissolubly to that of England. It is, however, important to remember that much of what was new in the Wales that emerged was not initiated during these years and that many of the changes that attended this emergence were the logical outcome of past events. For years before 1485 large tracts of Wales had been controlled by Englishmen, and Welshmen had in increasing numbers been anxious to acquire the rights and privileges enjoyed by their English neighbours.

This is not to deny the significance of the events which followed 1485. The means by which the inevitable was accomplished laid their own stamp upon the outcome, and modern Wales is the product almost as much of the way in which union was achieved as of union itself. Here again one must be careful, because political union was, from one point of view, not the implementation of a grand design so much as a rationalization of a series of experiments whose objective had been the better governance of Wales.

Union has, of course, cast its shadow over the period—if only because it was the springboard for so much else that took place. More immediately relevant, perhaps, to the majority of the Welsh people of the time were the changes which accompanied it. There were, for instance, the religious changes which led to the refashioning of the Church in Wales and exerted so profound an influence upon almost every form of activity. There was the transformation which occurred in the structure of Welsh society and the acceleration which took place in its economic growth. During these years many families built upon the foundations laid by earlier generations and established themselves in the front rank of Welsh society; others laid the foundations from which succeeding generations were to dominate the Welsh social scene. The rise of these county dynasties, like so much else in the period, is in itself a fascinating story and gains added interest from the light which it throws upon that complex of changes which constitutes this period of transition.

Horizons widened and opportunities multiplied. Individual Welshmen found it possible to fulfil themselves in a host of ways which had hitherto been closed to them. In the professions, in trade, even in maritime and overseas activities men bearing Welsh names were prominent. They ruled dioceses, taught at the universities, sat on the bench or pleaded at the bar, made fortunes in the world of business, entered the inner circle of royal favour, represented English as well as Welsh boroughs at Westminster and seized every available opportunity to advance themselves and their families among their neighbours nearer home.

But all this was bought at a price. The advancement of the minority, and the means by which this was achieved, produced a gulf in Welsh society which inevitably widened with the passage of the years. Between the few who had and the many who had not, sympathy and understanding declined as the gulf became wider, and it was this which lay at the root of much of the troubles in the Welsh countryside during the nineteenth century. This was no sudden, swiftly accomplished change; it was certainly not complete by the end of our period. But in their anxiety to win parity with their English counterparts many Welshmen of birth and intelligence turned their backs on things Welsh and abrogated their responsibilities as the natural leaders of Welsh cultural life. In their concern to make the most of their opportunities at home they sacrificed their heritage on the altar of progress and prosperity. Inevitably Welsh literary standards declined, the language degenerated, and religious experience waned. Revival and regeneration, when they came, owed little to them, and made deeper still the chasm that yawned between them and the *gwerin*. Ironically, their increasing involvement in English affairs eventually combined with the accident of birth and the coincidence of marriage to transfer much of their hard-won gains into the hands of the English families which they had courted so assiduously.

Profoundly important as are the events which separated the victory at Bosworth from the restoration of Charles II in the history of England, their impact upon the history of Wales is deeper and more revolutionary. In 1485 the Welsh people responded to one of their own in his bid for the crown of England, by 1660 individual Welshmen had tasted the fruits of that victory, Welsh society had been transformed, and Wales had been committed to partnership within a greater Britain.

SUGGESTED READING

The following books are recommended for constant reference:

David Williams: *A History of Modern Wales*. London, 1950.

W. Ogwen Williams: *Tudor Gwynedd*. Caernarvon, 1958.

A. H. Dodd: *Studies in Stuart Wales*. Cardiff, 1952.

William Rees: *A Historical Atlas of Wales*. Cardiff, 1951.

David J. Davies: *The Economic History of South Wales Prior to 1800*. Cardiff, 1933.

William Rees: *Industry Before the Industrial Revolution*. Cardiff, 1968.

A. J. Roderick (ed.): *Wales Through the Ages*, vols. I and II. Llandybie, 1959–60.

Y bywgraffiadur Cymreig hyd 1940. Llundain, 1953, or the English version: *The Dictionary of Welsh Biography Down to 1940*. London, 1959.

1. The Background to 1485

THE two centuries which separated the death of the last of the princes of Gwynedd and the accession to the English throne of the first of the Tudor monarchs witnessed important developments in every aspect of Welsh life. A brief examination of these is a necessary preliminary to any study of sixteenth-century Wales. They contain within themselves the key to any appreciation of the significance for the Welsh of Henry Tudor's victory at Bosworth. They also go far to explain the policies pursued by Henry and his descendants in Wales, and the reactions to this policy among the Welsh. For this reason, an appraisal of the significance of the Tudor period and its aftermath in Welsh history can only be attempted in the context of these developments.

Before 1282 change was already in the air, but the Edwardian conquest and the settlement that followed speeded up processes already under way, and the years which followed 1284 saw significant changes in the economic and social spheres of Welsh life. The native Welsh social and economic organization was subjected to a variety of pressures which modified the basic features of the old social organization. The practice of commuting labour dues had, for instance, already begun in the thirteenth century—it now proceeded more rapidly. Increasingly individual families were settling on defined plots of land or were acquiring, through grant or purchase, escheated land. The recurrent outbreaks of the plague during the fourteenth century increased the tempo of these changes and thereby hastened the collapse of the old order.

But change was a feature not only of those parts of Wales where the old indigenous order had been allowed to continue, for similar pressures were operating in those areas where Norman lords of the Middle Ages had introduced the manorial units with their non-tribal tenures and methods. During the thirteenth century the commutation of labour services for money rents was here too already far advanced: it proceeded even faster during the century that followed. There were also extensive sales of land, much letting of arable and pastoral land, and the farming out of mills. The lord of the manor was becoming, in South Wales especially, little more than a receiver of rents. In these areas too the Black Death and the outbreaks of the plague during the second half of the fourteenth century exercised a decisive impact. The heavy death-rate created on the one hand a surplus of land which the lords were more than willing to let, and on the other a relatively greater availability of money to the reduced population. The inevitable result was a fluid market in land, as a result of which old social divisions became blurred and social relationships were radically modified.

In addition to all this, and partly as a result of it, trade and industry, based increasingly on towns, were becoming more important to the economy. Towns developed, a trading section made its appearance, and individualism, alien to the collectivism of the old tribal society, was becoming a force in the social order.

Under these conditions there were those who prospered— and for them the ties of the old order were a nuisance. There were many who suffered—and among these discontent was bred. Inevitably, centuries-old usages, designed to protect the communities, were transformed to serve the purposes of individuals. *Commortha* became forced exaction, *galanas* became the cloak for perpetuating feuds, and *arddel* the instrument whereby men acquired the service of armed cut-throats to further their own ends. Against this confused background of the breakdown of a social system there emerged those individuals, bent on pursuing their own interests, who were able and willing to exploit the situation. Some of these compromised with the new order, others either would not or were not allowed to do so. Their conduct and the interaction between men of both groups go far to explain the form which events took in Wales during the period which preceded Bosworth.

One vital factor in all this was the involvement of the English. English marcher lords had long established themselves within the confines of Wales, had acquired land, built their castles, and exercised their jurisdictions—and they had penetrated far into Wales. English laws had, in substantial measure, replaced the 'gentle' laws of Hywel Dda even within those spheres where the old Welsh laws and practices had been permitted. Most of the administration in Wales was in the hands of Englishmen, some of whom were guilty of gross misuse of their authority. There were too those Welshmen who saw the advantages of throwing in their lot with the new order and so bound themselves to the English—though few of them achieved positions of consequence in the administrative hierarchy until the mid fifteenth century. Castles in Wales were nearly all commanded by English castellans and the towns virtually monopolized by English traders, many of whom competed with Welsh families for the land which was coming on to the market in the vicinity of the towns.

Rivalry and a sense of frustration created hostility among the leaders of society; exploitation and oppression produced discontent among the people. All this provided the combustible material which a chance incident could set alight; there were individuals in a position to exploit it; there was a natural target against which it might be directed; and the opportunities were not lacking for its expression.

'*The father of modern Welsh nationalism*'

Owain Glyn Dŵr achieved for a short period a remarkable position in Wales. When his quarrel with Reginald Grey sparked off his revolt Glyn Dŵr found ready supporters, first among the gentry of the north-east, later among Welshmen in every part of the country. Some of the reasons for this support are immediately apparent. Among a people for whom ancestry meant so much he occupied a unique position. He was directly descended through his father from the royal family of Powys; through his mother he was the representative of the premier line of the old royal family of Deheubarth; more distantly, he could also claim to be the nearest descendant of the royal line of Gwynedd. In his own person, then, he represented the three great ruling dynasties of medieval Wales. There was, too, the reaction in Wales to political events in England. The removal of Richard II from the throne in 1399 and his murder provoked anger and alarm among some of the Welsh. Some of the more prominent of them had held official positions under Richard; the royal family of York had the blood of the Welsh princes in its veins and so evoked an emotional loyalty; it had, also, many allies and friends among the lords of the Welsh march. To these men Henry of Lancaster was an usurper, no rightful king, one against whom revolt might not only be excused but be justified.

But Glyn Dŵr's protest could have achieved little had it not attracted to his side those Welshmen who resented the intrusion of the English and things English; who could not accept the permanence of English officialdom with its frequent instances of tyranny; who chafed at the subordination of the economic well-being of Welshmen to the interests of the English towns and plantations; who had been made acutely aware of the competition of Englishmen for land in Wales; who had lost or had not been able to find for themselves a lucrative niche in the hierarchy of the English administration in Wales. Nor would his revolt have sustained itself had it not given coherence and direction to the widespread confusion and discontent which attended the disintegration of the old economic and social bonds of a society in transition. This is precisely what Glyn Dŵr did by emphasizing the alien factor which had contributed to the profound changes which were taking place.

Glyn Dŵr struck another chord which, though different in kind, was in close harmony with the factors already noted. He gave practical expression to a particular kind of national aspiration which had never been far below the surface in Wales throughout the Middle Ages. No sooner had the Welsh been driven to the west than their bards and seers prophesied that their people would one day be delivered of the Saxon yoke. This had remained one of the significant themes in Welsh poetry, one to which Geoffrey of Monmouth had given a new lease of life in his *History of the Kings of Britain*. The poets of the thirteenth and fourteenth centuries had dreamed of the coming of a deliverer who would lead the Welsh in their bid for liberation. Glyn Dŵr's lineage, the stand which he took, and the temper of his countrymen combined to make him, in the eyes of many of his compatriots, this son of prophecy. That he was aware of this special mission is shown in a number of letters which he wrote. In one to Henry Dwn of Kidwelly he claimed to be the deliverer appointed by God to free the Welsh race from the bonds of its English enemies. In another he gave the King of Scotland

a short lesson in the early history of Wales, the real purpose of
which was to enlist support for his cause. After a rapid survey
which brought him to the three sons of Brutus, he went on,
'And the issue of the same Camber reigned royally down to Cad-
walladr who was the last crowned king of my people, and from
whom I, your simple cousin, am descended in direct line; after
whose decease, I and my ancestors and all my said people have
been, and are still, under the tyranny and bondage of mine and
your mortal enemies, the Saxons. . . . And from this tyranny
and bondage the prophecy saith that I shall be delivered by
the help and succour of your royal majesty.'[1]

Nor was Owain Glyn Dŵr merely an adventurer exploiting
this myth for his own ends. He and his advisers conceived of
a united Wales, independent of England both politically and
ecclesiastically, playing its part in the councils of Christendom.
His 'parliaments' at Machynlleth and Harlech brought together
for a common purpose men from all the commotes of Wales.
Whatever else their significance may have been, they must have
helped to counter that localism which was so characteristic of
Welsh life at that time. His relations with Henry IV's opponents in England in 1403 and 1405 were designed to separate
Wales from England, a Wales which would have encroached
far into the English border counties. To this end he also appealed
for assistance to his most redoubted lords and sovereign cousins,
the rulers of the Irish, the Scots, and the French.

He assumed the title and panoply of royal power. He had
himself crowned Prince of Wales in the presence of envoys from
France, Castille, and Scotland; he used the seals of state, great
and privy; he adopted the coat of arms of the royal house of
Gwynedd. He dispatched his envoys to the court of the French
king and bargained for the support which he was asked to give
to the French pope at Avignon. The conditions which he asked
for—expressed in the 'Pennal Policy' of 1406—constituted a
radical programme of ecclesiastical reform which has rightly
captured the imagination of succeeding generations of Welshmen. There was to be an independent Welsh Church, with St.
David's as the metropolitan see, which was to have among its
suffragans not only the Welsh bishops but also those of Exeter,

[1] Quoted in *The Chronicle of Adam of Usk* (ed. E. M. Thompson). London, 1876,
p. 194.

Bath, Hereford, Worcester, and Lichfield; only men familiar with the Welsh language were to be appointed to Welsh bishoprics and livings; all grants of Welsh parishes to English monasteries and colleges were to be annulled; two universities were to be founded in Wales, one in the north and one in the south, to educate the Welsh clergy in Wales. This was the ecclesiastical counterpart of the Welsh nation state envisaged by Glyn Dŵr in the Tripartite Indenture of the previous year—which also included substantial sections of English territory.

For a short while Glyn Dŵr, in his achievements and his aspirations, gave Welshmen a glimpse of a united, independent Wales freed from the shackles of an alien control.

The revolt exercised another powerful impact upon the Wales of the fifteenth century, for its story does not end with the disappearance of Glyn Dŵr and the collapse of his dreams. The harsh realities of the fighting left their mark upon Wales in general as they did on the market-place at Llanrwst where, according to Sir John Wynn, the green grass grew long after the fighting had ceased. Most obvious was the destruction of property which was in part the outcome of deliberate strategy by the rebels, in part of reprisals by the English soldiery. While Glyn Dŵr 'like a second Assyrian, the rod of God's anger, . . . did deeds of unheard-of tyranny with fire and sword', the English king 'laid waste the land and returned victoriously, with a countless spoil of cattle, into his own country'.[1] Less immediately apparent, but no less significant, were the new lease of life given to family feuds and the punishment meted out to some of Glyn Dŵr's more prominent supporters. All this accentuated and exacerbated the conditions which existed before the revolt—the poverty and unrest, the family hostilities, and the hatred of English control.

Of especial importance were the statutory measures taken by the Lancastrian government. Laws were passed which imposed further limitations upon the Welsh. No Englishman was to be convicted in Wales by a Welshman; no 'waster, rhymer, minstrel or vagabond' was to be allowed to maintain himself by 'making commorthas or gatherings upon the common people'; no unauthorized assemblies of Welshmen were to be permitted; no Welshmen who were not loyal to the king were to bear arms

[1] Ibid., p. 201.

or armour in any town, market, church assembly, or highway; no Welshmen were to be appointed to responsible public offices in Wales. These were some of the measures which reduced the Welsh to the status of second-class citizens. True, these laws were not enforced very often, but their very presence on the statute book provoked a sense of grievance which was to prove a powerful lever for future leaders anxious to win the support of the Welsh.

The Wars of the Roses

To Welshmen of the fifteenth century the Wars of the Roses were more than a dynastic struggle between the houses of York and Lancaster for the throne of England. Welsh involvement was inevitable for a variety of reasons. Lords marcher, holding land far into Wales, were deeply committed to one side or the other. In the early stages of the struggle the duke of York himself held the Mortimer estates which included much of the march land from Builth to Denbigh. On the same side there were the earl of Warwick who in 1449 had gained possession of the lordship of Glamorgan and the Nevilles who had acquired the lordship of Abergavenny. In the opposite camp the outstanding person was the duke of Buckingham, lord of Brecknock and of Newport. Then, some of the more prominent of the leaders on both sides were themselves Welshmen. From the first Jasper Tudor used his Welsh connections and his earldom of Pembroke to further the Lancastrian interest. William Herbert, also to become earl of Pembroke, played a waiting game until 1460 when he committed himself to supporting the house of York. He rose high in the service of Edward IV, and his death at the battle of Banbury in 1469 was accounted a national disaster by the Welsh poets. Other Welshmen were not slow to see the opportunity offered by the conflict to advance themselves and their families. In North Wales the Stanley family distinguished itself in this way, while in the south there were the Vaughan family of Tretower and the Dwnns of Kidwelly.

The details of the conflict do not concern us here, but it is necessary to remind ourselves of certain features which coloured attitudes in Wales and, in no small measure, determined the participation of Welshmen. There was, first, the widespread unrest and discontent which had been made the more acute by the revolt of Owain Glyn Dŵr. This made the Welsh an easy target for the propaganda of one side or the other and a fairly constant recruiting pool for their respective armies. And they must have been a valuable asset, for many Welshmen had won a considerable reputation for themselves in the French wars. Dafydd Gam had perished at Agincourt, Matthew Goch had died defending London against Jack Cade's rebels, but there were many among the Welsh of the mid fifteenth century who had gained experience in fighting and a taste for the life of the camp during the campaigns in France.

There was also the prevailing lawlessness and disorder. True, there is much disagreement as to the extent of this disorder, but of its existence there can be no doubt. Welsh writers of the late sixteenth and early seventeenth centuries, men like John Wynn of Gwydir, George Owen of Henllys, and Lord Herbert of Cherbury, may have had an axe to grind in stressing the turbulence of pre-union Wales. But there is abundant evidence in the official documents and literature of the fifteenth century to warrant the view that lawlessness on a considerable scale was one of the prevailing conditions in the Wales of the time. This was, of course, particularly true of the marches. Here feuds, murders, commorthas, organized raids upon towns, cattle stealing, kidnapping, attacks upon merchants, and piracy in the Severn estuary were some but not all of the catalogue of disorderly activities. That the problem existed and that it was sufficiently acute to warrant serious consideration is shown by the attention given to it. In 1437 a scheme was mooted of a special committee to deal solely with the problems of the Principality and the marches, but nothing came of it. In 1443, when lawless activity had been particularly acute, a conference of lords marcher was held to discuss the same question, but this again was barren of immediate results. Many Welshmen accompanied Humphrey, duke of Gloucester, to Bury, and the speed with which they were arrested shows the awareness of the government of the possible danger from Wales at that time. The problem of Wales continued to worry those in authority, and thirty years later, during the 1470s Edward IV created a business council for the affairs of the Principality. Out of this body grew the Council of Wales and the Marches.

The hostility towards the English which had long been

evident became more widespread and acute. This growing hostility is reflected in, and was certainly in part the product of, the prophetic poetry of the time. This age-old theme in Welsh literature had been given a new force by the revolt of Owain Glyn Dŵr and its aftermath. The Wars of the Roses triggered off a fresh outburst of these poems from bards like Tudur Penllyn, Lewis Glyn Cothi, and Guto'r Glyn. But the traditional prophecies, couched in traditional terms, now gave way to positive appeals to specific individuals and, in the works of poets like Dafydd Llwyd of Mathafarn, their tone became more strident, more bitterly anti-English. This comes through very clearly despite the fact that much of the poetry is unintelligible to the modern reader because of the allusions it contains and the animal symbolism which had long been a conventional device of the poets. How much of the poetry was a spontaneous out-burst: how much of it was inspired for propaganda purposes, it is difficult to say. It seems likely that Jasper Tudor enlisted the aid of the poets to win support in Wales for his cause, but William Herbert too received fervent appeals from the bards to 'make Glamorgan and Gwynedd, from Conway to Neath, a united whole'.[1] Banbury was a disaster for the Welsh, not because Edward IV was defeated, but because Herbert and a host of South Walians were killed in the battle.

The poetry not only reflected Welsh hopes and aspirations; it also helped to shape Welsh opinion. In the later stages of the struggle it ensured for Henry Tudor the role of Welsh liberator. By 1485 he had become the son of prophecy, able to exploit the awakened national feeling among the Welsh. That he made use of this emotional support there can be little doubt. This, together with the discontent and the grievances felt by the Welsh people, guaranteed for him widespread support through-out Wales. More than this, it gave his victory at Bosworth a special significance in the eyes of his fellow countrymen.

Who were the Tudors?

From the English point of view the rise of the Tudors is an interesting and romantic story. Early in the fifteenth century a handsome young man, Owen Tudor, had left his home in

[1] See Guto'r Glyn's *cywydd* to William Herbert (earl of Pembroke) in C. Ashton: *Gweithiau Iolo Goch*. Oswestry, 1896, pp. 262–6.

Anglesey to become a member of the household of Henry V. He became Clerk of the Wardrobe to Henry's queen and, after the king's death in 1422, continued to attend the queen mother. They fell in love, and some six years after her husband's death Catherine, the queen mother, married Owen. Four children were born to them, of whom Edmund and Jasper are the ones who will concern us. The young family passed through troubled times but at last gained the favour of the king, Henry VI, and in 1453 Edmund was made earl of Richmond and Jasper earl of Pembroke. Two years later Edmund was married to Margaret Beaufort, daughter and heiress of the duke of Somerset and descendant of John of Gaunt, the third son of Edward III. Edmund died in 1456 but in the following year his son Henry was born at Pembroke Castle. These were dangerous times and the young Henry spent his early years at Pembroke under the protection of his uncle Jasper.

In 1461, however, Pembroke Castle was taken by the Yorkists and for the next ten years the boy Henry lived at Raglan in the custody of Lord Herbert. That Herbert had by this time committed himself to support the house of York did not preclude his intention that the young Henry should marry his daughter Maud. Whatever his motives may have been, such a match would have offered a prospect not unpleasing to those who shared Guto'r Glyn's dream of a united Wales, freed from the tyranny of the English. Herbert's hopes were never realized, and after the events of 1471 Henry became at the age of fourteen the senior male representative of the house of Lancaster. With the Yorkist Edward IV on the throne, the outlook was far from promising for him, and so he was taken by his uncle Jasper first to Brittany and then to France. Finally, after fourteen years of exile he returned and on 22 August 1485 defeated Richard III to become King of England.

Henry's involvement in high politics was the outcome of his grandmother's marriage to Owen Tudor; whatever claim he had to the English throne came to him from his mother— hitherto his Welsh connections had not figured prominently in shaping his destiny. But Henry won the throne of England at Bosworth—and vital to his victory in 1485 was the support which he received from Wales. This support was in no small measure the result of his Welsh ancestry. For this reason alone the activities of Henry's antecedents in North Wales merit serious consideration. But in addition to this claim upon our attention the story of his family mirrors and illustrates the determining features of Welsh history during the latter part of the Middle Ages.

The relevant part of the family's story began with Ednyfed Fychan, steward to Llywelyn the Great, and one of the most prominent of those ministers and advisers who, through distinguished service to the princes of Gwynedd during the thirteenth century, were able to acquire estates and authority in North Wales. These were the pioneers of that section of the Welsh people which raised itself above its contemporaries during the later Middle Ages. It is among the members of this group that we find the roots of the gentry class which became so prominent a feature of the Welsh social scene during the sixteenth century. Ednyfed laid the basis of the family's future prosperity with the lands which were granted him by Llywelyn in Anglesey and Caernarvon and the estates in Cardigan which he acquired by his marriage with Gwenllian, daughter of the Lord Rhys of Deheubarth.

On the whole, his descendants behaved with circumspection during the critical years of the 1280s. True, one branch of the family did support the last Llywelyn and, having accepted the English king's overtures, lapsed again in 1294–5 when it became involved in the Madog rebellion. Thereafter, however, it gave its loyal support to the English Crown. During the fourteenth century the family prospered—though the erring branch of 1294–5 passed under a cloud during the 1340s and 1350s. The most prominent of the Tudors of the second half of the century was Goronwy ap Tudur who crowned a successful military career when he received the constableship of Beaumaris, a post which he received shortly before his death in 1382. Strangely enough, of his four brothers the one about whom least is known was Maredudd, the father of Owen Tudor and great-grandfather of Henry VII.

When Owain Glyn Dŵr raised his standard of revolt, he received loyal support from his kinsmen, the Tudors. Involvement in the revolt cost the family dearly—one member was executed in 1411 and the properties of the others were forfeited to the Crown. This temporary eclipse of the family fortunes may well have occasioned Owen Tudor's departure from the family home. The surprising thing is that he obtained a position at the court of Henry V.

The Tudor saga does not, however, end with Owen's departure for London. When he left Anglesey the family fortunes were at a low ebb; by 1485 they had been restored. This was in large measure the achievement of Gwilym ap Gruffydd who had married into the senior branch of the family. He had supported Owain Glyn Dŵr at the opening of the revolt, but in 1406 when it became apparent to him that the revolt was doomed to failure, he changed sides. He was thus able to obtain grants of land which had escheated to the Crown as a result of the revolt. He married twice, on the second occasion into the rising family of Sir William Stanley of Chester, and he and his son followed the lead of the astute Stanley family during the Wars of the Roses. Thus, they kept on the winning side, and so were able to acquire more escheated property and consolidate the family fortunes in North Wales.

By the third quarter of the fifteenth century the Tudor family had again established itself as one of the leading families of North Wales; it had created close family ties with one of the most influential of the march families; it could claim to have suffered in the cause of Wales under Owain Glyn Dŵr; it could boast its descent from among the most prominent of Llywelyn the Great's advisers; it could with some justice declare its ties of blood with the old ruling families of Wales. All this could not but evoke a response from the Welsh people when in 1485 the young earl of Richmond returned to the land of his fathers to claim the throne of England.

SUGGESTED READING

William Rees: *South Wales and the March 1284–1415*. Oxford, 1924, reprinted 1967.

E. A. Lewis: *The Medieval Boroughs of Snowdonia*. London, 1912.

W. H. Waters: *The Edwardian Settlement of North Wales 1284–1343*. Cardiff, 1935.

Glanmor Williams: *Owen Glendower*. Oxford, 1966.

T. H. Evans: *Wales and the Wars of the Roses*. Cambridge, 1915.

S. B. Chrimes: *Lancastrians, Yorkists and Henry VII*. London, 1964.

Glyn Roberts: *Aspects of Welsh history.* Cardiff, 1969.

Articles:

T. Jones Pierce: 'The Growth of Commutation in Gwynedd During the Thirteenth Century', *B.B.C.S.* x, 1939–41.

R. Rees Davies: 'Owain Glyn Dŵr and the Welsh Squirearchy', *Trans. Cymmr.*, 1968.

Glyn Roberts: 'Wales and England, Antipathy and Sympathy, 1282–1485', *W.H.R.*, vol. No. 4, 1963.

—— 'Teulu Penmynydd', *Trans. Cymmr.*, 1959.

2. Henry Tudor, Bosworth, and Wales

The Buckingham plot

THE Wars of the Roses entered their final stage when Richard of Gloucester advanced himself from the position of Protector of the realm to the throne of England. This action was dictated by a number of considerations, the most prominent of which were political expediency, dynastic necessity, and personal ambition. However necessary it may have been, and whatever the justification Richard was able to advance, the fact that legitimism had been set aside could not be concealed. Such a situation had in 1399 been the prelude to the Glyn Dŵr revolt; in 1483 it was to spark off the intrigue which focused attention on Henry Tudor.

Henry, duke of Buckingham, Richard III's henchman during his climb to supreme power in England, was in consequence of the rewards which he received the most powerful individual in Wales in 1483. The holder of vast estates in England and Wales, he was governor of all the king's castles in Wales, steward of all the royal manors in Shropshire and Hereford, chief justice and chamberlain of North and South Wales, as well as lord high constable of England. Here was an overmighty subject. But there was more—for he had royal blood in his veins. On his father's side he was descended from Anne, daughter of Thomas of Woodstock, the fifth son of Edward III; through his mother he was descended from John Beaufort, son of John of Gaunt. He stood perilously near the throne. Finally, despite the support which he had given Richard, he came of Lancastrian stock. His father had been killed at St. Albans in 1455 as had his mother's father; his other grandfather whom he succeeded had been killed at Wakefield—all fighting for the Red Rose. Moreover, his uncle Henry had until his death in 1471 been the husband of Henry Tudor's mother, Margaret Beaufort.

This was the man whom Richard chose to antagonize in 1483. He delayed granting him lands and offices to which Buckingham considered himself entitled and 'gave me such unkind words as though I had never furthered him'. The final breach occurred, so we are told, with the disappearance of the sons of Edward IV. For a while Buckingham toyed with the notion of attempting to win the crown himself, but finally decided against it because of the opposition which this would provoke from Lancastrians as well as Yorkists. He decided to promote the marriage of Henry Tudor and Elizabeth of York and to support the candidature of Henry to the throne. He and John Morton, Bishop of Ely, a prisoner whom Richard had committed to his charge, concocted a plot to this end at Brecon. While Henry was to invade England from France, Buckingham was to raise a revolt within the kingdom. He marched east from Brecon to meet the other rebels at Salisbury, but was delayed by the floods of the Severn. His followers, unpaid and dissatisfied, deserted, and Buckingham after attempting to seek refuge with friends was eventually betrayed and executed without trial at Salisbury. In the meantime, Henry Tudor's expedition which had approached the south coast of England had retired across the Channel when it was apparent that the plot had misfired.

For the time being victory lay with Richard, but the fiasco of 1483 was not without its importance. It revived interest in Henry Tudor's cause; it relieved him of the embarrassment of so powerful an ally—one who might well have tried to assume the role of a second kingmaker, and it prompted Richard to pursue a course of action which made imperative an early and determined attempt by Henry to win the throne.

The scene is set

Richard proceeded to strengthen his position in South Wales. Loyal supporters were placed in key positions—William Herbert, earl of Huntingdon, was made justiciar of South Wales, granted possession of the castles of the former duke of Buckingham, and the stewardship of numerous estates in southeast Wales. In the lordship of Brecknock the Vaughan family was firmly established; in the far south-west Richard Williams was made constable of Pembroke, Tenby, Cilgerran, Haverfordwest, and Manorbier; while Sir James Tyrell was placed in control of the upper reaches of the Towy valley and the lordship of Glamorgan. Strategic points were made ready—£113. 14*s*. 6*d*. was spent on strengthening Pembroke Castle and £60 on repairing the town walls of Brecknock. Richard himself was strong on the border—there was his own duchy of Gloucester, in the Middle March York had an unchallenged control, while in the north-east he had appointed that astute politician, Sir William Stanley, as chamberlain of Cheshire.

But there were very real weaknesses in Richard's position in Wales. Among his apparent friends there were those with very strong ties to the house of Lancaster. Members of the Tudor house still exercised a powerful hold in parts of Wales—Jasper in the south-west, the Penrhyn and Penmynydd branches in the north-west. Moreover, Henry Tudor's mother Margaret was now the wife of the head of the Stanley family, all powerful in the north-east. And, as a background to all this there was among the Welsh people widespread support for Henry, the promised redeemer of his people. Then in April 1484 Richard's position was drastically weakened. His son and heir died and the whole succession question was laid wide open once more; within the year his wife was dead. His opponents now saw their opportunity. Whether it was Richard's change of fortune or the measures he took to retrench his position—his attempts to secure the person of Henry Tudor, the proposals for his marriage to his niece Elizabeth of York—certainly the plot was now being formulated which was to lead inexorably to the battle at Bosworth.

Little is known about the actual details of the plot, but it seems certain that influential Welshmen were deeply committed to it and that others realized that something of the kind was in the wind. Various interpretations have been offered to explain the conduct of important Welshmen at this time. Their actions were undoubtedly dictated by an amalgam of considerations— self-interest, a determination to obtain the best possible terms for themselves, careful avoidance of being too obviously committed to either side, close family bonds and more general kinship ties, as well as a genuine sympathy with the aspirations of many of their fellow countrymen. It is not possible to see the picture clearly, and this is quite understandable when one remembers the secrecy which was so necessary for the success

Reinforcements
from N.W. Wales

Shrewsbury,
to Bosworth

Welshpool

Machynlleth

Newtown

Aberystwyth

Llanidloes

Wern Newydd

Llwyn Dafydd

Builth

Cardigan

Llandovery

Hadford
Bridge

Carew

Dale

Llandovery

Llangadog

Brecon

Carmarthen

— — — · The route of Henry Tudor   — — · — The route of Rhys ap Thomas

MAP I. The march to Bosworth

(Based on the map by Noel Jerman, 'The Routes of Henry Tudor and Rhys ap
Thomas through Wales to the Battle of Bosworth in 1485', in *Arch. Camb.*, 1937.)

of the conspiracy. But once leading Welshmen could be convinced of the success of their enterprise then individual self-interest would march in step with the more general wishes of the people.

On 7 August 1485 Henry Tudor, accompanied by his uncle Jasper and 2,000 Frenchmen, anchored near Dale in Pembrokeshire. Subsequent events have been coloured by local traditions: what is clear is that, despite the efforts of Richard Williams, the invading force was able to consolidate its position. Contact was made with Rhys ap Thomas; the plan of campaign was prepared. It was agreed that Henry should take his army north through Cardigan and move down the Severn valley while Rhys would march north-east and join forces with him near Shrewsbury. Why this plan was adopted it is difficult to say—it was certainly not without its dangers. It may have been thought wise to keep the two armies apart to prevent any disputes which might arise between them or to keep Richard guessing as to their objective; certainly it would have the advantage of attracting more recruits. On the 13th the two forces combined and were joined by men from the north-west; two days later Shrewsbury had thrown open its gates to them; and on the day following they were joined by Gilbert Talbot and his men. On the 17th Henry had the first of two meetings with the Stanleys to enlist their support. Less than a week later, on 22 August, Richard was killed, and his successful rival was crowned on the field of battle.

Victory and the Welsh

At last the dream had been realized—a Welshman ruled in London. For the bards the long yellow summer had come, the Boar was cold and the Bull of Anglesey had won the stone towers of three crowns. The psychological union had been achieved. But what does this mean? There can be little doubt that the support which Henry received from Wales was a major factor in his winning the throne, or that Henry appreciated this. On his coinage it was the dragon of Wales which shared with the Beaufort greyhound the privilege of supporting his crown. But some Welsh commentators have seen this as a challenge which Henry failed to resolve. He was the son of prophecy of whom so much had been expected, from whom so little was received. He was the heir of Owain Glyn Dŵr who had betrayed his inheritance, the cynic who had exploited the aspirations of his countrymen for his own ends. They had followed him to Bosworth to fulfil the dream of Welsh supremacy over the island of Britain: all they were offered were some sops to their pride and material rewards to the more prominent among them. In view of what we know of the later Henry this explanation of his conduct might not appear far from the truth.

But to leave the question there would be to ignore certain important facts. It is dangerous to be over-specific about the nationalism of the distant past; in 1485 the Welsh people responded not so much to an abstract idea of nationalism but to a leader who embodied its popular aspirations. Victory had been won—a Welshman did rule in London, and Henry was at pains to assert his Welsh origins. Genealogists were employed to trace or fabricate his descent from the great figures of the past of Wales; the dragon of Cadwaladr was incorporated in the royal standard and on the royal coins; his first-born son was named Arthur after the greatest of his people's heroes. He allowed little room for doubt that the throne was now occupied by one of Welsh blood and whose descent was therefore purer than a mere leader of a faction.

Henry's declared intentions before he landed in Wales were 'the adeption of the crown unto us of right appertaining'—the winning of what was rightfully his by inheritance; 'the oppression of that odious tyrant Richard late duke of Gloucester, usurper of our said right', and the reduction 'as well our said realm of England into his ancient estate honour and prosperity, as this our said principality of Wales, and the people of the same to their erst liberties, delivering them of such miserable servitudes as they have piteously long stand in'. To accomplish all this he trusted to 'the help of almighty God the assistance of our loving friends and true subjects', as well as 'the great confidence that we have to the nobles and commons of this our principality of Wales'.[1] Certainly he wished to restore to the Welsh rights of which they had been deprived; certainly he wished to repair the ravages of war; equally he was aware of the

---

[1] The text of the letter is printed in Sir John Wynn, *The History of the Gwydir Family*. Cardiff, 1927, p. 28.

support which he could expect from the Welsh. But this is not the language of the hero who has come to redeem his people; it is as much the appeal of a leader—determined to win what is rightfully his and aware that he embodies the hopes of his fellow countrymen—to the bonds of kindred and the self-interest of individuals.

It could be argued in general terms that Henry owed his victory to the support of Welshmen whose conduct was the result of one or other of two fundamentally different motives. There were, on the one hand, those who, inspired by the bards, had hoped for supremacy over the English, and, on the other, those whose major concern was to enjoy in their entirety the privileges of Englishmen. The hopes of the two groups were, of course, irreconcilable and while the members of the latter group were the more influential their ambitions were, too, the easier to realize. Not unnaturally, then, it was with their wishes in mind that Henry framed his policy towards Wales.

After victory had been won there was no grandiose declaration of the fulfilment of the prophecy. The foremost among Henry's supporters were richly rewarded—his uncle, Jasper, was created duke of Bedford and appointed Justiciar of South Wales and was later granted the lordship of Glamorgan. Rhys ap Thomas was knighted, was appointed steward and constable of the lordship of Brecknock, chamberlain of Carmarthen and Cardigan, and steward of the lordship of Builth. William Gruffudd was appointed chamberlain of North Wales. These were the most prominent in a long list of awards which included annuities, grants, and gifts, but also appointments to a host of local positions—shrievalties, constableships of castles, receiverships, coronerships, escheatorships, woodwardships, and bailiffdoms. Henry, it is true, was not creating a precedent in granting these positions to his fellow countrymen, but the scale on which these grants were made went far to hand over the administration of Wales at local level to Welshmen. More than this would have been impracticable, more perhaps than could justly be expected of Henry and, almost certainly, more than would be expected by those of his fellow countrymen who mattered.

Nor was it only in Wales that Bosworth opened doors for Welshmen on a scale unknown hitherto. The royal court and the city of London became the happy hunting-ground for ambitious Welshmen. They became members of the king's personal bodyguard, acquired positions at court and in the administration. They established themselves in the business life of the capital and, in increasing numbers, equipped themselves for the professions.

Wales at the opening of the Tudor period

Before we examine Henry's policy towards Wales, it is necessary to remind ourselves of the salient features of the Wales of the late fifteenth century. The first point to note is that Wales at this time was no more than a geographical expression; it was not a political or administrative unit. Parts of Wales were administered according to the English system, where English laws were enforced in the name of the King of England; there were those areas which were subject to the jurisdiction of the lords marcher; finally there were those districts, the Welshries, where native Welsh laws and customs were observed. In each case there were different sets of officials whose spheres of jurisdiction were strictly limited.

This was, of course, partly responsible for the parlous state of law and order in the country. The confusion of laws and legal systems, the multiplicity of administrative units all created opportunities for wrongdoers to evade the penalties of their crimes. But it is by no means the complete explanation. There was the widespread poverty which resulted from the devastation caused by the fighting of the fifteenth century. There were the family feuds which in part helped to shape and were in part the product of this fighting. There was the bitterness experienced by those who suffered from the profound social changes taking place as well as the friction caused by the conflicting ambitions of those able to exploit change. There was the hostility which existed between those native Welshmen who were pushing their way to the top and the English officials who stood in their way. There was, too, the sense of grievance which was the reaction to the harsh penal legislation of Henry IV. All this must be placed against the background of the breakdown of the old social system which led to the misuse of old customs and practices. Small wonder that Sir John Wynn reminded his readers that they were 'to understand that in those days and in that wild world every man stood upon his guard, and went not abroad but in sort and so armed as if he went to the field to encounter with his enemies'.[1]

It was a country where the strong and unscrupulous prospered, and these were the individuals who had supported Henry at Bosworth, whom Henry had to keep loyal. Those Welshmen who had accompanied Henry on the march to the Midlands were not the protagonists of lost causes; they were the go-ahead, forward-looking men who had seized the opportunities offered by the introduction of the English system in Wales and who had made the best of the Wars of the Roses. They were abandoning old Welsh customs like gavelkind, were anxious to use the processes of English law, and saw the advantages offered by the English administrative set-up. It was to accord with the wishes of these individuals that Henry shaped his policy in Wales.

Henry VII and Wales

If he did not realize his countrymen's dream Henry at least faced the harsh realities of life. During the first years of his reign Henry concerned himself with restoring order in the earldom of March which covered a wide tract of the border. Then in 1493 Arthur, who had already been made Prince of Wales three years earlier, was given wide judicial powers in Wales and the marches—to appoint commissions of oyer and terminer within the border counties, the marches, and the Principality, powers of array, of inquiry into liberties, and of investigating the flight of criminals. He was also granted a large number of the Crown's marcher lordships, including the whole of the earldom of March. There is little doubt that a council was established to administer his estates and to exercise his judicial authority. True, it was not until 1501 that this Council was formally appointed but there is no doubt that it was active during the 1490s. The removal of William Gruffudd from the Chamberlainship of North Wales marked the beginning of intensified administration in the Principality under the control of men higher in the king's confidence. In 1494 a thorough investigation was made into the rights possessed by the prince in the three north-western counties, especially into the sources of the prince's revenue. The demands for increased

[1] Wynn, op. cit., pp. 38–9.

C

revenue and the clash of interests between freemen and royal officials in respect of bond land caused much ill will and were responsible for the insurrection in Merioneth in 1498. Although Arthur died within a few months of the formal appointment of his Council, its work was carried on—shared between the king's Council and the commissioners in the marches. Nor was this all, for in 1504 Henry made the marcher lordships responsible to the Crown in one important aspect of the maintenance of law and order. He demanded an undertaking that they put a stop to criminals fleeing from one lordship into another in order to escape punishment for their crimes.

The special attention given to Wales and the marches by Henry's government was certainly as much the outcome of a desire for administrative efficiency as of concern for the Welsh. Ludlow Castle was to be the royal residence of the Prince of Wales; it was also to be the administrative capital of Wales. Law and order was to be enforced in Wales and the border, and some attempts were made to educate the Welsh gentry in the responsibilities of government.

Henry had, then, superimposed upon the existing system a Council whose purpose was to guarantee a much greater measure of law and order, and which could serve as a centre of royal influence in the area and as a focal point for regional unity. He had invaded the independent judicial authority of the lords marcher in the interests of efficiency. But march lordship had been the reward given to some among the more powerful of his supporters. A vast reorganization would have entailed a taking away with the left hand of what had been given by the right. Moreover, Henry's policy in other fields suggests that his real strength lay in his ability to breathe efficiency into an existing system rather than in the formulation of a radically new line of development. To expect Henry, therefore, to change the whole context of the marches at this time when his tenure of the throne was far from established and in view of the fact that the marches had themselves been the nerve centre of so much of the conflict of the fifteenth century would be to expect too much.

Where, however, he could formalize practice he did. During the last years of his reign he granted a series of charters, in 1505 to the lordships of Bromfield and Yale, in 1506 to Chirk and

Denbigh, in 1507 to Ceri and Cydewain and to the counties of Anglesey, Caernarvon, and Merioneth, and in 1508 to the lordship of Ruthin. These charters differ in detail, but essentially they were intended to remove the restrictions imposed upon Welshmen by the Lancastrian penal code and to rationalize the situation which had been created by the breakdown of the social and economic order of medieval Wales. Welshmen within the prescribed areas were, in consequence of the charters, able to 'purchase, have, receive, and hold any lands, lordships, manors, towns, townships, castles, rents, reversions, services, possessions and hereditaments whatever within England and in English boroughs and towns within Wales'. They were also entitled to hold 'the offices of sheriff, mayor, justice of the peace, bailiff, constable and other offices similar to them'. They could 'be held and reputed as burgesses' in English towns in Wales on precisely the same terms as Englishmen. Land and property which had hitherto been divisible among male heirs according to the old Welsh custom were henceforth to be subject to the law of primogeniture, 'according to the common law of England'. Inhabitants were granted immunity from compulsory service as officials. Finally, certain customs or dues, old Welsh dues which had been taken over by the lords marcher, were now 'destroyed and done away'. These, with variations, were the terms of the charters.[1]

The likelihood is that, in these charters, Henry was acceding, for a price, to the wishes of the progressive elements in Welsh society which were building up landed estates. As far back as 1439 William Gruffudd had petitioned Parliament to be 'made English' so that he might purchase and hold land according to English law, and 'enjoy all other liberties as other loyal Englishmen'. Welsh freemen had for generations been circumventing native law and custom in respect of land conveyance by the *prid* deed, whereby land was conveyed for successive periods of four years unless it were redeemed by the original proprietor. This device they hoped would be superseded by a change in the law relating to landownership, but their interests conflicted with those of the Crown which stood to lose revenue by such a change.

---

[1] For the text of the charter to Bromfield and Yale, see A. N. Palmer, *Y Cymmr.*, xlx, 1906.

The plagues of the fourteenth and fifteenth centuries, together with the devastation caused by the revolt of Owain Glyn Dŵr, had led to the depopulation of many bond townships. The Welsh estate builders had encroached upon the desolate lands which had been held by bond tenure: to change this tenure it was necessary to emancipate the bondmen. Henry was not the first to broach this problem, for his charter to the lordships of Ceri and Cydewain was no more than a confirmation of the grants of manumission to the bondmen of these lordships made by Richard, duke of York. For this Henry exacted his price— fines which together amounted to 1,600 marks. The three counties of North Wales received their first Charter of Liberties in 1504 as a result of negotiation and the payment of a substantial sum of money, £2,000 in fact. After further negotiation and the payment of another £300 there followed the Charter of 1507. The initiative lay with the acquisitive men of the localities whose oppression had been the most recent in a series of factors which depopulated the bond townships. Before Henry would regularize the situation it was necessary to compensate the Crown for the loss of revenue incurred.

The English settlers in the Principality did not take kindly to the terms of the Charters, and as a result of pressure exerted by them the king's Council in 1509 issued ordinances to the effect that the Welsh were to have in the Principality of North Wales only those liberties 'like as they of old times have used and occupied before any charters was to them granted'. These may well have cast doubt on the legality of the charters.

What place does Henry VII occupy in the history of Wales during this period? Certainly his winning of the throne in 1485 had a twofold significance. In his victory at Bosworth was realized the centuries-old dream of the Welsh people that a Welshman would wear the crown of England. This alone would guarantee Henry and his descendants the loyalty of the Welsh people and is one factor in explaining the docility of the Welsh during the sixteenth century. It was also inevitable that the bonds between the two countries were drawn closer after 1485— a Welsh king on the English throne made London a magnet which attracted many among the more adventurous of his fellow countrymen. Some of these occupied positions at court, others entered the business world of the capital. The success achieved by many of these established the attraction of London for future generations of Welshmen and the sixteenth century saw an ever-increasing body of London Welshmen. These, in their turn, made their new neighbours increasingly aware of Wales and things Welsh.

The rewards which Henry granted to his Welsh supporters were not unprecedented: the number of recipients was. One consequence was to tighten the bonds between the government at the centre and Welsh officialdom in the localities. The importance of Wales and the marches in the struggles of the fifteenth century had brought the problems of the area to the forefront of governmental attention and had ensured governmental intervention there once the effective authority of the central government was re-established.

Important, too, was the fact that Henry was able to retain his hold upon the throne, and to restore royal authority in England. The Wars of the Roses were at an end and, although we must be careful not to exaggerate the security of Henry's position, firm government now became both possible and desirable. The government could now face the task of establishing efficient administration, and this would inevitably mean focusing much attention upon Wales and the marches.

In the main, Henry pursued three general lines of policy— the establishment of some measure of uniformity in the system of administration; the granting of equality of rights and of legal standing—at a price; the formulation of some kind of alliance with the more progressive elements of Welsh society. These, together with the consideration which was given to Wales and the marches as a unit, were to figure prominently in later Tudor policy in Wales. Tradition has it that Henry on his death-bed urged his heir 'to have a care for the people of Wales'. In general, however, if we look for some bold declaration of principle or some flamboyant gesture of sentiment in the care which he himself exercised we shall be disappointed. But his winning of the throne and the policy which he pursued made Henry's reign a necessary preliminary to the changes which took place in the Wales of the sixteenth century.

SUGGESTED READING

The books and articles written by S. B. Chrimes and Glyn Roberts suggested for Chapter 1.

Articles:

W. Garmon Jones: 'Welsh Nationalism and Henry Tudor', *Trans. Cymmr.*, 1917–18.

J. Beverley Smith: 'Crown and Community in the Principality of North Wales in the Reign of Henry Tudor', *W.H.R.*, vol. 3, No. 2. 1966.

A. N. Palmer: 'Two Charters of Henry VII', *Y Cymmr.*, xlx, 1906.

C. A. J. Skeel: 'Wales under Henry VII', in *Tudor Studies* (ed. R. W. Seton-Watson). London, 1924.

3. Order out of Chaos

AT the opening of the sixteenth century Wales was administratively a complex of the Principality and of royal and marcher lordships. The Principality was composed of the territory in North Wales formerly held by Llywelyn the Last which had passed to the Crown after the conquest of 1282 and, in South Wales, of the Crown lands in Carmarthen and Cardigan. Some form of shire organization had been established in the southern section as early as 1241; in the north the Statute of Rhuddlan had created an administrative framework by forming the counties of Flint, Caernarvon, Merioneth, and Anglesey. The first of these counties had been placed under the jurisdiction of the king's Justice of Chester while the administration of the last three was made the responsibility of the newly created Justice of North Wales. In the south, Cardigan and Carmarthen, increased by territories won in 1282, were placed under the king's Justice of West Wales. While the Principality had never been part of the English realm, the English local government machinery had been introduced to conduct its affairs, English criminal law was administered in its courts, and its inhabitants were afforded opportunities of availing themselves of certain sections of English civil law.

The lordships of the march constituted the remainder of Wales. Each of these was a unit of government with its own administrative machinery and set of officials. A large number of them had by the early sixteenth century fallen into the hands of the Crown—either as Crown lordships or as lordships of the duchy of Lancaster. There were still, however, a substantial number in private hands. The Stanley family, for instance, had acquired the lordships of Knockin and Ellesmere through marriage, while the earl of Arundel held the lordship of Oswestry. The Grey family held the lordship of Powys which they had acquired as a result of the marriage early in the fifteenth century of Sir John Grey with Joan, daughter and co-heiress of Sir Edward Charleton, Lord Powys. Charles Somerset, created earl of Worcester in 1514, held the lordships of Gower and Kilvey, and from 1512 Abergavenny was in the possession of George Nevill, lord of Bergavenny. Finally, in the south-west the Bishop of St. David's held the lordships of Pebidiog, Llawhaden, Lamphey, Dyffryn Tywi, and Ystrad Tywi.

Among these private lords of the Welsh march two individuals stood head and shoulders above their fellows in prestige and wealth—the duke of Buckingham and the earl of Worcester. The first parliament of Henry VII's reign had reversed the attainder of Henry, the duke who had attempted the overthrow of Richard III in 1483, and restitution was made to his heir Edward. He at the time was seven years of age, so that the Buckingham estates remained in royal wardship until March 1498. This was the last of a number of wardships which they had endured during the fifteenth century, as a result of which their value had been considerably reduced. In spite of this Edward was undoubtedly an outstanding personage among the marcher lords of the early sixteenth century if only because of the extent of his possessions which included the lordships of Newport, Brecknock, Hay, Huntingdon, Caurs, Thornbury, and Bedmynster.

Charles Somerset, the future earl of Worcester, had, like his father, been a staunch supporter of the Lancastrian family. He had won the favour of Henry VII, by whom he was frequently employed on government business. His marriage in 1492 with Elizabeth Herbert, daughter of William Herbert, second earl of Pembroke, had brought him, among other lordships, those of Gower and Kilvey, Crickhowell and Tretower, English Talgarth, Chepstow, Tidenham, and Raglan. It was in virtue of his wife's claim that in 1504 he adopted the title Baron Herbert of Raglan, Chepstow, and Gower. Already in 1496 a commissioner of array for Wales, he acquired between 1503 and 1515 the stewardship of the most important Crown lordships as well as the shrievalty of Glamorgan and the office of chief forester of other lordships.

The contrast between these two giants is significant. One was a young, inexperienced man succeeding to a depleted inheritance, the other, in the fullness of his strength, acquiring estates and authority. The one received scant sympathy from the Crown for the problems which faced him, the other was almost overwhelmed by the rewards of a beneficent ruler. The one represented what the early Tudors most resented—a great magnate whose royal connections fostered grandiose dreams, the other was a loyal servant whose valuable services they recognized. But strangely enough there was one point at which the repercussions on the inhabitants of their respective lordships were not dissimilar. Buckingham in his earnest endeavours to recoup his losses and re-establish the family fortunes attempted to exercise to the full all the rights possessed by his ancestors; Worcester's manifold responsibilities made it impossible for him efficiently to supervise the conduct of his deputies and subordinates. In both cases the consequence was extortion and exploitation, and this in its turn produced resentment and unrest throughout their extensive lordships.

This apart, the very existence of so many administrative units within a comparatively limited area inevitably created its own problems, and these were accentuated by a number of other factors. There was, for instance, the chronic shortage of ready money which plagued a number of the marcher lords. Then, many of them were committed to a host of responsibilities—at court, on their estates in England, on royal service at home and abroad, in the marches themselves, and, in the case of some, there were also their ecclesiastical responsibilities. Finally, there were the difficulties involved in maintaining an effective hold upon lands which were scattered and often remote from the chief bases of those responsible for their administration. In addition to all this, there was the general unrest produced by the events of the fifteenth century.

The expedients adopted by the lords marcher to overcome their financial difficulties served only to worsen the situation. The duke of Buckingham, for instance, set up a council in 1500 to investigate his lordships in the march, the major purpose of which was to increase his revenues. Among the instructions which this council received from him was to obtain the maximum fines and rents possible for customary and other lands— 'as large fines to be made there for as may be driven'. The full exploitation of the duke's feudal rights was to be another feature —those holding by knight service, for instance, were to do homage to the duke 'or to be at fine for respite thereof'. A careful survey was to be made of the duke's lands 'so as it be not encroached upon any part'; his woods were to be viewed 'to see what thereof standeth in timber and what in underwood, and what sale without destruction might be made of the same and in what years'; his judicial rights were to be fully exercised and any outstanding fines to be paid.[1] This tightening of the duke's control, his revival of practices which had lapsed, and the increase of rents nourished resentment among the inhabitants of his lordships. There were serious disorders in the lordship of Brecon early in Henry VII's reign; the disturbed state continued and the duke himself lost popular support. He was fully aware of this and made use of it in a petition which he presented to Henry VIII, requesting an armed bodyguard for his journey to South Wales on the grounds 'that we can not to be there for our surety with out three or four hundred men'.

One source of revenue which the marcher lords could exploit lay in the judicial authority which they possessed. They exercised their criminal and civil jurisdictions in the chief courts of their lordships. These were held by their stewards every few weeks. But, in addition, they held the Great Sessions or sessions in eyre every three or five years. These operated as commissions of oyer and terminer concerning such crimes as felonies, rebellions, trespasses, and misprisions; they granted pardons and assessed fines, reversed false judgements in the courts of the lordship; they investigated the conduct of the lord's officials and asserted the lord's claims to revenue and jurisdiction both as feudal lord and as lord marcher. Since the revolt of Owain Glyn Dŵr, however, it had become increasingly common practice in South Wales for tenants to redeem these Great Sessions, that is, the lord would agree to forgo the Sessions in return for the payment of an agreed sum of money by the tenants. For the tenants, attendance at the Sessions was a nuisance, for they were obliged to attend for a week or more, frequently at busy times of the year. They were therefore pleased to obtain remission of the lord's claims to judicial penalties and profits and relieved to gain recognition of existing liberties and franchises. For the lords, on the other hand,

[1] For Buckingham's instructions to his council, 1500, see T. B. Pugh (ed.): *The Marcher Lordships of South Wales 1415–1536*. Cardiff, 1963, pp. 262–75.

there was the financial inducement of the fines which they received for the redemption—and these became a regular source of income. For both sides, then, there were short-term benefits.

But the practice of frequently redeeming the Great Sessions produced its ill effects. There was the resentment felt by the law-abiding inhabitants of the lordships who had to contribute to the redemption fine 'for to discharge felons, rioters and other misruled people'. Most serious was the encouragement it gave to criminals 'for that no justice should be ministered unto them if the said sessions should be so continually redeemed'.[1] It became increasingly apparent that this practice was one of the most serious causes of disorder in the marches. The Crown had already shown its concern about the conditions of law and order in the marches. Henry VII instructed the marcher lords to undertake that all their men be put under bonds to guarantee their good conduct and their appearance in court when sued or summoned. Despite instructions for the renewal of this undertaking in 1504 there was much negligence in its operation. One of the transgressors was the duke of Buckingham and he received a strongly worded reproof from the king in 1518 for his 'default and negligence' in this respect.

Attempts by the lords to compel their tenants to redeem the Great Sessions led to disputes between them and to protests, like that made on behalf of Buckingham's tenants in the lordship of Hay in 1518. Again the government interfered. It was decreed by Star Chamber that after 1521 Sessions were to be held twice a year and when held twice a year not to continue for more than eight days; tenants were not to be coerced into redeeming the Sessions which were not to be held between the middle of March and the end of September; if, however, the majority of the tenants were willing to redeem the sessions none were to be held—but for a period of three years only. The ordinance also imposed strict limitations upon the powers exercised by the lord's officers over the tenants.

In another case the lords' need for cash combined with their inability to supervise the lordships effectively to produce further unrest. Offices in the marcher lordship were farmed and the price at which they were sold took into account the

[1] Ibid., pp. 133–4.

opportunities for embezzlement which were offered the officials, especially in the case of those fines which were imposed for the pardoning of felons and other offenders. This was one only among the corrupt practices of these officials, for the system of farming of offices opened the door to all kinds of malpractices. There were cases of their taking bribes, failing to hold courts, extorting money from inhabitants, wrongful dispossession of tenants, embezzlement of fines imposed by the courts, and failure to levy some of the revenue for which they were liable. The earl of Worcester's deputy in the lordship of Gower, George Herbert, was accused of many of these offences; nor was he the only Herbert to come under fire in this respect. A certain Richard Fourde of the town of Montgomery presented a petition against Sir Richard Herbert, Worcester's deputy in those lordships which were later to form the eastern part of the county of Montgomery. Despite the acclaim which Sir Richard had won from people of consequence Fourde described him to the king as 'a solemn man of great subtlety and craft, to gather goods by extortion and polling of your subjects and poor tenants in those parts . . . and . . . for his own proper lucre and advantage, hindreth and minisheth the revenues and profits that should belong and of right ought to come unto your grace'.[1]

There was, of course, a powerful sting in the tail! There is no doubt that the government's primary concern was the contribution which this misgovernance made to the general disorder, but it was also deeply concerned with the loss of its revenues. In 1528 and 1535 ordinances were issued for the reform of financial administration in the lordship of Brecknock. These laid down that subordinate officers whom Worcester was entitled to appoint by letters patent were henceforth to be appointed by the king's receiver for the lordship, unless Worcester ensured that the officers entered into recognizances for the proper payment of the revenues.

The government also took steps to overcome the wider problem—'the matter of Wales' was very much in the minds of the king's ministers. In 1525 the Council was given a new lease of life when the king's only daughter, the Princess Mary, was dispatched to the marches. It was instructed to look into the

[1] For Fourde's petition, see *B.B.C.S.* xx, pt. 1, 1962, pp. 45–9.

change which had taken place in the 'Good Order, Quiet and Tranquillity of the Country', and reduce the area 'unto the pristine and sound Good estate and Order' which it had, presumably, enjoyed in the past. The Commissioners were given very full judicial powers and they received in addition supplementary instructions ordering them to bind holders of 'lordships Royal' by indentures 'after such form and manner as divers Lords and persons having such Lordships were bound in the King's days of blessed memory that dead is' and to institute *quo warranto* proceedings into any claims concerning sanctuaries and liberties.[1]

In the meantime two incidents had occurred whose impact upon the situation was considerable. In 1521 the duke of Buckingham was executed; ten years later Rhys ap Griffith, grandson of the mighty Sir Rhys ap Thomas, suffered the same fate. Between the two victims there were obvious similarities which, though they should not be pressed too far, are worthy of note. Both were young men of very considerable wealth who exercised no small influence in South Wales, and both were descended from men who had contributed substantially to the Tudor victory of 1485. Buckingham at forty-three years of age, the holder of vast estates from which he reputedly derived an income of £6,000 a year, was the greatest of the marcher lords. Rhys ap Griffith, some twenty years younger when he lost his life, had, so it was reported, a personal estate of £30,000 and an annual income of £10,000—though there is little doubt that this was a gross exaggeration. Moreover, the prestige of his family ensured for him a position of outstanding influence in south-west Wales. Buckingham's father had been responsible for the attempt to win for Henry Tudor the throne of England in 1483; Rhys ap Griffith's grandfather had been the key figure in guaranteeing for Henry the support of South Wales on his march to Bosworth in 1485. Ironically enough, there would have been, had Buckingham lived, a family connection, for both Buckingham's daughter and Rhys himself had married into the Norfolk family.

Buckingham, intensely proud and acutely aware of how near he stood to the throne, might well have hoped to succeed

[1] For the Instructions of 1525, see Skeel: *The Council in the Marches of Wales*. London, 1903, pp. 50–1.

Henry VIII if the latter died without heirs. Indeed, gossip had it that Buckingham, a student of astrology, had been led to believe that it was his destiny to wear the crown of England. Certainly the magnificence of his way of living and his love of ostentation gave credence to such a rumour. In 1517 and during the years that followed he sought the king's permission to take some hundreds of armed retainers to his lordships in South Wales. In 1520 he instructed his chancellor, Robert Gilbert, to present to Wolsey a request for permission that he be accompanied by a bodyguard of three or four hundred men on his visit to South Wales early in the following year, and that 'we have license to have our harness secretly conveyed with us and not have it worn but in time of need'. Buckingham justified his plea on the grounds of the threats to his personal safety, but it was interpreted as evidence of his plotting a rebellion to usurp the throne. There was little to give real weight to the charge, but Buckingham was found guilty and executed in 1521.

There is little doubt that Buckingham's fate was, in large measure, the result of the king's very real anxiety concerning the succession at this time. True, Buckingham and Wolsey were bitter enemies who had clashed on more than one occasion, and the Emperor Maximilian was not alone in attributing Buckingham's downfall to the 'butcher's dog'. But Buckingham's own conduct—his arrogance and ostentation—had been such as to arouse deep distrust, especially since he embodied all that the early Tudors most resented. His position in the March, moreover, made him especially vulnerable to the suspicions of a government which was particularly sensitive about this trouble spot. While it would be incorrect to attribute Buckingham's downfall to the government's plans for south-east Wales, the fact that it would make possible an extension of royal authority in the March would almost certainly have commended itself to the government.

Rhys ap Griffith was a much more shadowy figure. Heir to the great Sir Rhys ap Thomas, he had succeeded to his grandfather's estates and had become in consequence the most influential Welshman in the south-west. He was apparently offered the earldom of Essex, an offer which he declined. What he was not offered were his grandfather's public offices, the most important of which was the Chamberlainship of South

Wales. This was granted to Walter Devereux, Lord Ferrers, the most active member of the council established at Ludlow in 1525 for the Princess Mary. The latter's high-handed conduct and his steadily increasing influence doubtless aggravated the resentment felt by Rhys and his ambitious wife.

The situation in South Wales at the time was causing the government no small concern. There were, first of all, the reports of social unrest which royal officials were dispatching to London. This unrest was the product of a variety of factors—the oppressions of the great, the infiltration of English laws, and administrative practices. The far south-west presented another problem which must have created some alarm. The mid twenties had seen the immigration into south Pembrokeshire of large numbers of Anglo-Irish, driven from their homes in Ireland by the rebellion of the earl of Desmond. The town of Tenby, it was claimed, was 'almost clear Irish'. Such was the defiance shown to the king's officers by these immigrants that one correspondent considered it 'expedient and necessary that King's Highness with his most honourable Council should ponder the same, and devise some order to be taken'. The Tudor government had reason enough to consider Pembroke-shire an Achilles heel in its defence system—this was an area about which it was particularly apprehensive.

Then in June 1529 occurred the first incident which was to bring about the downfall of the greatest of the families of South Wales. A dispute concerning the lodging of their men in Carmarthen led to an open confrontation between Rhys ap Griffith and Ferrers as a result of which Rhys was arrested and placed in custody in Carmarthen Castle. This occasioned a riot, probably inspired by Rhys's wife, the Lady Catherine, which was made to appear more alarming than in fact it was. Rhys was released on bail of £1,000 and in November 1529 he was tried before Star Chamber. The case ended with an injunction to Rhys and Ferrers to make peace with one another and among their followers. During the months that followed Rhys, it seems likely, was living in London and he may well have been planning some form of revenge upon Ferrers. In October 1530 a warrant was issued for the arrest of his uncle, James ap Griffith ap Howell, and he himself was lodged in the Tower where he remained until June of the following year.

He was released on the grounds of ill health but was taken back into custody in September. The Emperor Charles V's ambassador reported to his master that Rhys was accused 'of having tried to procure means of escaping and going either to your Majesty's Court or into Scotland, where, owing to the credit and favour he enjoys in Wales, he hoped to be able to undertake something against the King.'

He was tried before the Court of King's Bench in November on a charge of having plotted and conspired to depose Henry and replace him by James V of Scotland, and of having adopted the name of Fitz Urien 'to the intent that under their fair pretence and title he might more worthily obtain the principality of Wales, which was the mark he assigned at after the conquest'.[1] The evidence against him was circumstantial and suspect, but he was found guilty and executed on 4 December. The government was determined that he should be removed, but whether it was because of what he did or because of what he was is a question which has never been satisfactorily resolved. Buckingham's fate had been attributed to Wolsey's influence; Rhys ap Griffith had made an enemy of Anne Boleyn. Certainly Henry's negotiations with the Church were at a critical juncture and Rhys's sympathies obviously lay with the old Church. His presence in the far south-west could well be an embarrassment to a king concerned with the good governance of the area—his fracas with Ferrers had already proved this. His Catholic sympathies could well have combined with the reported disorders in Pembrokeshire to create a dangerous situation for a government which was contemplating a breach with Rome. The time had come when the great house of Dinefwr should be humbled.

The prelude to Union

It is impossible to say whether the affair and ultimate execution of Rhys ap Gruffydd prompted or reflected the growing concern which Henry's government showed towards Wales. What does seem fairly certain is that Welshmen were trying to turn the king's attention to the state of their country. On 3 May 1532, for instance, Thomas Phillips presented a petition to Thomas Cromwell the burden of which was the disorderly

---

[1] For Rhys ap Griffith, see W. Llewelyn Williams: *Y Cymmr.*, xvl, 1902.

state of Wales and the urgent need for immediate action from the government. This was one of a number of similar petitions and whatever the motive which inspired them, of the growing concern there can be little doubt. On 1 September of the same year Henry took the unprecedented step of making 'Anne Rochford, one of the daughters of our well beloved cousin Thomas Earl of Wiltshire and of Ormond, keeper of our privy seal, to be Marchioness of Pembroke'. Anne Rochford was none other than his mistress and wife-to-be Anne Boleyn! One of the original points on the agenda for a meeting of the king's Council scheduled for 2 December 1533, was 'To reform the administration of Wales so that peace should be preserved and justice done'. In the event, this point, among others which had to do with the task of setting the realm in order, was removed from the agenda. It seems not unlikely that they were omitted because they were already being attended to. Another significant pointer occurred on 3 June 1534, when the king held an important conference with the marcher lords at Shrewsbury where they came to agreement concerning various reforms which were necessary.

Then Rowland Lee was created Bishop of Lichfield and Coventry and Lord President of the Council in the Marches of Wales. One of Thomas Cromwell's men, Lee had already gained experience of royal service. He certainly enjoyed the confidence of his master, for while the responsibilities which were delegated to him were enormous, the freedom of action permitted him was considerable. His instructions were the stern repression of crime, the establishment of order and the inculcation of respect for the law in the Principality and the marches. For such a commission no more suitable man could have been appointed. True, he had little love for the Welsh and his personal character left much to be desired in the eyes of his opponents—and there were many of them. 'You have', reported one of Cromwell's agents to his master, 'lately holpen an earthly beast, a mole, and an enemy to all godly learning into the office of his damnation.' He was sycophantic and brutal; he was also fearless and energetic, and much of the enmity which he provoked was the product of his utter lack of respect for rank and his single-mindedness in the performance of his duties.

Lee carried out his tasks with zeal and obvious zest, reporting

D

with relish the measures which he took to punish criminals.
Of his severity there can be no doubt—he boasted of hanging
'four of the best blood in the county of Shropshire' and revelled
in the atrocities which he perpetrated upon captured criminals.
His episcopal office did not deter him from using torture or
inflicting indignities upon his victims, nor was it allowed to
stand in the way of his passing the death sentence. The soldier
chronicler Ellis Griffith who was writing his chronicle at the
time reported that 'it is said that over 5,000 men were hanged
within the space of six years' during his Presidency—a gross
exaggeration doubtless, but one which indicates the profound
impression Lee made. All this understandably provoked much
opposition to him among the inhabitants of the area, not least
among the gentry of the border counties whom he treated with
such scant respect. So acute was this that at one time there was
some talk of his being replaced by Foxe, Bishop of Hereford.
The truth of the matter would appear to be that these reports of
his severity were exaggerated—and that Lee was content that
they should be.

What is certainly true is that his relentless pursuit of criminals
and his unflagging efforts to reduce crime did make their mark.
The success which he achieved impressed upon Welshmen and
the inhabitants of the marches a very healthy respect for the
law and a fear of the consequences of their crimes. Lee was well
aware of his success, nor was he content to hide his light under
a bushel: in 1536 he boasted to Cromwell that he might now
'boldly affirm that Wales is Redacte [reduced] to that state
that one thief taketh another, and one Cow keepeth another
for the most part'.

The three years which followed Lee's appointment saw the
passing of a number of laws, some of which were obviously
designed to assist him in his task. Statutory measures were taken
to limit the opportunities for the perpetration of crimes by
Welshmen in the border counties; the machinery of administration for the area was made more efficient by the resuscita-
tion of the Council and the consolidation of a large measure of
control in its hands; independent jurisdictions within the area
were limited by an attack upon the autonomy of the marcher
lords; some measure of uniformity in the administration was
achieved and, perhaps less to Lee's liking, some degree of

partnership with a section of the Welsh people was inaugurated. These, it seems, were the objectives of this series of laws. A brief survey of the laws will serve to confirm this. In 1534 an Act was passed to put an end to the common practice of suborning jurors; another was passed to set a limit to uncontrolled crossing of the Severn by night in order to put an end to the robbing and plundering raids of South Walians into the English border counties; the Bill concerning Councils made officials of marcher lordships answerable to the Council for unlawful punishment, prohibited the carrying of arms, declared illegal the exaction of old customary dues like *commortha*, bydale, and tenant's ale and the practice of *arddel*, transferred judicial authority over crimes and criminals in the marcher lordships to the justices of the peace of neighbouring English counties; a measure was passed against Welshmen and the inhabitants of the marches who committed assaults upon persons pursuing felons; and another limited benefit of clergy in cases of murder, petty treason, and felony.

In 1535 a most important measure was passed—an Act for the making of justices of the peace in Wales, i.e. in the counties of Chester, Flint, Anglesey, Caernarvon, Merioneth, Pembroke, Cardigan, Carmarthen, and Glamorgan. These officials were to be appointed by the Lord Chancellor or Lord Keeper of the Great Seal and they were to have the full powers 'to inquire hear and determine' all cases over which their English counterparts had authority. This was followed by an Act which provided safeguards for individuals in cases of trespass upon the forests of the king or marcher lords. Then was passed the statute whose purpose was to emphasize the royal source of legal authority. No person, it declared, was after 1 July 1536 to have the right to give pardons in respect of certain crimes except the king; only by letters patent under the king's Great Seal were justices to be appointed; and legal and judicial instructions were to be issued in the name of the king

The years 1534 and 1535 had witnessed a threefold attack upon the problem of disorder in Wales and the marches. The Council had been effectively restored, given a new vigorous President and had its authority strengthened. Specific measures had been passed whose purposes were to limit the opportunities for crime and to discourage its incidence. Finally, steps had been taken to establish a greater measure of unity within the administrative set-up in order to ensure more effective control by the Council over the lower ranks of the system. It was with this last feature that the key to any real success lay: the first two were attacking the problem from the outside, this last was a more positive reorganization from within. The problems created first by the independent jurisdictions of the marcher lords and, secondly, by the differences in the local administrative systems in the remainder of Wales were now being faced. Limitations had been imposed upon march independence and the first steps had been taken in the direction of administrative uniformity. But it must have become increasingly obvious that the logical conclusion was the abolition of these independent jurisdictions and the standardization of the machinery of administration. This, it might well be argued, was the conclusion which led inevitably to the 'Act for Laws and Justice to be Ministered in WALES in like Form as it is in this Realm' of 1536.

SUGGESTED READING

W. Llewelyn Williams: *The Making of Modern Wales*. London, 1919.

T. B. Pugh (ed.): *The Marcher Lordships of South Wales 1415–1536*. Cardiff, 1963.

C. A. J. Skeel: *The Council in the Marches of Wales*. London, 1903.

Articles:

T. B. Pugh: 'The Indenture for the Marches between Henry VII and Edward Stafford (1477–1521), Duke of Buckingham, *E.H.R.*, lxxi, 1956.

—— and W. R. Robinson: 'Sessions in Eyre in a Marcher Lordship, etc.', *S. Wales and Mon. Rec. Soc. Pubns.*, lv, 1957.

W. Llewelyn Williams: 'A Welsh Insurrection', *Y Cymmr.*, xvi, 1902.

4. The Union of England and Wales

The question of motive

THE intentions of the government as declared in the preamble of the Act of 1536 were to bring the Welsh people 'to the perfect Order Notice and Knowledge' of the laws of England to remove any 'sinister Usages and Customs' which differed from these laws, and to establish 'an amicable Concord and Unity' between the king's English and Welsh subjects. The king was said to be inspired by the 'singular Zeal Love and Favour' that he bore towards the Welsh people to remove the 'Distinction and Diversity', together with their attendant hostility, which allegedly existed between his English and Welsh subjects. This was the explanation which the government thought fit to offer for the Act whose purpose was made explicit in its title. This, had it been complete, would have accorded well enough with the new spirit which, it has been asserted, was responsible for the Act. Further evidence for the existence of such a new approach is seen by some commentators in the strong objections which Rowland Lee voiced to the terms of the Act. It would have found approval among many of the Welsh gentry of the late sixteenth and early seventeenth centuries. It is arguable, however, that too much emphasis should not be placed upon the radical nature of the policy implicit in the Act. Rowland Lee is certainly not unique in misliking the outcome of a course of action in whose conduct he had played no small part. The later Welsh gentry were clearly not the most objective witnesses to a development which had brought such marked benefits to themselves and the class to which they belonged.

To accept this interpretation of the government's intention would be to ignore a basic factor and thereby confuse the significance of the Act. The objective was, after all, the good governance of Wales and the marches; and harsh reality had shown that permanent success could only be achieved by massive reorganization and an invasion of privilege. The corollary of this was the deliberate extension of royal authority over the area. This was the only remedy—other measures could cure the symptoms, but would leave the disease untouched.

Conditions in the Wales of the time favoured such a course of action. It would almost certainly be popular with at least one section in the area—and that a very significant one. The petition which Sir John Price reportedly presented on behalf of the people of Wales, requesting that they might 'be received and adopted into the same laws and privileges which other subjects enjoy', may well have been inspired. Sir John was, after all, an agent of the Tudor government and related by marriage to Thomas Cromwell. Nevertheless there is little doubt but that it reflected the wishes of many of that influential section which was pushing its way to the top of Welsh society. These had for years been availing themselves of the opportunities afforded by the English administration in Wales and enjoying many of the privileges to which, according to the statute book, they were not entitled. A statutory declaration of their right to these would obviously be popular, as would the increased scope offered by the extension of royal administration. The ultimate guarantee of these would be a common body of laws which were uniformly administered. But this required the extension of royal authority, it required union.

Nor must we underestimate the significance of members of this group. It would not be difficult to draw unfavourable comparisons between them and their English counterparts in respect of the value of their estates and the gold in their coffers. But many were men of substance who had experience of office in the administrations of the king and the marcher lords, while nearer home they could exploit the bonds of kinship to ensure a following for themselves. There were those among them who had received legal training and had managed the affairs of the monastic houses. Small fry they may have appeared to Rowland Lee but many of them were not unworthy to be considered as partners at local level by a central government which was venturing on such a policy; and the experience acquired by many of them in the practical business of administration would certainly enhance the value of their partnership.

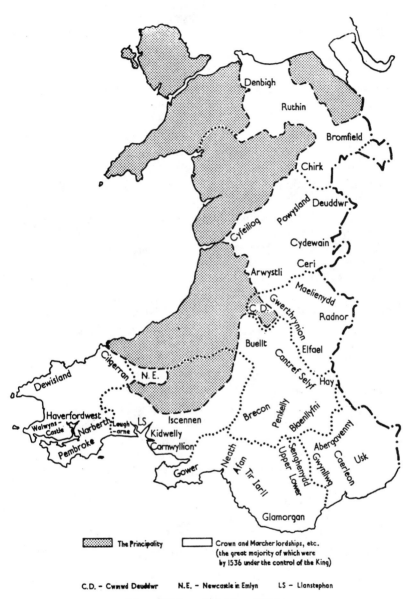

Denbigh

Ruthin

Bromfield

Chirk

Powysland Deuddwr

Cyfeiliog

Cydewain

Ceri

Arwystli

Maelienydd

C. D. Gwerthrynion

Radnor

Buellt

Elfael

Cilgerran

N. E.

Dewisland

Cantref Selyf

Hay

Haverforwest

LS

Walwyns
Castle

Loughlarne

Iscennen

Brecon

Penkelly

Blaenllyfni

Narberth

Kidwelly

Abergavenny

Pembroke

Carnwyllion

Neath

Senghenydd

Gwynllwg

Caerleon

Usk

Gower

Afan

Tir Iarll

Upper Lower

Glamorgan

░░░ The Principality   ▢ Crown and Marcher lordships, etc.
(the great majority of which were
by 1536 under the control of the King)

C.D. – Cwmwd Deuddwr   N.E. – Newcastle in Emlyn   LS – Llanstephan

MAP 2. Wales and the Act of Union

(For full comments on the composition of the new counties, see William Rees, 'The Union of England and Wales' in *Trans. Cymmr.*, 1937, especially the explanatory footnotes on pp. 85–95. Based on maps (Plates 55 and 56) in William Rees, *An Historical Atlas of Wales*, by kind permission of the author.)

There was, too, the strength of the king's position in the marches. Changes of fortune during the Wars of the Roses had brought many of the marcher lordships into the hands of the Crown, the vast Mortimer estates, and the lordships of the Duchy of Lancaster. Many lordships escheated to the Crown through the failure of heirs. And the process did not cease in 1485. It was perhaps inevitable that some of the marcher lords should be involved in the plots which were hatched to dispossess Henry VII of the crown which he had won at Bosworth. Equally inevitable was the heavy price which they had to pay for such entanglements. Sir William Stanley's support of Warbeck cost him his life and added the lordships of Holt, Chirk, Bromfield, and Yale to the Crown's territories in the marches. In 1495 Arwystli and Cyfeiliog were acquired by purchase. The attainder of Buckingham in 1521 brought the lordships of Brecon, Hay, Huntingdon, and Gwynllwg into the royal net. The king was the outstanding lord of the march: by the 1530s by far the greater part of Wales belonged either to the Principality, the Crown lordships, or those of the Duchy of Lancaster.[1] The time had come when a rationalization of the situation was both necessary and desirable.

The situation within Wales then favoured such a policy. Important also was the fact that at the centre of government there were those whose political thinking led them to precisely the same conclusion. Among the king's ministers there was a more rational, more modern approach—a determination to consolidate the territory over which the king governed under the exclusive sovereignty of the king in parliament. The new national state which was in the making was, on the one hand, the antithesis of the private jurisdictions of the marcher lords; it was, on the other, an advance from the personal control of the king, which was the basis of his authority in Wales, to royal authority based on permanent institutions designed to consolidate it. To the men responsible for this new thinking the perpetuation of the old order in Wales and the marches was as unthinkable as the disorder which was so prominent a feature of it.

The general situation in the mid 1530s was such as to demand positive action. Wales was economically backward, the mass of

[1] See W. Llewelyn Williams: *The Making of Modern Wales*. London, 1919, p. 73, note.

the people conservative. South-west Wales had already been disturbed by the fate of Rhys ap Gruffydd. There was a large measure of popular sympathy for the old church. A number of treasonable utterances against the religious changes had been reported to the government. Royal agents like Lee and Barlow commented upon the increasing tension of these years. Others were more explicit—Sir Richard Bulkeley, sheriff of Anglesey, reported that unless measures were speedily taken to suppress the discontent, there would be as much to do in North Wales as in Ireland. And here there was a complicating factor. The rebel Kildare was still holding out in Ireland and there was a very real fear that, with conditions as they were, an Irish invading force would receive assistance from the Welsh. Even if all these royal agents in Wales had a personal axe to grind by stressing existing tensions, their fears were far from being groundless. There was also the possibility that Catholic Europe might launch a crusade against England—and if this occurred there was a real danger that an invasion might be launched against west Wales. Near-by Ireland was one obvious base of operations and the Welsh coast offered numerous landing-places far removed from the centre of government. Threats such as these must have impressed upon the king and his ministers the urgent need for an overhaul of the system in Wales. The defence of the coast and the maintenance of order required direct governmental control, effective local administration, and partners in the area.

The Act of 1536 was the logical solution to a fundamental problem; its accomplishment was made possible by favourable conditions and desirable by a new thinking among the king's ministers; its timing was dictated by quite another contingency —the possible repercussions to Henry's Reformation. It is perhaps to this last that we must look for the explanation for the haste with which the Act was drawn up, and it was this haste which made necessary the reservations which it contained. The 1536 Act enunciated the principles of union but much remained to be done. There were many i's to dot and t's to cross and some anomalies to be ironed out. These were not accomplished until the Act of 1542.

The whole emphasis of the 1536 Act was upon unity: Wales was to be incorporated, united, and annexed to England;

Welshmen were to enjoy the freedoms, rights, liberties, privileges, and laws of England; land was to be inherited 'after the English tenure without division or partition'; English laws were to 'be had, used, practised and executed' in Wales; lordships marcher were to be formed into new counties or attached to existing counties English as well as Welsh; courts of law were to be conducted in the one language—English, a knowledge of which was a necessary prerequisite for the holding of office in the local administration in Wales; Wales was to be represented at Westminster. Certain safeguards were allowed to individuals and the king was given the authority to make whatever modifications were considered necessary during the course of the succeeding three years.

The problems of establishing the new administrative machinery were enormous and it is not surprising that there were delays in implementing the provisions of the Act of 1536. At the end of the three years allowed the king for the making of any changes little had been achieved, and in 1539 an Act was passed extending this period for another three years. The king, it was explained, 'hath had such great affairs and urgent causes to do concerning the state and wealth of this Realm, that by occasion thereof his Majesty hath had no convenient time nor leisure to accomplish and execute the power and authority committed to his Highness by the said Act'. During this period the existing officers continued to exercise their responsibilities subject to the supervision of the Council of Wales and the Marches. In July 1540 an Act was passed which laid down that grants of certain offices for term of life or lives were to be void on 1 September 1540. The main purpose of this measure, it seems, was to annul all existing appointments of sheriffs in order to make possible the appointment in November 1540 of new sheriffs in all the Welsh counties for one year only. This was followed on 28 June 1541 by the appointment of four justices, one for each of the four circuits which were to be established in Wales. This was the end of the safeguard allowed Ferrers and Worcester for the continued exercise of their judicial offices. The final step in the establishment of the new administrative system was taken with the appointment of justices of the peace, some before and during 1542.

Then was passed the Act of 1542. In this again the king

claimed to be acting of 'his tender Zeal and Affection' towards the Welsh people. His declared intention was that 'good Rule and Order . . . be from henceforth kept and maintained . . . whereby his said subjects may grow and arise to more Wealth and Prosperity'. By its terms the king was given the authority to make whatever additions or modifications he thought necessary to the original Act. Changes were made in the territorial arrangements of 1536—by the transfer of certain districts to other counties and the making of Haverfordwest into a county borough 'of it self'. The Court of Great Sessions was formally established. This court was to be independent of the high courts at Westminster, and Wales was divided into four circuits of three counties each—the north-west, south-west, north-east, and south-east. The procedure of the courts was modelled on that of the Sessions of North Wales established by Edward I. Two sessions, each of six days' duration, were to be held annually in each county to try 'all manner of pleas of the Crown in as large and ample a manner as the King's Chief Justice in England'. Each circuit was to have its own complement of officials and the law to be administered was the Common Law of England. The hundred courts were still to be held fortnightly by the Sheriff. Finally, the Council of Wales and the Marches, formerly a prerogative court, was placed on a constitutional footing and given the responsibility of carrying out the new administration.

The significance of the union

The impact exerted by the union upon the history of Wales is a subject which has provoked more than a little disagreement. To see the union in its proper perspective it is necessary to examine it in the context not only of other aspects of Tudor policy as they applied to Wales but also of developments which were taking place in the Wales of the time. The union was, it could be argued, the rationalization of a policy which had been pursued piecemeal for years before 1536. While its successful implementation could only be achieved by the fostering of changes—social, economic, and religious—many of whose roots lay far in the past, its influence can only be correctly assessed in conjunction with the fulfilment of those developments which were taking place independently of it. To ignore these is to run the risk of misinterpreting the function which the union was intended to perform and the measure of its responsibility for the changes which occurred during the years that followed.

The union represents one aspect of Tudor policy in Wales in its determination to achieve uniformity in the essentials without attempting complete assimilation. The government was determined that institutions in both countries should be basically the same; but it was not wholly unwilling to make some allowance for the special conditions in Wales. The care which the government took to provide for the special conditions in Wales is amply illustrated. A uniform system of administration was established but the responsibility for its efficient working was delegated to the Council of Wales and the Marches; a uniform body of laws was introduced but the Court of Great Sessions was created to enforce them; Wales was to be represented at Westminster on much the same lines as was England but special provisions were made for the Welsh borough constituencies whose poverty would make the payment of their representatives a burden to them. Although integrated, Wales, it seems, was not to lose its identity completely. Then, the terms of the union struck no discordant note with the changes which had been and were taking place in Wales. In fact, it might almost be said that, rather than anticipating the changes, they were giving statutory recognition to those changes which were already taking place or were a response to the wishes of those Welshmen who were directly involved in them. The implication of this was, of course, that the policy of union was acceptable to the politically significant elements of Welsh society.

The conclusion to be drawn, therefore, was that the union did not initiate the changes which were so characteristic a feature of sixteenth-century Wales. From 1284 Welshmen had shown a willingness to co-operate with the new order, had seen the advantages of close personal contact with the king and his court, had been associated with the administrative set-up in the royal possessions in North and South Wales, had performed official responsibilities in the march. These had been significant factors in the emergence of the future gentry class. Moreover, the later Middle Ages had seen the integration of English families settled in Wales and native Welsh families. There had been very considerable intermarriage between them, and it is possible to see the emergence of a social group which was recognized as an element in Welsh society. Progressive Welsh families had, on the one hand, adopted things English in their official capacities, and on the other, had established close personal ties with English families in Wales. During the fifteenth century this tendency became very much more marked as the result of the involvement of far-seeing Welshmen in English affairs.

Members of this group had exercised authority within the administration in Wales either as officials themselves or as deputies for important absentee holders of official positions. They had taken advantage of English laws to further their own ends. They had dispatched their sons to the courts of the king or the marcher lords to be educated. This inevitably implied the assimilation of English attitudes and a mastery of the English language. A few enrolled their sons at English schools, at the universities of Oxford or Cambridge, and at the Inns of Court, where they completed their education with the study of English law. All this could not fail to leave its mark upon the attitudes of the most capable and ambitious among the Welsh. While their influence and prestige should not be exaggerated, they did constitute a ready made group of partners for the central government.

To this extent then, the significance of the union lay not so much in the new direction which it marked out for developments in Wales, but in the acceleration which it gave them along lines which had already been laid down. This it did in a variety of ways. As a result of union the whole hierarchy of local administration was open to Welshmen, and the opportunities for bettering themselves and their families were thereby substantially increased. Some of the new laws together with the improved state of law and order which followed upon the more efficient administration of justice helped to create an environment in which economic expansion was possible. This was further improved by the closer and easier contact between England and Wales—English markets became more accessible to Welsh produce and Welsh industries received a transfusion of capital from England. But another, quite distinct, factor contributed to this economic expansion which should not be confused with the union. This was the rapid increase in prices which occurred during the sixteenth and early seventeenth centuries, especially in the basic agricultural products, and provided the incentive for primary producers to extend the scale of their undertakings. Prices were artificially inflated by poor harvests—and these were not infrequent during the second half of our period—but even when these have been taken into account, the general increase is striking. The average price for all grains multiplied by over seven, cattle by almost six, dairy produce by almost four, and wool by over four. This naturally created a situation where landowners and farmers were encouraged to produce more.

Economic expansion was reflected in social change, and here again the union made its contribution. The law of primogeniture made possible the consolidation of landed estates, the statutory abolition of the limitations imposed upon Welshmen provided a wide scope for individual initiative. The result of this was a busy market in land—and landownership reflected a person's status in society. Established families added to their acres and increased their social influence. Yeomen climbed into the ranks of the squirearchy, while traders and professional men invested their money in landed estates. This was not a new phenomenon, but the tempo and scale on which it occurred were, and for these latter the union was in large measure responsible. All this could only be achieved by some at the price of a marked deterioration in the economic, and therefore social, position of others. The outcome of this was a substantial mobility within society, but one must be careful not to attribute this solely to the impact of the union. There was a steady increase in population during the period—partly natural and partly the result of the influx of Englishmen into the counties of the north-east—which added significantly to the pace of social change.

The anglicization of the gentry class is another development to which the union made its contribution. It has already been noted that individual Welshmen had long seen the advantage of a knowledge of English and that there already existed an Anglo-Welsh element within the landowning section of Welsh society. Union did, however, place a premium upon a mastery of English and did make for freer and closer contact between

Welsh and English. It is this feature of the union which has been censured most severely by certain Welsh writers of the twentieth century. There is no doubt that the Tudors did on more than one occasion explicitly declare their concern that as many of the Welsh people as could should acquire a mastery of the English language. But one should be careful neither to exaggerate the speed with which their hopes were fulfilled nor to assume that the learning of English was of necessity incompatible with a continuing sympathy for things Welsh. It is likely, too, that in this context expediency weighed more heavily with the Tudors than any maliciously conceived plan to alienate the leaders of Welsh society from their homeland or their cultural heritage. Nevertheless, the circumstances and events of the sixteenth century, of which the union was one of the most significant, did hurry along this process by which the social leaders of Wales became English in speech, attitudes, and outlook.

To suggest that the union was one only of a number of factors which shaped the course of developments in Wales is not in any way to minimize its importance. It was decisive but it alone did not initiate; its objective was to solve existing problems not to create a new Wales, but the means it adopted could not but open a new chapter in Welsh history.

SUGGESTED READING

William Rees: 'The Union of England and Wales', *Trans. Cymmr.*, 1937; reprinted Cardiff, 1967.

W. Llewelyn Williams: 'The Union of England and Wales', *Trans. Cymmr.*, 1907–8.

J. F. Rees: *Tudor Policy in Wales*, Historical Association pamphlet No. 101; 1935; reprinted in *Studies in Welsh History*. Cardiff.

R. T. Jenkins: 'Y newid yng Nghymru yng nghyfnod y Tuduriaid', *Y Beirniad* vl, 1; a vl, 2; reprinted in *Yr Apêl at Hanes*. Wrecsam, 1933.

D. Myrddin Lloyd (ed.): *The Historical Basis of Welsh Nationalism*. Cardiff, 1950, pp. 60–99.

Peter R. Roberts: 'The "Act of Union" in Welsh History', *Trans. Cymmr.*, 1972.

5. The New Order

Government and administration

WELSH commentators of the late sixteenth and early seventeenth centuries were unanimous in their approval of the machinery established for the administration of the country by the union. George Owen, for instance, could claim that 'comparing the present government of Wales with the government of the rest of this Realm I find ourselves now in far better estate than any other part thereof governed with more ease and less charge'.[1] True, some qualifications were made, but criticism was always tempered by the rapturous appreciation of the achievements of the new system. It was to this factor more than any other that they attributed the improvement in the state of law and order in the Wales of their time. Whatever reservations it may be necessary to make there is no disputing the progress which was achieved by the new order in the governing of Wales.

The Council of Wales and the Marches

The marches had been a source of embarrassment to the government for centuries. As early as 1291 Edward I had held courts at Llanddew, near Brecon, and at Abergavenny to put an end to the hostilities between the marcher lords. He had imprisoned two earls, confiscated their estates and abolished their privileges; more important he had set a limit to the independent jurisdiction of the marcher lords. This strong policy was not, however, continued, and the lords of the march were later able to resume their former privileges and powers.

But in the middle decades of the fifteenth century the government had turned its attention to the problem of disorder in

---

[1] For sixteenth-century views on the Council of Wales and the Marches, see the letters and discourses printed in *Y Cymmr.*, xüi, 1900, Appendices A–F, pp. 125–163, and George Owen's *The Dialogue of the Government of Wales*, published in his *The Description of Pembrokeshire*, Part III, *Cymmrodorion Record Series*, No. 1, 1906.

Wales. Certain measures were taken which, ineffective as they were, show this awareness on the part of the government. Then in 1471 the future Edward V was created Prince of Wales, and soon after a council was established to supervise the education and manage the household of the young prince. This was followed in 1473 by the appointment of a business council to control the affairs of the Principality and soon after the prince was sent to Ludlow to keep court. Three years later the prince was appointed Justiciar of Wales and given power to appoint other justices in the Principality and the marches, responsibilities which, it appears, were to be exercised by his council. There is, however, very little real evidence of any activity on the part of the council in these early years.

The next step was taken in 1493 when Henry VII sent his eldest son, Arthur, to Ludlow and established a council for him, with Bishop William Smyth as its President. The prince was granted a variety of powers—judicial authority, powers of array, of inquiry into liberties, and of investigating the flight of criminals—all of which were probably administered by the Council. Although it was not until 1501 that the Council was formally appointed, it seems likely that it was active during the 1490s. Henry, it would appear, intended to establish at Ludlow the administrative and judicial centre for Wales and the marches. Arthur's death marked the end of this design, for although the Council continued its nominal existence, there is little evidence of any positive action on its part. Henry VIII sent his daughter, Mary, to Ludlow in the fullness of time. Lords President were appointed, Blythe in 1514 and Veysey in 1525, but there was precious little else. Nevertheless, the government's activity in other directions showed that the problem of order in Wales and the marches continued to exercise its attention. Then in 1534 it was decided that the Council should control its efforts in the area.

Rowland Lee was appointed Lord President with instructions to establish the authority of the Council and to repress crime. Under his driving leadership the former was achieved and a measure of law and order was established without which later developments would have been impossible. The importance of his endeavours and the success which attended them did not pass unobserved. In 1576 William Gerard, in a letter which expressed general satisfaction with the state of law and order in

E

Wales but pointed out the weaknesses of the Council in his own day, had this to say: 'This stout bishop's Dealing . . . within three of four years generally so terrified them, as the very fear of punishment rather than the Desire or love that the people had to change their Welshry wrought first in them the obedience they now be grown into.' Lee would have been well content with this verdict on his efforts.

In 1542 the Council of Wales and the Marches received statutory recognition—'That there shall be and remain a President and Council in the said Dominion and Principality of Wales, and the Marches of the same'. But the Act, detailed as it was in its organization of the administration of Wales, was vague and unspecific in its definition of the authority of the Council. It declared that the President and Council should have power to hear and determine 'such Causes and Matters as be or hereto fore hath been accustomed and used'. This vagueness as to the Council's powers and responsibilities continued throughout the century, for George Owen, writing in the 1590s, had to confess that its authority and jurisdiction 'is not certainly known'.

The Council was composed of the Lord President and his deputy, with twenty members nominated by the Crown. These included some *ex officio* members, certain members of the royal household, some of the bishops of Wales and the justices of the Great Sessions. In addition there were the salaried officials—the attorneys, clerks, and court officials. Inevitably the bulk of the work fell upon the President and his deputy and a few ordinary members, and as the volume of the work increased so too did the number of officials in attendance. The area of the Council's jurisdiction covered the thirteen counties of Wales and the border counties of Hereford, Gloucester, Worcester, Shropshire, and Cheshire. This did not remain constant, for Bristol was exempted from its jurisdiction in 1562 and Cheshire followed suit in 1569. Worcester attempted to free itself in 1576, but without success. These reflected the growing unwillingness of the English counties to accept the jurisdiction of the Council.

The Welsh element, significant though it was, was never very strong among the members. An examination of the membership list during Elizabeth's reign shows that of the hundred members appointed during her reign there were twenty from Wales.

True, there were the two earls of Pembroke whose ties with Wales were very close and a few more who were of Welsh descent. Among the others were twenty-six justices of one or other of the Welsh circuits, two who were attorneys for parts of Wales, one who was the steward of Arwystli and Cyfeiliog, and one who had represented a Welsh constituency. The majority of the others were from the English border counties.

The Council's judicial functions as defined in the Instructions of 1553 and 1574 were certainly very wide. It was to hear all suits, civil and criminal, which were brought by individuals too poor to sue at common law; it was to try all cases of murder, felony, piracy, wrecking, and such crimes as were likely to disturb the peace; it was to investigate charges of misgovernment by royal and local officials and the false verdicts of juries; it was to enforce the laws against livery and maintenance, to punish rumour mongers and adulterers, and to deal with disputes concerning enclosures, villein service, and manorial questions. All this fell within its sphere of responsibility as well as the administration of the laws of England which included the ever-increasing body of legislation dealing with religion. It heard appeals from the common law courts and filled in the gaps in the processes at common law. 'And generally' according to George Owen 'it is the very place of refuge for the poor oppressed of this Country of Wales to fly unto'.

It supervised the working of the Court of Great Sessions and the holding of assizes and quarter sessions courts. The local officials were nominated by the Lord President and were responsible to him for the proper execution of their duties. The Council exercised police functions in the apprehension of criminals and pirates, and in the taking of precautionary measures to maintain the peace. It supervised the local officials —in 1585, for instance, Sir Henry Sidney ordered the justices of the peace in each shire to assemble the quarter sessions in order to work out a system for investigating and reporting crimes within their districts. It regulated certain aspects of economic activity—taking emergency measures in time of scarcity, seeing to bridges, and settling problems arising out of common rights. The Lord President as *ex officio* Lord Lieutenant of Wales was responsible for the military organization of the country. This work was delegated to the Council which, in consequence, exercised powers over the militia and preparations for defence. Finally, it was the intermediary for the transmission of the orders of the Privy Council in respect of Wales and the marches.

Broadly it might be said to operate on two levels. There was first its ordinary routine work which it carried out in virtue of the powers and responsibilities defined for it by statute and the instructions which were issued from time to time. Secondly it was the local representative of the Crown, conducting, supervising, or transmitting to local officials the instructions of the Crown, the Privy Council, or the higher courts. Small wonder that in the Instructions of 1574 the Council was described as necessary for 'the continuance of quietness and good government of the people and inhabitants within the Dominion and Principality of Wales and the Marches of the same'.

There is little detailed information of the Council's work during the middle decades of the sixteenth century. This was the time of its greatest achievement, when it was the main instrument in the establishment of law and order in Wales and the marches. During Elizabeth's reign its authority seems to have declined in some respects but the records show that it was the linchpin of the administration of the Principality. It had still much to do before it became 'useless to the subjects of the thirteen Counties'. The cases with which it dealt were less important but more numerous and, particularly in the spheres of defence and religious conformity, its responsibilities were accumulating.

The second half of Elizabeth's reign saw its difficulties increase. In some respects it now became the victim of the success which it had achieved and the popularity which it had justly won. It was reprimanded and criticized, exploited and defied. The reprimands came from the Privy Council for its failure to ensure that the latter's orders were efficiently carried out at local level, from the Courts at Westminster, especially the Court of the Exchequer, for the undue extension of its judicial authority to the damage of the local courts and thus the royal revenues from these courts. The criticisms came from its own members, from dissatisfied clients and impartial commentators. They were many and varied: Lords President and judges were not so energetic or effective as Lee and Englefield had been; they were not in constant attendance; the Bench was despised by counsellors at the bar. There were too many councillors, and too many of them were concerned with lining their own pockets. Inadequate precautions were taken against the bringing of malicious suits; there was overmuch elaboration in its procedure. There were too many petty suits 'meter for a mean under Steward at a Leet or lawday to be decided'. The Council was exploited by those who conducted their feuds in the courtroom and the consequence was 'many frivolous suits grounded more upon malice than good matter'. Finally, it was defied by prominent gentlemen who were not infrequently themselves local officials and even members of the Council. One of the most illuminating instances of this was the defiance shown by the Sheriff of Glamorgan in 1570 to the Council's instructions for the election of new coroners for the county.

Valid as much of this criticism undoubtedly was, two factors must be borne in mind. The first is that a close reading of the available evidence does suggest that the Council was doing its work with reasonable efficiency, more efficiently and disinterestedly than it has been given credit for. Then, many of its shortcomings were, to no inconsiderable extent, the product of the very success which the Council had achieved and the outcome of certain social features over which it could have little control. Unfortunate as many of these were, it must be remembered that some did perform a useful function. Many of the trivial suits gave poor people in Wales some protection at a time when social and economic change threatened their interests. Many of the malicious suits were a valuable catharsis—better that individuals fought their duels on the floor of the courtroom than settle their disputes with violence as their forebears had done.

It must also be remembered that the Council suffered from a chronic shortage of money which, on the one hand, made it difficult to attract really able men into its service, and, on the other, made its officials dependent upon the fees which they could obtain from cases. There were, too, the heavy demands made by the Crown upon the Presidents which occasioned their absence for long periods. This was especially true in the case of Sir Henry Sidney, one of the most understanding of all the Presidents. The Council's effectiveness was also hampered by the friction between the President and some of its members.

The earl of Pembroke and Lord Zouch both antagonized important sections within the Council, the former by his disregard of established interests, the latter by his lack of sympathy with the lawyers. It should, however, be remembered that such weaknesses as these were not peculiar to the Council of the Marches. Other councils, like that of the North, showed precisely the same flaws. Perhaps the basic factor was that by the seventeenth century the conditions for which they had been established no longer prevailed, the *raison d'être* of their existence had all but disappeared. Inevitably they were exploited, inevitably they were challenged. But theirs had been an important contribution to the new social and political system that developed during the sixteenth century.

The Court of Great Sessions

'That there shall be holden and kept Sessions twice in every Year, in every of the said Shires in the said Dominion and Principality of Wales.' The Act of 1542 grouped the counties of Wales into four circuits, one under the Justice of Chester, another under the Justice of North Wales, one Justice was to be appointed for the counties of Radnor, Brecon, and Glamorgan and another for the counties of Cardigan, Pembroke, and Carmarthen. Monmouthshire was attached to an English circuit. The sessions were to be held for six days twice a year in each shire, following upon proclamations issued in the shire towns at least fifteen days before the sessions declaring when and where they were to be held.

Each circuit was to have its own set of officials. There was to be a Prenotary, who was the recorder of the court; a Marshal and Crier to attend the justices; and the officials who carried on the business of the courts—Attorney-General, Chamberlain, Chancellor. The sessions were authorized to exercise almost all the powers of the king's justices at Westminster. Briefly their responsibilities were to inquire, hear and determine cases of treason, petty treason, murder, robbery, felony, riot, rout, extortion, embracery (the bringing of pressure to bear on a jury); to hold pleas of the Crown 'in as large and ample a manner as the Lord Chief Justice of England and other Justices of the King's Bench'; to hold pleas of assizes 'in as large and ample a manner as the Chief Justice of the Common Pleas in England', and finally to hold a Chancery Court to determine cases of equity 'in sort as do the Chancery in England or Council of the Marches'.

Welshmen made full use of the courts for both civil and criminal cases. They were efficient and therefore popular. So much so, in fact, that a petition was presented to Elizabeth during the 1560s requesting that the number of justices should be doubled. An Act of 1576 laid down that the queen should appoint two or more judges for each circuit in Wales. Proceedings were conducted in English, a language which was foreign to the majority of the Welsh people, but there are good reasons for believing that the courts did what they could to overcome the difficulties created by this. Interpreters were used, and since this practice had obvious weaknesses, Sir William Gerard, a member of the Council of Wales and the Marches and a Judge of the Great Sessions in South Wales, recommended that 'it were very convenient that one of the Justices of assizes did understand the Welsh tongue'. That this problem was overcome is suggested by the popularity of the courts. What seems to have impressed George Owen was the sympathy shown by the judges in the performance of their duties—'the guilty condemned with pity, and the Innocent delivered by Justice', and the impartiality of the treatment offered to rich and poor—'the like care and pains was used for both'.

Nevertheless, there were certain complaints. The Welsh judges, it was alleged by some, were not drawn from the most able of those qualified. They were allowed to continue practising at the bar in England, so that their circuits were often fixed to avoid interference with their English commitments. This might well cause inconvenience and hardship to Welsh litigants. It seems also that the efficiency of the courts was impaired by the very considerable number of cases which were settled out of court, without the court's being informed of these settlements.

The lesser courts

The most important of these were the Courts of Quarter Sessions which were held four times a year by the justices of the peace of every shire. They were concerned with a multitude of matters, legal and administrative. Those bound to keep the peace were called to appear before them; indictments of various kinds were heard, felonies were presented, heard, and the accused sent for trial at the Court of Great Sessions; indictments for all forms of trespass, assaults, affrays, riots, routs, unlawful assemblies, embraceries, and maintenance were heard. In addition to their judicial functions they performed a variety of administrative responsibilities which multiplied enormously during the period. Among other tasks they controlled alehouses, they punished those involved in the playing of unlawful games; they controlled servants' and labourers' wages and covenants.

Then there were the base courts—chief of which was the County Court, which was held monthly by the sheriff. It determined small causes of less than forty shillings—involving debt, trespass, detaining of goods, distress (the right of a landlord to distrain on the goods of a tenant for non-payment of rent). The judges were the freeholders of the shire and it was here, too, that they elected members of Parliament for the county and the coroners. Next in order of importance were the hundred courts which were held every fifteen days. They conducted much of the business of the county courts. Finally, twice a year, there were the sheriff's tourns, attended by the land-holders of the district. Here were presented to the sheriff the offences committed within the district and he then arrested the individuals concerned.

Government in the shires

The most important of the hierarchy of officials on whom devolved the responsibility of local administration was the sheriff. He was 'the chief officer of trust and credit in the shire'. Appointed by the Crown on the nomination of the Lord President, the Council of Wales and the Marches, and the Justices of the Great Sessions, he was associated with the justices of the peace for much of their work. Among his many duties he was responsible for executing all processes out of the courts of law, both central and local, as well as those from the local officials, which were directed to him. He returned all juries for the trial of civil and criminal cases as well as the members of the great Inquest. He had charge of the gaol and prisoners, and executed the decisions of the courts. He executed all lawful processes from the Lord President and the justices of the peace and collected all the extracts sent to him from the various courts. He was responsible to the king for the goods of felons, outlaws, waifs and strays, for forfeitures, and for all escheats. This was not all. Particular responsibilities could be delegated to him by the Council. On occasion he was given the task of inquiring into cases of 'overcharging' the shires with cattle or instructed to pursue felons into neighbouring counties. He was responsible for the publication of proclamations, and for making the arrangements for the visits of the Judges of Assize and for the holding of the courts. In addition, he acted as returning officer in parliamentary elections—a duty which became increasingly difficult as the century wore on.

It was this multiplicity of his responsibilities which made the sheriff a key figure in all aspects of the life of the county. His fee of £5 a year seems scant reward for doing so much, and yet men were not found wanting to undertake these heavy burdens.

The union also established in all the Welsh counties the justices of the peace, justices of the quorum and of gaol delivery who had been functioning in some of the counties before. These were to be appointed by the Lord Chancellor on the recommendation of the Lord President, the Council of Wales and the Marches, and the Justices of Great Sessions. There were, according to the terms of the Act, not to be more than eight for each shire and they were to be 'of good Name and Fame', even though the property qualification of an annual income of £20 from land and a familiarity with the laws of the land were not insisted upon in Wales as they were in England. Their powers and responsibilities were to be the same as those of their English counterparts.

The functions which they were called upon to perform covered the whole range of local government—legal and judicial, police and administrative; and between these very different responsibilities no precise line was, or indeed could be, drawn. In their Quarter Sessions they heard the presentments and indictments of the Grand Jury in respect of offences ranging from robbery and vagabondage to plots and riots. They tried and sentenced the offenders. At their special sessions they dealt with everything except the actual trial of offences requiring a jury or a Grand Inquest. As individual justices they committed suspects and persons obstructing the course of justice, they punished offenders for vagrancy, drunkenness and profanity, for non-attendance at church or attendance at bull-baiting.

On the whole, they performed their judicial responsibilities with reasonable efficiency; and no small measure of the credit for the improvement in the general state of law and order is theirs—despite the criticisms that were and have been levelled at them. By twentieth-century standards the law was administered with great severity—one frequent punishment was a public whipping inflicted upon men and women indiscriminately. It is to the credit of the justices that they tempered justice with humanity, thereby, however, provoking the wrath of some of their contemporaries who attributed their conduct to negligence. George Owen made much of their failure to ascertain all the facts relating to many of the cases which were brought before them—that they failed to discover the real value of stolen articles or the precise details of time and place of certain criminal offences. This, it seems likely, was the result not so much of carelessness but of a deliberate attempt on the part of the justices to reduce the seriousness of the charge in order that they might impose less severe penalties.

Their administrative duties were heavy and became increasingly so as the period advanced. In their sessions they were responsible for the repair and maintenance of bridges, gaols, and houses of correction; they regulated prices, wages, and contracts between master and man; they inspected weights and measures and the quality of manufactured goods; they licensed alehouses and suppressed disorderly houses. Their heaviest single responsibility was the organization of poor relief in their districts—from 1597 two justices met annually to appoint Overseers of the Poor for their parishes and to pass the accounts of these officials.

Their manifold responsibilities made it inevitable that the statutory maximum of eight justices for each county should be ignored—by 1575 Denbigh and Caernarvon had seventeen each. Radnor had sixteen; six years later the number of justices in Carmarthenshire had risen to twenty-five and in Flintshire to nineteen. What is surprising is that there were so many who were anxious to occupy the office, for they received no payment other than the five shillings a day allowance for their services under the Statute of Labourers of 1593. The answer to this lies, no doubt, in the status and authority which the office bestowed upon its holder, and in some cases the opportunities which it offered to abuse this authority.

From the beginning Rowland Lee had been against the policy of handing over administration at local level to Welshmen. His objections were based on the small number of those who possessed the necessary worldly wealth to make them impartial, the lack of educated men with some knowledge of the law, and his general mistrust of Welshmen. It would not be difficult to find evidence to support Lee's fears in the conduct of local administration during the hundred years that followed his first response to this part of the union. The sheriffs, justices, and coroners were, after all, amateurs and part-timers, and it could well be argued that they only put their hearts into the work when it really suited them. Certainly they were not impartial in their handling of legal cases brought before them nor did they show overmuch efficiency in implementing instructions which did not accord with their interests. The earl of Pembroke, writing to Sir Edward Stradling and William Matthew of Glamorgan in 1587, did not mince his words—'I do not find such singularity in the upright administration of justice that I may justly think you each way faultless'. There were frequent complaints from the Council of their failure to carry out its instructions in the suppression of crimes and the punishment of offenders, in preparations for defence and the training of the local levies, in the punishment of recusancy and the curbing of piracy.

Worse than this, there is evidence of the positive misuse by the justices of their authority for their own profit. George Owen complained of the 'Men of no substance nor of credit made sheriffs and Justices of the peace which must live by polling and pilling'. He has been followed by later commentators, one of whom has seen the local government of Wales of the time as a happy hunting-ground for the Welsh gentry and upstarts. The records of the Star Chamber and the Council of Wales and the Marches provide a good deal of evidence in support of this contention. At the same time it would be a mistake to make too sweeping a denunciation based on the strength of such evidence. All this legal testimony tends to be strongly partisan and highly coloured. Frequently one is able to hear only one side of the story, many complaints were the results of family feuds and, of course, there is no mention of those who performed their duties honestly and conscientiously.

The unit of local government with which the majority of the people became increasingly familiar was the parish. Originally concerned only with ecclesiastical administration, it was given the responsibility for executing many of the functions hitherto performed through its elected officers, the churchwardens, whose responsibilities reflected the current reluctance to compartmentalize rigidly as between ecclesiastical and secular administration. They continued to exercise their original task of controlling expenditure on the upkeep of the fabric of the church, the supply of the accessories of worship, and the costs incurred in the discharge of clerical business. Theirs was the responsibility for providing the church with copies of the Scriptures and Service Books as laid down by law, and the register book for recording births, marriages, and burials after 1597. From 1604 it was also their duty to provide the bread and the wine for the communion service.

The most onerous of their secular responsibilities was the relief of the poor. Already they had performed the church's work of helping the destitute, and the statutes of the sixteenth century superimposed upon this the performance at local level of the increasing responsibilities of the state in this sphere. From 1536 they organized the collection of voluntary alms given for this purpose on Sundays and holy days. As the result of later legislation the churchwardens and two to four substantial householders of the parish were nominated as overseers of the poor by the local justices of the peace and fulfilled the statutory obligation of relieving the sick and aged poor, setting the able bodied paupers to work and apprenticing pauper children. This was financed by a compulsory poor-rate on all the inhabitants of the parish, for the collection of which and the expenditure of the moneys so made available the overseers were responsible to the justices of the peace.

Statutes of 1533 and 1566 made them responsible for the extinction of vermin and from Mary's reign the roads of the parish were made their concern. The churchwardens and constables of each parish were empowered to elect annually

two persons to act as surveyors of the highways and to provide
statute labour for unpaid service on the roads. Included in this
part of their work was the maintenance of the small bridges of
the parish. Finally, they were responsible for the organization
of the beating of the parish bounds—a ceremony not without
its purpose at a time when maps were scarce.

This, in brief, was the pattern of administration of the
countryside—at a time when towns in Wales were small and
few. It remained for long the basis of local government, and its
inadequacies in the face of later social changes should not blind
us to the fact that it worked with reasonable efficiency under the
conditions for which it was designed. It also offered the opportunity for men of widely differing means to play their part in
the governing of the country. The good governance of Wales
may have necessitated the introduction of English laws and
the English administrative machinery—but they were implemented by Welshmen.

The administration of the towns

Towns corporate were governed under the terms of charters,
granted by the Crown or the nobleman within whose lordship
the towns stood. Despite the wide variety in the details of these
charters, authority within the boroughs was generally vested in
a senior citizen, who bore the title of Mayor, Portreeve or
Bailiff, the aldermen, and a common council. The mayor was
ex officio the Lord President's Deputy-Lieutenant within the
borough; he also acted as coroner, escheator, clerk of the
market, admiral, and justice of the peace within the town.
The mayor was elected annually, and his year of office began
around Michaelmas, either at the first hundred court or from
the first Monday after the feast.

There was too an establishment of officials—a recorder, town
clerk, two chamberlains or bailiffs whose responsibility it was to
collect the rents and tolls of the town and to pay the fee farm
rents of the town into the Exchequer at May and Michaelmas.
There were two sergeants at mace who attended the mayor at
the borough courts and civic functions; to them also fell the
more onerous tasks of collecting fines and carrying out the
penalties which were imposed in the borough courts. The task
of maintaining order was the responsibility of the constables

who were allocated to the wards into which the town was divided. Finally, there were the beadle, often supplied with an official uniform, and the town crier who received a fee for the performance of his duties.

Boroughs in their corporate capacity exercised a variety of powers of self government. They had a council chamber, often within the guild hall, where meetings were held; they were authorized to make by-laws for the administration of the municipality; to lay down rules for the regulation of trade, to make and determine rates and assessments, to punish law-breakers, to hold a regular court of record, to receive and levy for their own use fines imposed upon the inhabitants, to have a common gaol, to hold view of frankpledge (that is, to hear the reports of the tithings or groups whose members were each responsible for the others' good conduct), to apprehend and try criminals for crimes committed within their jurisdiction and to have returns of writs. Finally, the borough was allowed its quota of weekly markets and annual fairs.

The borough had its specific financial resources. There were the chamber rents—the fines collected for the pardon of felons, the licences collected from brewers and bakers, the rents from lands and houses, and the castle rents—which included rent in respect of chantry lands and escheat lands. There were the tolls —the small tolls and the market tolls which were farmed out by the corporation, and others, such as the toll of 'byffes' from the shambles at Haverfordwest, which were collected on market days and on other special days in the year. From the trade corporations it received the tonnage on imported goods; from the courts it received the fines which were imposed upon offenders and collected by the sergeants, and the fines paid by those who refused municipal office.

It also had its commitments. There was the fee farm which had to be paid twice a year to the Exchequer; the fund which had to be organized for the purchase of a new lease or the payment for the renewal of its charter. It was responsible for the maintenance of public buildings and of institutions which it had taken under its wing, for the cleansing of publicly owned trading areas and public highways. It was in performance of this function that the corporation of Swansea passed one regulation to prohibit women and servants from washing 'clothes skins inwards of beasts or any other filth near to any winch or well in this town'; and another which instructed that 'no dung nor filth of their houses or streets' be thrown 'in any place (on) the strand side except they cast it without the marks that shall be limited to them by the portreeve and aldermen'. Finally there was the periodic expenditure on the entertainment provided to afford a civic welcome to important individuals.

Among its responsibilities were the maintenance of law and order and the general supervision of the economic activity which took place within the bounds of its jurisdiction. At Neath, for instance, the constable, portreeve, and burgesses drew up on 25 January 1542 a set of by-laws which laid down regulations concerning the behaviour of private individuals within the town and of the traders and craftsmen who conducted the business of the town. The bakers were to bake good and wholesome bread in loaves of two sizes, innkeepers were to have a sign above their doorways, no innkeeper was to refuse to sell ale to any inhabitant if he had three bottles or more in stock. Safeguards were laid down to prevent commercial sharp practice—there was to be no cornering of the market in goods, no forestalling or regrating (no buying up of goods to retail later at profit, and no purchase of some goods before they came on to the market). The protection of the town and its property, the prevention of what today would be termed nuisances, the punishment of those who provoked discord among the townspeople—these, too, were the concern of the boroughs in their corporate capacity. At Neath every burgess was to have the arms necessary to assist in the defence of the town and its officials; no inhabitant was to fence off part of the town's common land for his own use, nor to erect an outhouse or pigsty in his garden 'to the annoyance of his neighbour', and the punishment for scolds was stipulated in detail.

In the towns, as in the countryside, the efficiency of local government depended upon the participation of amateur part-timers. Standards, therefore, varied considerably, but by and large the system worked well enough until the resources of the towns were strained to breaking-point by profound changes which took place in the economic and social life of the country —but these are outside the province of this study.

Private charities

One interesting development of the time was the growing concern shown by the well-to-do for their less fortunate neighbours which reflected itself in the provision of various social services which have since become the concern of the state and of local administration. Though we should not exaggerate the extent of this private charity, the fact remains that during the sixteenth and more especially the seventeenth centuries an ever-increasing number among the gentry, the prosperous yeomen, and those who had made their fortunes in trade gave or bequeathed property and money to be used for the spiritual, intellectual, and material advantage of the inhabitants of their native districts. Lands, ecclesiastical revenues, rents of houses, and sums of money were handed over in trust to town officials, churchwardens, overseers of the poor, and private individuals to be put to charitable uses.

The value of these benefactions varied considerably as did the purposes for which they were intended. Many of the grammar schools—at Beaumaris, Ruthin, Monmouth, and Presteigne to mention but four—owed much to private benefactors. But there were others—Thomas Lloyd, for instance, in 1613 conveyed substantial properties in Haverfordwest for the establishment and maintenance of a Free Grammar School in the town; Sir John Davy in 1624 bequeathed an annual £40 from the revenues of the church at Abernant and its chapel at Conwil for the erection and support of an almshouse and a free school in the parish of Defynnog, Breconshire; John Matthews of Llangollen in 1630 made provision for the maintenance of boys of the district at school and university.

Others were more immediately concerned with the services and appearance of their districts. Sir John Perrott in 1580 granted lands and properties in the town of Haverfordwest for the maintenance and improvement of the town's roads, bridges, and public buildings. Sir John Williams of Gwernyfed in Breconshire directed that part of the great tithes of the parish of Gwenddwr in the same county should be used for the repair of local roads and bridges. Nor was the spiritual welfare of the recipients of their charity ignored. A number of individuals provided for sermons to be preached on specified occasions in churches with which they had connections and for the purchase of Bibles to be distributed among the poor.

The item for which most gifts and bequests were intended was the relief of the poor. Some provided for almshouses, others for the distribution of money or food or clothes among the poor. Many of these bequests involved substantial sums of money, many were of relatively small amounts. But together they must have been a useful supplement to the relief administered by the parishes from money collected from the poor-rate.

Though the cynical might impute ulterior motives to these private benefactions, they are worthy of attention. They did perform useful functions in that they went part of the way to fill gaps in the provision of a variety of services at local level. They do repair to some degree the tarnished reputations of those whose less desirable attributes have received their fair share of attention. Finally, they illustrate certain general conclusions concerning the pattern of social developments in the Wales of the time. The number of properties involved in the bequests which were situated in London, Bristol, and Shrewsbury give some indication of the centres in England to which certain Welshmen gravitated in search of fame and fortune.

Wales and the Parliament at Westminster

Before 1536 there is record of only two occasions when Wales was represented in the English Parliament. These were in 1322 when twenty-four representatives were summoned from South Wales and the same number from North Wales to the Parliament at York which affirmed the principle that all legislative changes required the assent of the three estates of the realm. Then in 1327 forty-eight Welsh representatives attended the Parliament at Westminster which deposed Edward II. But these two occasions had not established a precedent and it would not be true to say that the Welsh people as such were represented in them. It was not until 1536 that Wales was given formal parliamentary representation—as an essential part of the policy of integrating Wales and England and of firmly establishing the new concept of Crown in Parliament as the supreme authority through the king's domains.

The Act laid down that for the existing and all future

F

Parliaments, one knight was to be elected to represent each of the counties of Wales and one burgess every borough which was a shire town. There were two exceptions to this general rule— the county of Monmouth was to have two members and the shire town of Merioneth was to be unrepresented. The election of the members for these Welsh constituencies was to be 'in like Manner Form and Order' as in England, and the Welsh members were to have 'like Dignity Pre-eminence and Privilege', and were to be allowed the same fees as their English counterparts. The moneys for the payment of the members' fees were to be levied upon the commons of the shire which they represented in the case of the county members, and upon the shire towns and 'all other ancient Boroughs within the same Shires' in the case of the borough members.

The Act of 1542 clarified certain issues and modified some of the arrangements made in 1536. It established the responsibility of the Welsh to abide by the financial decisions of Parliament— they 'shall be charged and chargeable to all subsidies and other charges to be granted by the Commons of any of the said Parliaments'. Haverfordwest was declared to be a county in its own right and therefore entitled to elect a member to represent itself in Parliament. The Act of 1543 laid down the arrangements for the payment of the members' fees—Welsh members were to receive the same fees as the English members, four shillings a day in the case of the county member, two shillings in that of the borough member. These were to be paid for the duration of the parliamentary session and for a reasonable period before and after the meeting of Parliament in order to cover the expense of the journey to and from Westminster. The sheriff was given the responsibility of collecting and paying these fees in the counties and the mayor or chief official in the boroughs. Since many of the Welsh boroughs were poor and would find the expense of returning a member heavy, special provision was made whereby boroughs 'not finding Burgesses for the Parliament themselves' were to contribute their due share to the borough member's fee. In return for their contribution the burgesses of these boroughs were to take part in the elections in which they were to 'have like voice and authority to elect, name and choose the Burgesses of every of the said Shire towns, like and in such manner as the Burgesses of the said Shire towns have and use'. Two justices of the peace were to make the necessary assessments upon the boroughs for the payment of the members, the rates to be paid by each inhabitant in the boroughs were to be calculated by discreet and substantial burgesses named by the mayor who was made responsible for the collection and payment to the member.

The situation in general terms was that Wales was granted twenty-seven members, fourteen of whom represented the county constituencies and thirteen the boroughs. These were to be elected in the same manner as their English counterparts, that is, in the county and borough courts on a limited franchise. In the county constituencies the right to vote was exercised by the forty-shilling freeholder, in the boroughs by the freemen. This latter was not simply based on an inherent right by birth or by apprenticeship—almost certainly it was the result of arbitrary election at the borough court. Nor was there any uniformity in the conditions imposed upon these freemen—in some boroughs the franchise was restricted to resident freemen, in the majority this rule did not apply, and in these latter there was on occasion a good deal of manipulation of freeman status for partisan interests. Originally the borough member was elected by the freemen of the county town, but this was changed in 1543 when the system of contributory boroughs came into operation. So small were the towns throughout Wales that this system operated in almost every county. Here again there was no uniformity—the member for Carmarthen, for example, was until 1604 elected by the freemen of Kidwelly, Llanelli, Newton, and Dryslwyn as well as those of Carmarthen. The freemen of Cowbridge, Llantrisant, Neath, Aberafan, Kenfig, Swansea, and Loughor joined with their fellows in Cardiff to elect the member for Cardiff. In some cases boroughs were either unwilling or incapable of bearing their share of the expense and so they took no part in the elections. Llanidloes, Llanfyllin, and Welshpool joined with Montgomery in the election of its member, but Caersws, Machynlleth, and Newtown took no part even though they were corporate boroughs and therefore entitled to do so. There were, too, some instances of boroughs which shared occasionally in the election of the borough member, but which either did not achieve or did not want permanent participation. This seems to have been the case of Chirk which took part in the Denbigh election of 1572 but in no other.

During the hundred years that followed the union, two features become increasingly discernible. The first was the growing awareness among certain Welshmen of the importance of the House of Commons and the increasing part which the Welsh members took in the conduct of its business. Secondly, there was the growing consciousness among the rising Welsh families of the importance which membership of the House bestowed upon them in their localities.

Before 1567 Welsh members made very little impact at Westminster despite the fact that there was a good deal of legislation concerning Wales during these years. Neither among the Welsh members themselves nor among those whom they represented does there seem to have been very much awareness of the former's representative responsibilities and little regard seems to have been paid to the importance of the lower House. There is no other explanation for the action of the inhabitants of one county who entrusted the promotion of one of their projects to a member for another county; or for that petition by the inhabitants of Wales and Chester concerning the non-payment of subsidies when mises were being collected, which they presented not to the House of Commons but to the upper House. The attitude of the represented is reflected in the conduct of their members. Where the names of Welsh members did find a place in the records of the House it was usually that they were demanding one or other of the privileges which membership conferred upon them—more often than not that of freedom from arrest for their unruly servants. Frequent also were their requests for leave of absence from their parliamentary responsibilities, usually on the grounds of illness, the distance involved in their attendance at Westminster, or the pressure of their other duties. Membership of Parliament certainly had some prestige value even in these early years, but it seems that the full import of this part of the union had not yet aroused any real response in Wales.

The last thirty years of the sixteenth century saw a significant change in the role of the Welsh members. These were the years during which the committee procedure was developing in the House of Commons, and among the lists of the committee members the names of Welsh representatives become increasingly prominent. It was quite natural that they should serve on committees dealing with Welsh questions, like that which dealt with the Reformation of Errors in Fines and Recoveries in Wales or that which considered the inclusion of the lordship of Llandovery in the county of Carmarthen. More significant was their appearance on committees which had responsibility for matters which were not exclusively Welsh. Even when Welsh members' names do not appear it is apparent that some have been busy behind the scenes, in the move, for instance, to amend one part of the Poor Law of 1572 to omit minstrels from the list of vagabonds who were to be punished. There is a substantial drop in the requests for leave of absence from Welsh members, fewer non-Welsh names appear among the lists of those representing Welsh constituencies and there was an increasing body of legislation affecting Wales. Welshmen were making their presence felt at Westminster—they were learning the procedure of the lower House and taking an increasing part in the conduct of its business. Representation at Westminster had become a meaningful reality to a section of Welsh society.

At local level too membership of Parliament was becoming an important issue. In Wales to a greater extent perhaps than in England reactions to national issues were decided by local considerations. True, a number of the Welsh counties may have been of recent origin, but the forces of localism and particularism were not; bonds of kinship and inherited feuds were uniting and divisive forces which had operated on a local scale for centuries. Membership of Parliament, especially as the county representative, bestowed upon the individual and his family a local pre-eminence of which people became more aware as Parliament gained prestige in Wales and the Welsh became more politically conscious. In some counties it was for a succession of parliaments the monopoly of the one outstanding family, in others it was a distinction which circulated among the members of a small group of families. But in some it was a prize which was fought for by contending factions, not simply for its own sake but for the evidence which it provided of one or other's local supremacy. The 1571 election in Merioneth, for instance, resolved itself into a struggle between the families of Llwyn and Rug, another stage in the struggle between these families which was occasioned by John Salusbury's attempt to obtain a reversion of the royal grant of the township of Dolgelly, then in the hands of John Lewis Owen of Llwyn. The 1597 election in Radnorshire was a similar struggle between the Vaughans of Clyro and the Prices of Monachty—one in which the sheriff flagrently misused his authority to declare James Price returned for the county. Under these circumstances almost any form of stratagem was possible and there are four particularly well-known disputed elections in Wales during the reign of Elizabeth which illustrate the tactics of the opposing sides—the Montgomeryshire election of 1588, those for Denbighshire in 1588 and 1601, and the double return for Cardiganshire in the same year.

In this context parliamentary representation reflects the growing prestige of the new families, who when they had gained the pinacle of the county seat could feel that they had well and truly arrived. In the case of Breconshire, for example, the county seat was virtually monopolized from the union to 1614 by two families long established in the county. These were the Games family of Newton, with its cadet branches at Aberbran and Buckland, and the Vaughan family of Porthamal. Only on three occasions was this stranglehold broken—by Sir John Price of the Priory, Brecon, in 1547 and by Watkin Herbert of Crickhowell in two of Mary's parliaments. True, the county member for the last three of Elizabeth's reign and the first of her successor's was Sir Robert Knollys, but he was the son-in-law of Rowland Vaughan. Second in importance to the county seat was that of the borough, and this too had until 1584 been monopolized by the two great families—only once had there been an intruder, William Awbrey of Cantref. But in 1584 a new star appeared in the person of David Williams, the son of a small landholder of Ystradfellte who had made a fortune at the bar. He became the borough member in this year and again four years later. The Williams family continued to flourish, Sir David's son Henry succeeded to the borough seat in 1601 and to the county seat in 1620 which he shared with Sir Charles Vaughan and John Price of the Priory until William Morgan appeared on the scene in 1640.

The parliamentary history of the period reflects the increasing measure of integration between England and Wales.

Initially, Welsh members had represented Welsh constituencies. Then some Welsh families who had climbed to the topmost rung of the social and political ladder moved their centres of influence to England, but preserved their patronage in Wales. Outstanding among these was the earl of Pembroke, head of the great Herbert family, who shared control of the county and the borough seats in both Glamorgan and Montgomeryshire. He also exercised a determining voice in the representation of constituencies in Wiltshire and Cornwall. The result of his influence is seen in Old Sarum's being represented by William Price, or in the case of Matthew Davies who gave up Cardiff in 1620 but returned to Westminster in 1624 as member for one of the Wiltshire seats. Sir Thomas Morgan of Ruperra also sat for Wilton, and among the members for Cornish boroughs were the two Trevors, Sir Robert Mansel and Sir John Stradling. It is true that these men did not identify themselves with their constituents to the same degree as does the modern member. But there is no doubt that as members for these English boroughs they established contacts and acquired interests which helped to make union a living reality.

SUGGESTED READING

C. A. J. Skeel: as for Chapter 3.

Penry Williams: *The Council in the Marches of Wales under Elizabeth I*. Cardiff, 1958.

Sir John Neale: *The Elizabethan House of Commons*. London, 1949. Chapter 5.

Articles:

T. H. Lewis: 'The Justice of the Peace in Wales', *Trans. Cymmr.*, 1943–4.

—— 'The Administration of Justice in the Welsh County in its Relation to other Organs of Justice, Higher and Lower', ibid., 1945.

W. Llewelyn Williams: 'The King's Court of Great Sessions in Wales', *Y Cymmr.*, xxvl, 1916.

Penry Williams: 'The Welsh Borderland under Queen Elizabeth', *W.H.R.*, vol. 1, No. 1, 1960.

Glyn Roberts: 'The Parliamentary Representation of the Welsh Boroughs', *B.B.C.S.*, lv, 1929.

A. H. Dodd: 'Wales's Parliamentary Apprenticeship (1536–1625)', *Trans. Cymmr.*, 1942.

B. G. Charles (ed.): 'Haverfordwest Accounts, 1563–1620', *N.L.W. Journal*, lx, 1955–6.

6. The Changes in Religion

How prepared were the Welsh for change?

THERE is no lack of evidence for the low standards which characterized the Roman Catholic hierarchy in Europe on the eve of the Reformation, nor is there any reason to think that in Wales conditions were any better. Here the Church had been subjected to the same pressures as elsewhere, in some cases in a more acute and complex form. At the top, for instance, the leaders of the Church were in Wales, more so than in most countries, unqualified to fulfil their responsibilities, for the appointment of Welsh bishops and upper clergy was dictated by political expediency and the interests of the English Crown. For this reason Welsh clerics were infrequently promoted to the episcopal bench and the Englishmen who were appointed possessed little knowledge and less understanding of their dioceses. Moreover, in many instances, they considered their Welsh bishoprics merely as the lower rungs on the ladder of episcopal promotion. Not only did this deny the Church positive leadership, but of necessity it created a divergence of interests and sympathy between the upper and lower clergy—a divergence which was reflected in the different reactions of each section to the religious changes when they occurred.

Among the lower clergy too a variety of forces had undermined efficiency. The recurrent plagues of the second half of the fourteenth century had taken a heavy toll of the clergy as well as the laity, and the depletions in the clerical ranks had been made worse as a result of the revolt of Owain Glyn Dŵr and the Wars of the Roses. The outcome was vacant parishes, rapid transfers from one parish to another, and a general lowering of standards of recruitment. This was made all the more acute by the general poverty which characterized the Welsh Church of the time. Many church buildings which had been ruined during the troubles of the fifteenth century had remained in this condition for long periods. More significant was the fact that clerical stipends were, on the whole, pitifully inadequate—the vast majority varied between £5 and £15 a year, while a considerable number were less than £5. Small wonder that the ordinary parish priests were men of little education and training—few had been to a grammar school, fewer still to university. It follows, therefore, that despite the improvements achieved in the late fifteenth and early sixteenth centuries the majority of Welsh parishes were either without spiritual leadership, or were served by priests of inferior ability and insufficient training.

This malaise was even more apparent among the regular clergy. Religious houses, markedly undermanned by inmates who were, to say the least, ineffective, had become the prey of powerful local families. The conduct of some of the religious provoked scandals—there was Abbot Salusbury of Valle Crucis who achieved notoriety as a robber and bandit, while the Pennant abbots of Basingwerk earned for themselves an unenviable reputation—they ignored their vows of chastity, were guilty of nepotism, used force to obtain their wishes, and plundered the property of their monastery. Among too many others practice failed to match ideal, conduct did not fulfil vows which had been taken.

More general than the scandals, and for this reason more ominous, were the inadequacies of monks and parish priests as spiritual guides and mentors. The Welsh people could expect little from those to whom had been entrusted the care of their souls. Inevitably, therefore, the later Middle Ages had seen an increasing emphasis upon the more superficial aspects of religious experience and more frequent exploitation of the superstition and credulity of an uneducated people. As late as 1567 Nicholas Robinson could report that he had 'found since I came to this country Images and altars standing in churches undefaced, lewd and indecent vigils and watches observed, much pilgrimage going, many candles set up to the honour of saints, some relics yet carried about, and all the countries full of beads and knots'.[1] And this in spite of the efforts of the leaders of Protestantism!

Powerful though the impact of this superficial element may have been and sincere though the adherence of many Welshmen

[1] For Nicholas Robinson, see A. E. Owen, *Y Cymmr.*, xxxlx, 1928.

certainly was to the teachings of the Church, they did not protect the clergy from attack. They themselves were satirized and their conduct severely criticized by the laymen—all ranks were lampooned in the poetry of the time and there were shrill protests against the less savoury of clerical practices. The people of Carmarthen and Haverfordwest registered their complaint against the sale of indulgences when in 1474 they reported that 'of late days divers persons have come in to our coasts usurping upon them by feigned and coloured writings great power to assoil a pena et a culpa, and afterwards found fickle and untrue'. A clash occurred at Neath in 1521 between some merchants and monks, occasioned by the former's resentment of what they considered to be the unwarranted interference in their trading activities by the Abbot of Neath Abbey. Nor was there such respect for the Church as to safeguard its property from unlawful intrusion. Richard, earl of Warwick, had occasion to write to his sheriff in Glamorgan that he had received complaints from the Abbot of Margam of oppression by 'certain of our bailiffs and ministers with a great multitude of men and horses'.

The Welsh Church on the eve of the Reformation was then in no condition to resist serious challenge. It was served by a clergy among whose lower ranks standards were poor, pluralism and absenteeism rife, ignorance widespread. It was bereft of that leadership and unity which alone make possible any concerted action in times of crisis. It was crippled by its own ineffectiveness and paralysed by the animosity which existed between the upper clergy and members of the laity. The Church, it would seem, could do little to defend itself, and many among the laity would do even less to protect it. But this does not mean that the Welsh people were ready for any radical change in religion. Forces which exerted so powerful an impact elsewhere had not made themselves felt in Wales. Lollardy may well have had some influence upon the people of the border counties, and contacts with English ports may have led to some instances of anti-clericalism in Pembrokeshire, but there can have been little if any heresy among the mass of the Welsh people. Moreover, those non-religious factors which played so important a part in shaping the Protestant Reformation in England and Europe were still of too tender a growth to exercise a decisive influence in Wales. In fact, they may well have had the reverse effect.

A growing sense of national identity certainly made some Englishmen impatient of papal control and thus won for the king a measure of support in his attack upon the papacy: for the Welsh Roman Catholicism was the faith which they had observed in the days of independence. More than this, some of its leaders had identified themselves with the aspirations of the Welsh people on those occasions when they had attempted to win freedom from the control of the English. The Welsh gentry class had reached a stage in its growth when some of its members might exploit individual churches and monasteries, but it was not equipped to challenge the Church itself. The monasteries which were the subject of such bitter hostility elsewhere were in many parts of Wales, as in the economically backward parts of England, reasonably popular. The New Learning which in other countries had done so much to undermine the faith of thinking people in the Church had not made itself felt in the Wales of the early sixteenth century. On the contrary, the prevailing widespread ignorance strengthened the hold of those outward forms of religious devotion to which the people were accustomed. Nor was this made any the less difficult for the reformers by the problem of the language. Protestant propaganda, which drew its inspiration from England and expressed itself in the English language, could elicit very little response among the mass of a people who were monoglot Welsh.

Finally, Wales was a remote, sparsely populated country, largely dependent upon a pastoral economy, whose towns were few and small, whose trading elements insignificant. This was not the background for a great change in religious belief: its natural product was conservatism. Wales was a country where there were no growing points of opposition to the Church, among whose inhabitants existed no machinery for the expression of any such opposition. The wonder is that the religious changes, when they did occur, failed to provoke more vehement opposition.

Doctrinal controversy could, then, have had little immediate relevance for many Welshmen. For them the first major stage of the religious revolution must have been the disappearance of the monasteries.

The dissolution of the monasteries

The regular orders had forty-seven religious houses in Wales
on the eve of the Reformation—thirty-four monasteries, three
nunneries, and ten friaries. The largest single monastic order
was the Cistercian with thirteen houses while the Benedictines
had eight and the Augustinian Canons had six. Half the friaries
belonged to the Dominican order, three to the Franciscan, and
the Carmelites and Austin Friars had one each. The majority
of these houses had been established during the two centuries
that followed the Norman Conquest of England in 1066 and
coincided with the penetration of Wales by the marcher lords.
Many were established by these latter, constituted as cells of
English monasteries and endowed with churches, lands, and
tithes in England and Wales. The Benedictine houses were the
first to be established, then followed those of the Cistercians and
Augustinians, while the friaries were for the most part founded
during the second half of the thirteenth century. They were,
with few exceptions, located near the coast and in the rich river
valleys, and it was from the lowland areas that they drew the
bulk of their incomes.

The Welsh houses were, by comparison with those in England, poor and ill endowed. Their combined net annual
income in 1535 was some £3,178—less than that enjoyed by
the very wealthiest of the great English monasteries. Not one
had an income of £200—there were seven which received
between £150 and £200, eight between £100 and £150,
eleven between £50 and £100, four between £25 and £50,
while the income of six was below £25 a year. The wealthiest
order was the Cistercian whose thirteen houses had an aggregate
income of £1,487. On the other hand, within the Welsh
Church the monasteries enjoyed a relatively strong financial
position. Nearly half the total wealth of the diocese of Llandaff
was in the hands of the monasteries, and there were several
abbots whose incomes were larger than those of the Welsh
bishops, St. David's alone excepted. Nevertheless, one of the
decisive features of monastic life in Wales in the early sixteenth
century was its poverty.

Equally prominent was the degree to which the houses were
undermanned. The numbers of the inmates had been seriously

Penmon
Llanfaes x⊗ +
        ⊖ Conway   Rhuddlan +
  + Bangor   Basingwerk ⊖
                        ⊠ Denbigh

  ⊗ Beddgelert   ⊖ Valle Crucis

◑⊗ Bardsey

        ⊖ Cymer

                  ⊖ Strata Marcella
                ⊠ Llanllugan

              ⊖ Cwm-hir

        ⊖ Strata Florida
      ⊠ Llanllyr

        ■ ● Cardigan
    St. Dogmael's

              □ Talley

                  + ●   Llanthony Prima
                  Brecon   ⊗

                      Abergavenny
                          ●   ⊖ ● Monmouth
                          Grace Dieu

  Haverfordwest   ⊖ Tintern
    ⊗+ ▼ Slebech ⊖ Whitland x Carmarthen   □ St. Kynemark
  ● Pill   ⊗   Chepstow
  ■   ● Kidwelly   Usk ⊡ ●
                                              ●
Pembroke ○■ Caldy   ⊖ Neath Llantarnam ⊖
                              ⊖ Margam   ● Malpas
                      ⊖ Neath
                          Newport △
                      Cardiff + x
                  ● Ewenni

  ● Benedictine   ⊗ Augustinian Canons   ⊠ Carmelite Friars
  ○ Cluniac   □ Premonstratensian Canons △ Austin Friars
  ■ Tironian   + Dominican Friars   ▼ Knights Hospitallers
  ⊖ Cistercian   X Franciscan Friars   ⊡ Benedictine Nunnery
              ⊠ Cistercian Nunneries

MAP 3. The religious houses in Wales at the end of the Middle Ages

(Based on information in Glanmor Williams, *The Welsh Church from Conquest to Reformation.*)

reduced by the disasters of the fourteenth and early fifteenth centuries and recruitment had been handicapped by the declining attraction exerted by the ascetic ideal. All thirteen Cistercian houses could together muster only eighty-four monks —Tintern alone had the required complement of thirteen to perform its religious obligations properly. The friaries were little better—the Dominicans had five houses which, with the exception of Bangor for which no numbers are available, contained thirty regulars while the three Franciscan houses could claim only twenty-seven. The inadequacy of these numbers was in part the product of the deterioration which had overtaken the monastic life; it also placed insuperable barriers in the path of any attempt at revitalization and reform.

Unfortunate in its consequences too was the growing intrusion of secular influences and control into monastic life. This is, perhaps, seen most clearly in the administration of the sources of monastic revenue. Many of these, both spiritualities and temporalities, had been farmed out to laymen since the fourteenth century. The monasteries kept direct control over only a small portion of their land, usually the demesne on the home grange. The remainder, organized into manors or granges each containing a number of farms or tenements, was leased to tenants who recognized the authority of the bailiff appointed by the monastery. In addition to the bailiffs who were each responsible for a particular manor, the monasteries also appointed a steward or seneschal who exercised an over-all supervision of the administration of their estates. Both steward and bailiffs were drawn from the ranks of the landowning gentry class; the former especially were men whose influence was such as to guarantee the monastery protection and security.

The Benedictine priory of St. John at Brecon had been endowed by its founder Robert Newmarch with property in Wales, the border counties, and the south-west of England. It had leased the tithes of the near-by parish of Battle to Thomas Walton, Evan Day, and Thomas ap Ieuan at an annual rent of £10. 6s. 1d. and those of Berrington in Herefordshire to a certain Roger Parsons and his wife Matilda. At Berrington too it had leased two messuages to William Rowberry and his wife Jane, while certain spiritual and temporal tithes of the chapel of Mouncton had been demised to John Walbeof of Llanhamlach at a yearly rent of £10. At the time of the dissolution all nine churches appropriated to it had been leased while the priory lands in and around the town of Brecon brought in a total rent of £113. 0s. 1d.

The majority of those holding lands of the monasteries had been tenants-at-will, but increasingly after the 1480s these tenancies were converted into leaseholds, many of them let for long periods. This was particularly the case on the very eve of dissolution—fifty-one of Neath's seventy-one leases were drawn up later than the end of 1535, while all of Whitland's 138 were. These were obviously precautionary measures on the part of the tenants to safeguard their hold upon their monastic lands. Already many among the laity had lucrative interests in the monasteries, appreciated the opportunities which they offered, and were anxious to consolidate the hold which they had already acquired. There is no doubt that many were able to accomplish this by exerting pressures of various kinds upon the monasteries—pressures to which the latter had made themselves vulnerable by their dealings with and reliance upon members of the laity. Nor was this the only unfortunate consequence of the increasing influence exercised by laymen upon monastic houses. These men were constantly in attendance at the monasteries and were frequently entertained by the monks. They brought into the monasteries their own worldly standards and destroyed the concept of isolation from the world which was at the very heart of the monastic ideal. Moreover, the special position enjoyed by some of the laymen gave them opportunities of exercising a measure of control over the affairs of the monasteries. Not only did they insist upon being entertained by the monks in such a way as to strain the resources of the houses, they exercised a control upon the business of the monasteries especially in the elections of the heads of the houses. The Trevors exerted considerable influence over the affairs of Valle Crucis, the Pennants over Basingwerk, the Bulkeleys over the priory of Penmon, and the Gruffydd family of Penrhyn over the friary of Bangor.

It is hardly to be wondered at that the monasteries and their occupants were falling far short of the standard set by their founders and failing abysmally to fulfil their obligations. The religious services were not, indeed could not be, properly conducted; good works in many cases took second place to good living—there was, for instance, a marked imbalance between monastic expenditure on food and entertainment on the one hand and charity on the other. Monasteries employed servants and labourers to perform the onerous physical work while the monks were in receipt of wages which varied from 13s. 4d. to £2. 13s. 4d. a year. In the case of most houses their poverty made it impossible to maintain the fabric in a reasonable state of repair, while indifference caused them to neglect their responsibilities for the maintenance of the churches appropriated to them. The intrusion of secular influences created an atmosphere of worldliness and destroyed any sense of vocation. The poets praise some houses for their lavish entertainment and their heads for the patronage which they offered to scholars and writers; the records reveal much indiscipline and disregard of monastic vows. Scandals there were also—such as those in which Abbot John Griffiths of Margam was involved and Richard Smith of Strata Florida and Abbot Salusbury of Valle Crucis.

It was a much tarnished image that the monasteries presented to the interested sections of public opinion in the 1530s. The scandals apart—and too much should not be made of these—there were their inadequacy and growing irrelevance; they had abrogated their responsibilities and surrendered to the control of powerful local families. They were victims ripe for the plucking and there were many who had already staked out their claims on the carcase.

The fate of the monasteries

Once the king had finally broken with Rome events moved rapidly. In 1534 governmental visitors were dispatched to enforce upon the monks the oath acknowledging royal supremacy—an oath which no Welsh monk in Wales is known to have refused; in the following year a record of monastic income, the Valor Ecclesiasticus, was drawn up, and 1536 saw a second visitation of the monasteries, whose reports were intended to justify their dissolution. John Vaughan, for instance, presented a very gloomy report on Monmouth Priory and added, 'I intend to suppress the said house for it is the voice of the country that whilst you have monks there you shall have neither good rule nor good order'.[1] Then followed the Act for the suppression of houses with an annual income of less than £200 a year. Since all Welsh monasteries fell into this category they should have been dissolved, but some were able to postpone the inevitable. Three houses, Neath, Whitland, and Strata Florida, were allowed to pay fines to the Crown to escape; others like Ewenni and Malpas, which were daughter monasteries of larger English houses, survived until the mother house was dissolved. Centres of other religious organizations followed in the wake of the monasteries—the friaries disappeared in 1538, the Commandery of the Knights of St. John at Slebech and the possessions of the Order in North Wales continued only until 1540, and the chantries were appropriated in 1549.

Older monks were generally given pensions; others were granted benefices and became parish priests; and some reverted to the secular life. Some monastic churches were used for parish worship; others—at Brecon, Carmarthen, and Abergavenny—to establish schools; and a number were allowed to fall into ruin. But the repercussions of the dissolution were felt as much in the economic as in the religious sphere. The suppression of the monasteries released for lay exploitation and speculation a very considerable quantity of land. Leases, even those which had been granted after 1535, were for the most part confirmed by the Crown, and many of these continued into the seventeenth century. The Crown gave away a small fraction of monastic property—in 1537 for instance, the earl of Worcester received the site and the possessions of Tintern Abbey. It also leased monastic possessions, vacant sites, demesne lands, and rectories not already farmed, to those in contact with the royal household. Those men who had conducted royal visitations were, of course, ideally situated and made the most of their opportunity—John Price leased substantial portions of Brecon Priory, Edward Carne of Ewenni, and John Vaughan of Grace Dieu, Whitland, and Pembroke. The rents in these instances were based on the assessment of 1535 and the leases were for terms of twenty-one years.

Then in 1539 the Crown began to sell monastic property. In 1540, for example, John Cavendish bought Cardigan Priory

[1] Quoted in Glanmor Williams, *The Welsh Church from Conquest to Reformation*, p. 387.

G

and three of its rectories at twenty years' purchase. These early sales were, for the greater part, of small, isolated tenements and the terms and conditions of purchase were not light. But the need for ready cash, especially in the middle 1540s, forced the Crown to sell more and on easier terms. This continued during the reigns of Edward VI and Mary, and by the beginning of Elizabeth's reign all that remained in the hands of the Crown from the former monastic possessions were the rectories and tithes. The purchase of the estates of Margam Abbey in Glamorgan by Rice Mansell affords an interesting illustration of the way in which monastic property was acquired by the go-ahead elements of Welsh society. In 1538 he obtained a lease of twenty-one years on the site of the monastery and a small portion of the demesne. Two years later, in June 1540, he bought the site of the Abbey, the church, the bell-tower, cemetery, a water mill, the fishery in the Afan, together with a number of granges, lands, and tithes for £938. 6s. 8d. He paid the Crown in instalments, and when he had cleared the first purchase, he bought more granges, lands, tenements, woods, and water mills in August 1543 for £642. 9s. 8d. Three years later he acquired a further portion of the estates of the former abbey for £678. 1s. 6d., and finally in December 1557 he made the final purchase of the remainder for £223. 15s. 3d. Altogether he paid a total of £2,482. 13s. 1d. for the abbey's very considerable estates.

There was a busy market in Welsh monastic property during the second half of the sixteenth century. The possessions of many of the former monasteries passed through a number of hands, many of them English, before finally being acquired by local families. In North Wales, for instance, the possessions of Beddgelert passed first of all to Anne of Cleves; Bangor Friary passed from a local family, the Gruffydds of Penrhyn, to Londoners before being acquired by Geoffrey Glynne, the founder of Friars' School. The Priory of Penmon and the possessions of Bardsey was likewise subjected to the intrusion of outsiders and similar changes in ownership.

Directly or indirectly, however, the greater part of the monastic property came into the hands of those Welsh landed families, whose members had the necessary money available. This money had been acquired in a variety of ways—in the service of the Crown, during a successful legal career, or by trade, to mention a few. The purchasers were not discouraged by existing leases from investing in monastic properties. In the diocese of Llandaff, for instance, less than a quarter of these remained in royal hands by 1559. The desirability for the Crown of creating a vested interest in the Reformation did not lead to any large-scale grants or cheap sales and leases. The lands and properties of the former monasteries were bought for cash estimated at twenty years' purchase or more. Leases were granted initially for twenty-one years in return for an entry fee calculated on four to six years' rent. True, the Crown was vulnerable to the vagaries of the economic situation and, after 1580 especially, the market hardened against it. This caused a lowering of entry fines and a lengthening of leases, so that by the last decade of the sixteenth century entry fines were down to one year's rent and leases were granted for three lives. But the suppression of the monasteries was not in Wales, any more than in England, the occasion for indiscriminate bounty on the part of a beneficent government to its associates in the attack upon the Church. It did, however, afford the acquisitive with an opportunity of adding to their estates and establishing their control over certain aspects of ecclesiastical affairs. As such it was an important factor in determining the evolution of a new social pattern in modern Wales.

Protestantism introduced

The diocese of St. David's was the scene of the first stage of the Protestant offensive in Wales. The presence of William Barlow, first as prior at Haverfordwest and then as bishop from 1536, was in itself sufficient to explain a determined effort to establish the new faith, for he was the first wholehearted Protestant to hold a position of authority in the Church in Wales. And he was not entirely without allies, even though there was the barrier of the special position enjoyed by St. David's to be overcome. There were the ports of the South Wales coast whose traders were in constant touch with Bristol and other English towns; there were quite a number of English-speaking people in the region, for whom the propaganda of the opponents of the old Church would not be alien and incomprehensible. It was no accident that what slight evidence there is of heresy in medieval Wales suggests that it showed itself in south-west Wales, and that there was more anti-clericalism here than elsewhere. Moreover, Barlow could rely on the support of one interested party who was very close to the king—Anne Boleyn, marchioness of Pembroke—and who could exert some pressure on his behalf in the area.

Barlow opened his campaign in 1534 with a series of anti-papal sermons which provoked considerable opposition. He answered his opponents with a vigorous onslaught upon the clergy of the diocese. None preached God's word, he claimed, and very few were in favour of it; immorality and idolatry were common and no diocese he supposed, was 'more corrupted nor none so far out of frame, without hope of reformation'. He urged upon Thomas Cromwell with whom he was in close contact the pressing need for a strong Protestant champion in the diocese—he had set his own sights on the bishopric, and this he achieved in 1536 after some other commissions which included a very short spell as Bishop of St. Asaph.

His return to St. David's in July 1536 marked the reopening of his attack upon the forces of reaction within the diocese—an attack which was conducted with vigour and enthusiasm. His plan was, on the face of it, sensible enough. First, his authority as bishop was to be extended by himself becoming the head of the cathedral chapter and confirmed by the support of staunch Protestants. Some of these, men like Young, Meyrick, and Green, he introduced into the chapter, others, members of his own family especially, received valuable benefices. Then a severe blow was to be struck at the old religion by the removal of the see from St. David's to St. Peter's, Carmarthen. This would sever the emotional hold evoked by the old cathedral, sanctified by its associations with the most revered of the old Welsh saints and hallowed by the pilgrimages of countless generations of Welshmen. Finally, schools and Protestant preaching were to be endowed from the proceeds of suppressed colleges and friaries. Protestant propaganda was to be given some guarantee of success by creating an educated clergy and a literate section among the laity. An echo of this is to be found in the licence granted to Barlow for the foundation of the grammar school at Brecon in 1541. 'Our subjects in South Wales are so poor that they cannot give their sons a good education; nor is there any school of letters in those parts; wherefore not only are clergy and laity of every age and condition rude and ignorant of their duty towards God and their obedience to ourselves, but have no skill in the English tongue, so that they are unable to observe or to understand our statutes, which they are bound to keep.' A break with the past, a frontal assault upon the teachings and practices of the old faith and the preparation of the ground for the seed of the new religion. This seems to have been Barlow's grand design.

But both the plan and the means adopted for its execution provoked as much, perhaps more, opposition than did their objective. There were vested interests at stake which could best be preserved by the maintenance of the *status quo*, while senior clergy resented the extension of episcopal authority which threatened the clerical balance of power within the diocese. Moreover, Barlow's methods—his preferment of some of his own family to well-endowed livings and the support which he gave to other members in promoting their secular interests— laid him open to attack. Finally, he had to hurry slowly—he was a convinced Protestant whose religious convictions were more radical than those favoured by the government, a fact which had not passed unobserved among his enemies. His frequent quarrels with his clerical opponents led to suits in Star Chamber and Chancery in which Barlow did not have it all his own way. Cromwell received numerous complaints about his protégé, the burden of one of which at least was that he held unorthodox religious beliefs. Self-interest and his hopes for the ultimate Protestant triumph restrained Barlow, for he dared not outstrip the supreme head of his Church. This might have disastrous consequences for himself and for the cause which he championed.

Barlow gained for himself a somewhat unsavoury reputation but there can be no doubting either the sincerity of his Protestant convictions or his intentions in the determined efforts he made to root out superstitions and the relics of the old religion. He was, it is true, ignorant of the people whom he set out to convert, but he was a champion of the New Learning who tried to improve not only the training of his clergy, but also the financial position of the less well paid. Barlow was, however, not his own master and had to temper his zeal with moderation. In

1539 a halt was called to the general religious changes and in the following year his patron, Thomas Cromwell, fell from power. These two events strengthened the hands of his opponents within the diocese and he had to proceed more carefully. But this did not stop his plans on behalf of Protestantism and he struggled manfully until he was translated to Bath and Wells in 1548.

Barlow's successor at St. David's was the Yorkshireman Robert Ferrar who had already acquired some experience of Wales as one of the royal visitors for the Welsh and the border counties in 1547. Ferrar was not the nepotist his predecessor had been; he certainly had more sympathy with the Welsh, and he was to show a much more realistic appreciation of the situation by his willingness to compromise with the old order. Despite this, the conflict which had marred so much of Barlow's episcopate was apparent from the outset of Ferrar's. His attempt to increase the authority of the bishop provoked opposition from the cathedral chapter, within which the hard core was Barlow's former enemies. His endeavours to recover Church estates and rights, alienated to laymen during his predecessor's time, aroused the hostility of powerful clergy and laymen in South Wales. Charges were brought against him, some trivial while others were patently unjust, but a number were serious. A commission was set up in 1552 to examine these charges and Ferrar was found guilty of some of them. He was imprisoned, and was released only to suffer a martyr's death at Carmarthen in 1555. His death certainly created a profound and long-lasting impression, but essentially his efforts met with failure. He had been unable to overcome the problems which faced the Protestant reformers in Wales; he had failed to contain or to overcome the opposition of powerful elements, clerical and lay, and the quarrels between him and his opponents had done considerable harm to the Protestant cause in the region.

In North Wales there was little to parallel Barlow's efforts in St. David's. The bishop of Bangor, John Salcot, was not cast in the same mould as his South Wales counterpart and was frequently absent from his diocese. The front of the stage was, therefore, occupied by men whose motives were much more the result of self-interest than any reforming zeal. There were quarrels, bitter and protracted, such as those between Sir

Richard Bulkeley on the one hand and William Glyn and Edward Gruffydd on the other, which were the result of the conflicting ambitions of rival families. Small wonder that in 1537 the government expressed its dissatisfaction with the progress being made in the religious changes.

The dissolution of the monasteries provoked little or no opposition. Very different, however, was the reaction to the suppression of shrines and pilgrimages which had willing champions in North Wales. Winifred's Well at Holywell, the image of Derfel Gadarn at Llandderfel in Merionethshire, and the relic preserved at the friary in Bangor were objects of special veneration. Equally unpopular were the attacks on Church property which took place during the reign of Edward VI. The expropriation of the collegiate churches, chantries, and guilds, the confiscation of church plate and vestments, the destruction of images, rood screens, and lofts—all these caused grave offence among a people to whom the reformers could offer little in compensation. Their efforts to disseminate the new beliefs foundered on the rocks of the language difficulty.

In North Wales, then, no more than in the South, had the Reformation made any positive impact upon the Welsh people before Mary ascended the throne in 1553.

The reaction under Mary

Mary's restoration of the old religion provoked no general opposition in Wales. There were, for instance, three martyrdoms only in the country—those of Robert Ferrar, Rawlins White, and William Nichol. It is true that many among the names of those who suffered martyrdom in England suggest the Welsh origins of their owners and that Ferrar's death did leave a very deep impression upon the people of the south-west. But the new cause did not draw much strength in Wales from the blood of its martyrs during the years of Mary's persecution. It is less easy to discover the number of those who were deprived for heresy, but here again the indications are that it was very small. Those Welshmen who left the country to escape persecution numbered some half a dozen, and of these the most prominent, Richard Davies, had not held a living in Wales.

It was the issue of clerical marriage which produced the most positive impact in Wales. Marriage had been a fairly general practice among Welsh priests for centuries, and many had taken advantage of the laws passed in 1549 permitting clerical marriage to regularize existing relationships. These laws were repealed in Mary's first Parliament and a decree followed which prohibited a priest to minister and to say Mass after 20 December 1553 if he were married. This did lead to a substantial number of deprivations in both St. David's and Bangor. Again precise numbers are unobtainable but it has been suggested that in St. David's about sixty-five and in Bangor some fifteen priests lost their livings on this issue.

On the face of it, then, it would seem that in Wales Mary's policy met with a considerable measure of success; nor would it be difficult to advance an explanation for this. But the permanence of the success can be measured by the reaction of the Welsh clergy to the Elizabethan settlement. Among the upper clergy this occasioned significant changes—of the four bishoprics two were vacant—Bangor and St. Asaph; Henry Morgan, Bishop of St. David's, was deprived. Morris Clynnog, who was elected but not consecrated Bishop of Bangor, had gone into exile when Mary died. Anthony Kitchin of Llandaff was able to stretch his conscience sufficiently to accept the new order. There were numerous deprivations among the upper clergy, many of whom had been Marian appointments. In St. David's, for instance, six of these lost their livings—among them the Precentor of the Cathedral and the Archdeacon of Brecon; in St. Asaph the same fate befell the Dean, John Lloyd. The mass of the lower clergy, however, seem to have accepted the settlement with little or no difficulty. Mary's restoration of Roman Catholicism produced little protest; her sister's restoration of the Protestant faith occasioned no more, less in fact from the lower clergy among whom there was nothing like the upheaval caused by the penalties imposed by Mary upon the married clergy. Among the holders of key positions in the Church too there were a few who although Catholic like Leveson, Archdeacon of Carmarthen, remained in office under Elizabeth, while others like Thomas Davies, elected Bishop of St. Asaph in 1561, and Thomas Huet, later Precentor of St. David's, accepted all the religious changes of Henry VIII's children with no apparent qualms.

The Welsh people and the religious changes

Profound change usually prompts heroic action. The story of
the Reformation in sixteenth-century Europe is an amalgam
of heroism and sacrifice, cruelty, and horror. Conviction and
zeal dictated men's conduct and inspired deeds of supreme
courage and terrible savagery. In Wales, however, such was not
the case. Lower clergy and laity accepted one change after
another with comparatively little outward show of favour or
hostility. The rejection of papal supremacy under Henry VIII,
the doctrinal changes under his son, Mary's reversal of their
revolution and her sister's compromise settlement—none of these
seems to have aroused in the Welsh the passions felt by their
European, or even English, contemporaries. All this poses a
number of questions. If the Welsh were, as is generally accepted,
not ready for the Reformation, why did they not show more
spirit in the defence of their old Church? If, as is agreed, the
monasteries were popular in many parts of the country, why
was there no organized protest at their dissolution? If it was the
age-old ritual which bound the Welsh to the old faith, why did
they not object to its destruction? If they were truly Catholic
at heart, why did so many among their clergy abandon their
vocation rather than sacrifice the comforts of married life?
The apparent inference must surely be that either the Welsh
were not so well grounded in the Catholic faith as has been
thought or that they were not of the stuff of which heroes are
made. Either there was too little for which they were prepared
to offer their lives or there was among them a more than
ordinary reluctance to risk their lives. There is, however, no
straightforward answer to such difficult questions.

Those factors which predisposed Welshmen against religious
change have already been noted. There were, however, some
whose convictions, though they may not have been such as to
produce agitation for change, would allow them to accept the
changes which took place during the first phase of the Reformation. In the literature of the middle decades of the century it is
possible to detect reformist undertones and favourable reactions
to the religious changes. More significant, perhaps, was the
popularity which the early Tudors were able to command in
Wales. There was the emotional connection which was, no

doubt, exploited to the full and helped to guarantee the loyalty
of the Welsh. The changes in religion coincided with a more
positive attempt at the effective administration of Wales and
could well have been considered an integral part of this latter
by some Welshmen of the time. These would approve whole-
heartedly the reflection at local level of the Erastian principle
which was so apparent in the political thinking at the centre
of government. Moreover, the government was not unaware
of the climate of opinion in Wales—certainly not that of the
politically significant. Thomas Cromwell received from his
agents, nominees, and correspondents in Wales reports which
guaranteed this.

There were, in addition, other non-ecclesiastical factors in
operation. Much of the land of the Church was already leased
out to individual laymen—there were the estates of the Abbey
of Whitland, for instance, which before the Reformation were
leased for a term of ninety-nine years. Some had been able to
secularize Church property—the Carne family had done this to
the manor of Nash in Glamorgan. So firm a hold had some lay
officials established on ecclesiastical property that they treated
it as their own. Important in this context was the fact that the
natural leaders of the old order, the feudal aristocracy, who had
exercised control over many aspects of Church life and who
would be more positively opposed to royal control over the
Church, had been more effectively destroyed in Wales than in
England. In Wales, the leaders were the new men, allies of the
Crown and supporters of any change which would benefit
themselves.

Finally, there were those more apparently relevant conditions.
The Church itself in Wales cannot have been in a condition to
defend itself effectively—its leaders were aliens, the rank and
file of its clergy for a great part but ill qualified to fulfil their
responsibilities, and between them both there was a wide
cleavage—economic, cultural, and linguistic. The hold of the
Church upon an illiterate peasantry bore a direct relationship
to the impact exercised upon them by its clergy. There was
little hope that these could rally the people of Wales to the
defence of the Church. Then there was the quality of the
religious experience of the mass of the Welsh people. In this
respect the weaknesses of the pre-Reformation Church had

produced a superficiality in which credulity and superstition were some of the most notable ingredients. Not unnaturally, it was the attacks upon their images and shrines which elicited a response from the people. But they were not such as to evoke martyrdom, if only because in a remote, sparsely populated country it was comparatively easy to continue undetected the age-old practices which constituted the greater part of popular religion in Wales.

These were the factors which predetermined the response of the Welsh people to the religious changes initiated by Henry VIII. But, significantly enough, while they paralysed any possible defence of the old religion, they did not guarantee any success for the new. The first phase of the Reformation in Wales was a failure. It failed partly because the people were not ready for it, partly because its leaders were unable to overcome the problems created by the social and cultural conditions which prevailed in Wales. There were too the clash of personalities among those involved and the conflicts provoked by the methods adopted by the champions of the new religion. Chapter politics made impossible concerted action from inside the Church and the limitations imposed by the secular leaders of society upon their allegiance to the new religion minimized pressure from outside. The controversy and conflict which all this produced bewildered and affronted a people who failed to understand why 'Jesus had been made the occasion of wrangling'.

The prospect of Mary's successful restoration of the old religion may well have appeared likely. In the event she failed, not as in England because her methods produced opposition and created resentment, but because she too was unable to make a strong enough impact upon the people. Her Church failed to provide the necessary drive and zeal, for many among its lower clergy were unconvinced and uninvolved. Among a people to many of whom points of theology meant little or nothing, her turnabout made confusion worse, or was irrelevant. They followed the lead of their betters, the degree of whose religious attachment was tempered by their own self-interest. The gentry families had acquired a vested interest in the Protestant Church: however real their innermost loyalties were to the old faith, they were not prepared to risk the gains which the religious revolution had offered them by shaping their conduct to conform to these.

Finally, the settlement by Elizabeth succeeded partly because there was, indeed there could be, no frenzied revolution. Elizabeth could not be too exacting in the matter of doctrinal orthodoxy during her early years. Such was the scarcity of clergy that bishops were compelled to accept men of whose religious views they did not really approve; such was the ignorance among many of them that deep convictions would not be expected. Moreover, clergy and people were given time to adjust themselves for they were not presented with the immediate problem of divided loyalty. Elizabeth's settlement had to face no declaration of papal displeasure for some years, not in fact until 1570; and this meant that the Elizabethan bishops in Wales were given the opportunity to establish the new Church. But this does not imply any early success, for the task of consolidation and of winning the Welsh over to Protestantism was to prove an arduous undertaking, one which was not to be accomplished without the expenditure of much time, care, and effort.

SUGGESTED READING

Glanmor Williams: *The Welsh Church from Conquest to Reformation*. Cardiff, 1962.

—— *Welsh Reformation Essays*. Cardiff, 1968 (contains some of the many valuable articles written by Professor Williams on various aspects of the Reformation in Wales).

A. H. Dodd: *The Church in Wales in the Age of the Reformation*. Welsh Church Congress handbook, 1935.

M. V. J. Seaborne: *The Reformation in Wales*. London, 1952.

W. Ambrose Bebb: *Machlud y Mynachlogydd*. Aberystwyth, 1937.

7. The Religious Settlement Implemented and Defended

ELIZABETH's religious settlement of 1559 was based upon the Acts of Supremacy and Uniformity. The former imposed much narrower limits upon royal authority over the Church than had been exercised by Elizabeth's father and brother. The title of Supreme Governor which she adopted reflected this new interpretation of the powers which she exercised, for they were jurisdictional only—but it did establish royal supremacy. The second of the Acts enjoined the use of the Prayer Book which differed substantially from that of 1552 and was intended to be more acceptable to the conservative elements among the English people than its predecessor had been. On the one hand she insisted upon identifying her Church with the State, on the other she resisted the demands of the returned exiles who hoped for a more radical Protestant Church. By so doing, she guaranteed support for her Church from the moderate majority among her subjects, but inevitably provoked the opposition of convinced Roman Catholics and committed Protestant extremists.

In Wales, as in England, the new Church came under fire from its own supporters as well as from dissident elements. There were the critics who were obsessed by the failure of the Church to establish itself and its faith among the Welsh, by its inability to provide the teaching and guidance which would alone safeguard the spiritual health of the people. Some of the most severe of these were to be found in the ranks of the clergy themselves, and the leaders of the young Church were often appalled by the task that confronted them. They drew attention to the inadequacies of the Church—the ruinous state of some of its buildings was perhaps one of the most obvious. William Bleddyn, Bishop of Llandaff, for instance, went so far as to say that 'Horses graze and, alas, pigs are fattened in the houses once dedicated to God'.[1] Equally apparent were the paucity of clergymen and the low standards and absence of a sense of vocation which characterized too many of them. Bishop Richard Davies's report of 1569–70 on the state of his diocese makes sorry reading. He observed that 'some priests in the diocese have remained a whole twelvemonth together incorrigible, some in fornication and some against all Injunctions to the contrary, taking upon them to serve three or four yea sometimes five cures; but never one aright'. Of many of the churches he commented that they 'for the most part of this time have not whole Service once in a year; but upon Sundays and holy days the Epistle and the Gospel or suffrages only' and that they were served by 'a priest that shall come thither galloping from another parish, which for such pains shall have xls a year, iiij or marks or iiij li the best'.[2] Then there was the crippling effect of poverty, the paralysis produced by excessive secular influence, and the frustration caused by the obstructionism of many among the local government officials. To these reasons were attributed the low standards of spiritual life in Wales, the lack of popular respect for the Church and the perpetuation of the relics of popery, all of which were prominent features of the Wales of the late sixteenth and early seventeenth centuries.

There is no doubt that all these weaknesses did exist, but the general conclusion which was drawn is more open to question. The shortcomings of the Church do constitute one major reason for its failure to exercise the desired impact, but they certainly do not provide the complete explanation. There were enormous difficulties to be overcome—difficulties which had existed from its inception. The task of inculcating a new set of religious beliefs among a people the social and economic conditions of whose lives predisposed them to conservatism was complicated by the fact that the new faith required a measure of understanding denied to its uneducated majority. The production of a body of religious literature in a language which the people could understand was in itself a major undertaking, but one whose value was minimized by the fact that the vast majority of the people would be unable to read it. This placed a heavy

---

[1] For the speeches of William Bleddyn, see J. A. Bradney: *Y Cymmr.*, xxxl, 1921.
[2] For Richard Davies's Report of 1569/70, see D. R. Thomas: *Davies and Salesbury*, pp. 37–44.

burden of responsibility upon the parish clergy, recruitment into whose ranks was no easy matter in a country where grammar schools were few and the general poverty such as to impose strict limits upon the numbers of their pupils. These were the problems which, unless they could be overcome, made an easy victory for the new Church impossible. But the Church—even had it been free of those weaknesses which its critics were quick to note—could not solve these problems alone. Under the circumstances, all that it could reasonably hope for was that its efforts would hasten the process of familiarizing the people with a new faith, and wean them away from one to which they had clung for centuries. This of necessity was a slow and arduous process. The Church's failure has received ample comment, the measure of its success has perhaps been given less than its due attention.

The provision of religious literature

Despite the claims of Richard Davies and William Salesbury, it is most unlikely that there had been any extensive translation of the Scriptures into Welsh before the sixteenth century. Certain important passages had been translated and there did exist at least one book in Welsh which contained the history of the Jews as told in the Old Testament. For more than this there existed neither the religious incentive nor the interest. It was the peculiar conditions of the Tudor period which made a translation both possible and desirable. The higher standard of linguistic scholarship combined with the possibility of large-scale publishing and the particular need for a vernacular version of the Scriptures by the new Protestant faith to make a translation a practicable proposition. That it was needed had been emphasized by the failure of the first attempt to establish the Protestant Church in Wales.

The years before Mary's Catholic reaction had seen some attempt to meet this need. In 1547 Sir John Price was responsible for the publication of a book which contained Welsh versions of parts of the Scriptures. In the same year, too, was published William Salesbury's *Oll Synnwyr Pen Cymro* (The Welshman's Common Sense), a collection of proverbs which was designed to help in the work of translating the Scriptures into Welsh. Then in 1551 followed Salesbury's *Cynnifer Llith a Ban o'r Ysgrythur lan*[1] which contained translations of the epistles and gospels which were read in churches at Communions, on Sundays and holy days. This was the nearest Welsh equivalent to the English Prayer Book and was used when the Bishop of St. Asaph, Thomas Davies, in 1561 ordered that the epistles and the gospels were to be read in Welsh in the churches of his diocese. During Mary's reign Salesbury was in hiding, probably busying himself with the translation of the New Testament. Elizabeth's accession prompted the return of the Protestant exiles from Geneva and Germany, and among them was Richard Davies whose appointment as Bishop of St. Asaph brought him without doubt into contact with Salesbury. Together these two were to lay the sure foundations of a Welsh version of the Scriptures.

In 1563 the Act was passed ordering the translation of the Scriptures into Welsh. How much of the credit for this Act should be given to Richard Davies it is difficult to say—it is significant that he alone of the Welsh bishops was present in the House of Lords for all three readings of the Bill. The work of translating the Bible and the Book of Common Prayer was to be accomplished within three years and was to be the joint responsibility of the four bishops of Wales together with the Bishop of Hereford. As soon as this was accomplished the whole of the divine service in the Welsh-speaking parts of the country was to be conducted in the Welsh language. In the meantime, the epistle and gospel of the day was to be read in Welsh at every Communion service, and once a week the clergy were to read to their parishioners the Lord's Prayer, the Articles of the Christian Faith, the Ten Commandments, the Litany, and such other part of the Divine Service as the bishop of the diocese should decide. English and Welsh versions of the Bible and the Book of Common Prayer were to be placed in every church throughout Wales, and made available to everyone who wished to read them. Despite its weaknesses—the inadequate arrangements made for financing the work and the insufficient time allowed for its completion—the Act of 1563 was a significant advance. It was, after all, the first formal recognition by the

[1] The full title of the book may be translated as: 'As many passages of Holy Scripture as are read in Church on Sundays and Holy Days throughout the year.'

government of the right to use the Welsh language in public worship.

Richard Davies, who had been translated to St. David's in 1561, invited Salesbury to join him at St. David's and from 1565 they were engaged in their great task. Then in 1567 the New Testament and the Book of Common Prayer were published in Welsh. Salesbury shouldered the greater part of the burden—it was he who translated the Prayer Book and the major portion of the New Testament. Of the latter Richard Davies's contribution was the first Epistle to Timothy, that to the Hebrews, the first two epistles of Peter and that of James, while Thomas Huet, Precentor of St. David's, translated the Book of Revelation. The oddities of Salesbury's orthography provoked some hostile criticism, but on all counts the work of translation was a remarkable achievement. Davies and Salesbury had intended that it should be followed by a Welsh version of the Old Testament, but their important partnership came to an end with a quarrel of whose cause little or nothing is known. It was not until 1588 that a Welsh version of the Bible was published.

This was the work of William Morgan, who did the greater part of the translating while vicar of Llanrhaeadr-ym-mochnant, to which living he was appointed in 1578. It was a remarkable achievement for in addition to the demands of his pastoral responsibilities he was harassed throughout this time by bitter quarrels with some of his parishioners. Even more remarkable was the quality of the work, in which was combined the purity of language of traditional Welsh literature and the greater flexibility of more recent usage. It would be difficult to exaggerate the impact which William Morgan's Bible has exerted upon the history of the Welsh people. It, more than any other single factor, has been responsible for the continued existence of the Welsh language; its prose became the model for subsequent Welsh writers. It opened a new era in the literature of Wales; to the people it offered the means whereby they could identify themselves as a nation. And contemporaries were quick to appreciate the importance of William Morgan's translation—Maurice Kyffin, for instance, asserted that he had placed the Welsh people for ever in his debt. Thus was accomplished the first major phase in the task of making the Scriptures available

H

to the Welsh people in the language which they could understand.

The translation of 1588 was revised, and a new edition appeared in 1620 under the name of Richard Parry, Bishop of St. Asaph, although it appears that Dr. John Davies, Mallwyd, was responsible for most of the preparatory work. Then in 1630 appeared the first cheap edition of the Bible in Welsh, 'y beibl bach coron', the cost of whose publication was borne by a group of London Welshmen of whom Sir Thomas Myddleton and Rowland Heylin were the most prominent. In the meantime, William Morgan had published his translation of the Psalms in Welsh in the same year as his Bible had appeared. Their potential as a means of involving the congregation in divine service was realized when first William Midleton and then Edmwnd Prys produced their metrical versions. These filled the role which hymns were later to occupy in the services of the church.

Complementary to the versions of the Scriptures were the service books which were published. Here again the pioneer was William Salesbury whose *Cynniver Llith a Ban* was intended to give Welsh people a version of the Book of Common Prayer published in English in 1549. He also contributed substantially to the first official Prayer Book of 1567, of which other editions appeared at regular intervals. The needs of the parish priests were also met by the frequent reprinting of the Book of Matins (*Llyfr Plygain*) which appeared consistently during the late sixteenth and early seventeenth centuries, and by the publication in 1606 of Edward James's Book of Homilies (*Llyfr yr Homiliau*).

In addition to all this, many English theological works were translated into Welsh whose intention was to present the Anglican case to the Welsh people. In 1595 appeared two important works—Maurice Kyffin's translation of Jewel's *Apologia* under the title *Deffyniad Ffydd Eglwys Loegr* and Huw Lewys's *Perl mewn Adfyd*, a translation of Coverdale's *A Spiritual and Most Precious Pearl*. Two works again appeared in 1630— Rowland Vaughan's *Yr Ymarfer o Dduwioldeb* and Robert Llwyd's *Llwybr hyffordd yn cyfarwyddo yr anghyfarwydd i'r nefoedd*, the first a translation of Lewis Bayley's *Practice of Piety* and the second of Dent's *Plain Pathway to Heaven*. The major concern of all these was the religious and moral well-being of the Welsh people which could best be served by Bible-reading. It was to this end that the Church leaders urged the cause of education, laying particular emphasis on the ability to read in Welsh, for the most immediately effective step was the creation of a Welsh Bible-reading public. This explains the emphasis which was laid upon the antiquity and excellence of the Welsh language—a proper pride in their language would be the most effective incentive for the people to learn to read it. It would, moreover, help to overcome the objections that the new faith was an alien religion in a foreign guise.

The immediate impact of the Welsh version of the Scripture could only be measured in terms of the reading public of Wales, and there can be little doubt that before the mid eighteenth century this was very limited. It is true that Sir John Price claimed in 1547 that there were many Welsh people who could read in Welsh, but this seems to be more the result of wishful thinking than of real knowledge of the situation. Vicar Prichard writing in the early seventeenth century asserted that less than one in a hundred was capable of so doing. Moreover, it must be remembered that the cheap edition of 1630 cost as much as did a sheep, so that it was still out of the reach of the vast majority of the people. The value of the translation lay in the fact that it was now possible for services to be conducted in Welsh and that the congregations could hear the Bible read to them in a language which they understood. There were the few who could now go to the parish church to read the Scriptures and no doubt there were others who found in the existence of a Welsh version an incentive to master the skill of reading.

One feature of the work of translation was the opportunity which it provided for the spread of Protestant propaganda. Richard Davies, for instance, in his preface to the New Testament argued at length that the Reformation was the restoration of the old Church of the Welsh purified of the grossness which had been imposed upon it after the triumph of the Roman Church. This was more than a mere counterblast to the charge that Protestantism was an imported English faith. It was an appeal to the sense of nationalism of the Welsh, an appeal which derived strength from the fact that the new religion could now be presented to them in their own language. Too much must not, of course, be made of the efficacy of this propaganda, but it does serve to show the awareness which existed among the leaders of the new Church of the need to 'sell' their Church and their efforts in this direction.

The provision of a body of religious literature was the outstanding, but by no means the only, achievement of the established Church during the reigns of Elizabeth and her successors. One of its most striking features was the better leadership which it enjoyed. The bishops were, many of them, in contrast to a number of their predecessors, men of learning, who resided within their dioceses and enjoyed the advantage of local family connections. They were energetic and courageous: they set themselves high standards and were acutely aware of their own failings and their Church's shortcomings. At St. David's Richard Davies's chief claim to fame was his part in the translation of the New Testament, at Bangor Nicholas Robinson earned for himself the reputation of 'persecutor' by the zeal which he showed in crushing recusancy. But both laboured prodigiously in many other directions to establish their Church in the affections of their fellow countrymen. At St. Asaph there were the Davieses, first Richard, then Thomas who did much to improve the administration of the diocese; at Llandaff, occupied for so long by Anthony Kitchin, William Blethyn could claim that 'More than all others I have laboured and toiled for ten years, travelling about, according to the pressing need, that I may preach the Gospel'. Their successors, for the most part, struggled manfully in the face of tremendous difficulties to build on the foundations which these men laid.

The bishops succeeded in raising the standard of recruitment into the Church. Gradually the ranks of the upper clergy were increasingly filled by men of ability, who were Welsh by birth and resident in their benefices; in growing numbers, too, the younger sons of the gentry and freeholders of substance were attracted to the service of the Church. Most of these had been educated at the grammar schools which were being founded in Wales, and a number of them at one or other of the older universities. Of the hundred and thirty or so Pembrokeshire families which Dwnn considered sufficiently well born to merit attention from the King-at-Arms thirty-one were those of beneficed clergymen. What was true of St. David's was also a feature of the other Welsh dioceses. Many of them were able to offer their parishioners spiritual guidance in the language which they could understand, others were patrons of local bards or themselves poets of modest merit, while others busied themselves with one or other aspect of the New Learning.

This is not to say that the Church found eager applicants for holy orders. The paucity of preaching clergymen was a difficulty for which the poverty of the Church made a satisfactory solution impossible. Nevertheless, there were determined efforts to make a career in the Church more attractive to the sons of the well-to-do. These were aided by the working of economic forces, for in the majority of livings a substantial portion of the clerical income was made up of returns in kind from the glebe and the tithe. During a period of rising prices this operated in favour of the clergymen. Between 1535 and 1583 the incomes of the clergy of St. David's had, according to Bishop Middleton, trebled in value. This price trend was doubly advantageous for the many among the clergy who supplemented their incomes by farming. The result of this is seen in the increasing prosperity of many of the Welsh clergy during the late sixteenth and early seventeenth centuries. William Myryck, vicar of Beguildy in Radnorshire, for instance, who died in 1577, left an estate which comprised livestock to the value of £13. 18s. 8d. and household stuff valued at £4. This would seem to indicate a standard of living comparable to that enjoyed by a fairly well-to-do small farmer.

At the same time, the bishops made the best use of their slender resources. William Morgan in 1601 arranged that forty-four sermons should be preached annually by members of the cathedral chapter at St. Asaph. One of his successors, Bishop Owen, instructed that Welsh sermons be preached in the parish church of St. Asaph on the first Sunday in each month by those members of the cathedral chapter who received a portion of their stipends from the tithes of the parish. Nor was it only the leaders of the Church who appreciated the importance of this new element in the church service. Prosperous laymen also made provision for the preaching of sermons. Sir William Meredith of Stansty left £30 'for the wages of a Preacher at Wrexham for one year'; Sir John Hanmer in 1624 bequeathed the corn tithes of Bettisfield to pay a learned and painful preacher give a sermon twice every Sabbath day in the parish church. Among his other charitable bequests, Sir David Williams of Gwernyfed in Breconshire allowed for three annual sums of ten shillings from the great tithes of the parish of Gwenddwr to endow sermons at Glasbury on Palm Sunday, at Ystradfellte on Whit-Sunday, and at Aberllynfi on Trinity Sunday. Thomas Atkins, alderman of Carmarthen, provided in his will for two sermons to be preached in the town annually, on Christmas day and Ascension day, ten shillings to be paid for each sermon. These and other similar bequests did not, of course, meet the requirements of Wales but they did help in some measure to fill some gaps.

The government, too, made some effort to raise the general standard of efficiency of the Church. The thirty-fourth canon of 1604 laid down minimum requirements in respect of the learning and education demanded of the clergy, specified the conditions as to age of entry, and insisted upon the testimony of grave ministers upon the aspiring ordinands. The Archbishop of Canterbury's letter of the following year expressed the royal disapproval of pluralism, required the names of those holding more than one living and the distances between these livings, and requested reports on those whose curates were poorly paid and insufficient. In 1633 royal instructions were issued insisting that bishops should reside at one or other of their episcopal houses. Attempts to limit the control of the laity were also made —in 1632 Charles I emphasized the need to recover for the Crown the patronage of livings which had fallen into other hands and in 1634 an instruction was issued urging the reversal of the practice of lengthening the leases on Church property.

Impressive as is the record of the Church between 1559 and 1640 there is, nevertheless, no denying that its efforts were insufficient either to establish itself in the affections of the people, or to provide the spiritual leadership which it was its duty to afford. This was partly the result of its own inadequacies; but no small measure of responsibility for the failure must be laid at the door of the Church's natural allies, the Crown and its local agents, as well as the more grasping among the gentry. Over and above all these, were the enormous problems posed by the nature of Welsh society which predetermined the response of the Welsh people to religious change.

The Catholic reaction

The majority of the Welsh people both clergy and laity conformed to the Settlement of Religion of Elizabeth, though their acceptance of it was frequently the product more of self-interest than of any real conviction. Their outward conformity did not prevent a number of the clergy from saying mass in secret, nor many among the gentry from showing a marked lack of concern in persecuting recusancy, nor the continuance among the people of pilgrimage-going and of shrine-worshipping. It may well have been indeed that a discreet closing of the eye in official quarters to such practices constituted one important reason for the general acceptance of the new Church, and helps to explain why there was in Wales hardly an echo of the rising of the northern earls in 1569. But neither the bishops nor the government can have been satisfied with the state of religion in Wales. As early as 1563 the persistence of relics and the superstitious observances of the old faith elicited the complaint that Wales was 'in an evil condition as to religion'. This official dissatisfaction was to become more apparent with the passage of time—when Catholic plots were hatched against the queen, when reports of Catholic activity became more frequent and when the government took a firmer line with the champions of the old faith.

There seems to have been very little Catholic recusancy during the early years of Elizabeth's reign. In the diocese of Bangor was reported, only one persistent recusant though there was a refusal to attend church on the part of some men living in Llŷn and Eifionydd; in St. Asaph there was no one and in St. David's only one old man, living in Radnorshire. In Llandaff, however, there were thirteen recusants of whom eleven were inhabitants of Monmouthshire and their number included one justice of the peace, Thomas Carne of Ewenni. It is doubtful whether anyone really believed that this was a true reflection of Welsh sympathies. If so, it changed. The energetic Whitgift who for a period was Vice-President of the Council of Wales and the Marches during the absence of the more tolerant Sidney, complained in 1577 of the secret masses being held in private houses, of clandestine baptisms, and of the burials at night to avoid the funeral service.

Among the factors responsible for the persistence of the old faith in various parts of Wales one of the most interesting was the influence of the prominent families. In the Creuddyn, for instance, part of which lies within the diocese of St. Asaph, there was a group of twelve recusants, the nucleus of which was the influential family of the Pughs. Members of two prominent North Wales families, Thomas Salusbury of Llyweni and Edward Jones of Plas Cadwgan, were implicated in the Babington conspiracy and were executed. In east Montgomeryshire there were two bodies of recusants, at Welshpool and Guildsfield, of whom members of the Herbert family were the most important, and it seems not unlikely that they had the sympathy of Sir Edward Herbert. In Glamorgan the local power of the Turberville family explains the recusants of the parishes of Colwinston and Penlline, while in Monmouthshire, notorious for its recusancy, the Morgan family of Llantarnam, the Wolfs of Werngochyn and later the Herberts of Raglan exerted their influence to such effect that their tenants' allegiance to the old Church was considered a part of their copyhold. Roman Catholic groups also survived in the districts near old centres of the faith; it was fairly strong in Flintshire especially in those parishes near Holywell where the well of St. Winifred had for so long been a popular pilgrimage centre. This seems also to have been true of parts of Carmarthenshire, for the Council of Wales and the Marches reported in 1592 that 'Divers people in Carmarthenshire repair in the night time and in daytime to certain places where in the past there have been pilgrimages, images and offerings'. There was also a revival of recusancy in the parts of Wales nearest England and therefore more accessible to those English recusants who were trying to shake off their persecutors. From the Council in 1601 came the report that 'there is great backsliding in Religion in these parts and especially in the confines of the shires between England and Wales as Monmouthshire and the skirts of the shires of Wales bounding upon them'. These and the activity of the Catholic priests were responsible for the survival and, during the 1580s especially, a general increase of recusancy in Wales.

In 1578 a Roman Catholic clique was unearthed among the gentry of Llŷn, the leader of whom appears to have been Thomas Owen of Plas Du—a family which supplied a number of stalwarts to the Catholic cause at this time. The investigation and the subsequent prosecutions did cause a panic among the recusants of the area and this, together with Bishop Robinson's tireless efforts, achieved for a time a higher measure of conformity. In 1582 he claimed that there were only six recusants in his diocese, but in the following year he reported eleven persons to the Great Sessions. In Denbighshire too their number was increasing—to forty-eight in 1592, while in Llandaff recusancy which from the early days of Elizabeth had been fairly strong was by the late 1580s causing some alarm—in the Vale of Glamorgan alone there were forty-two recusants in 1587. There does appear to be some substance to the claim that Roman Catholicism was recovering its hold upon the inhabitants of certain districts. It must, however, be emphasized that recovery was achieved on only a small scale. By the last year of Elizabeth's reign the total number of recusants in Wales amounted to a mere 808, and this out of an approximate population of some 212,450. Their distribution is quite interesting—32 in the diocese of Bangor, 250 in St. Asaph, 381 in Llandaff, and 145 in St. David's. Of these the vast majority were members of the yeoman class; the gentry families had few representatives. Official information concerning recusancy among the latter may, however, be somewhat misleading in that the local officials, themselves drawn from the gentry families, would have been reluctant to report friends and relatives. Nevertheless, it was observed at the time that the recusants did on the whole belong to the socially less significant elements of Welsh society.

Of those Welshmen who refused to accept the Elizabethan settlement the most prominent were Dr. Morgan Phillips, the Precentor of St. David's, Owen Lewis who became the Bishop of Cassano, Rhosier Smyth, Morris Clynnog, Bishop-designate of Bangor in 1558, who became the Warden of the English College at Rome, and Dr. Gruffydd Robert, appointed Archdeacon of Anglesey in 1558, who became Canon of Milan Cathedral. These men played an active part in the religious developments on the Continent during the second half of the sixteenth century. Phillips and Lewis with William Allen founded the College at Douay to train priests for the reconversion of England—in the ten years following 1568 the College dispatched some hundred priests to England.

Though the Catholic missionaries in Wales failed to win back the Welsh to their faith, their courage and self-sacrifice created a deep impression upon those among whom they worked. The schoolmaster Richard Gwyn of Llanidloes in Montgomeryshire who taught in the Wrexham district was in 1584 the first Welsh Catholic to die a martyr's death. It was William Davies of Colwyn in Denbighshire who brought with him from the Continent a copy of Gruffydd Robert's book, *Y Drych Cristionogawl* (The Christian Mirror). This was re-printed at Rhiwledyn, where the group of Roman Catholics, to whose spiritual needs William Davies ministered, had set up a secret press. Despite the protection of Robert Pugh of Penrhyn Creuddyn, Davies was captured and, after unsuccessful attempts by the authorities to persuade him to abandon his faith, was hanged in 1593. Morris Clynnog himself officiated at the mass celebrated in an old chapel near the home of David ap Jevan of Margam in 1591, which was attended by some 180 people. The Jesuit Robert Jones's tireless efforts in Monmouth-shire earned him the reputation of being 'the firebrand of all'. There were Welsh Catholics, too, who worked in England—and suffered for it—men like John (or Griffith) Jones of Clynnog who died a martyr's death in 1598, John Roberts of Trawsfynydd and Philip Powell of Breconshire who met the same fate in 1610 and 1648 respectively.

In 1578 an English College was established at Rome with Morris Clynnog, who had in 1568 published his *Athravaeth Cristnogawl* (Christian Doctrine), as its first warden. Clynnog's alleged partiality to Welsh students at the College sparked off a quarrel between the Welsh Catholics on the Continent and the powerful Jesuits. The latter represented the physical force element in the Counter Reformation while the Welsh exiles, for the most part, favoured spiritual force. They believed that the people could be 'secretly persuaded' to remain loyal to Catholicism on the grounds that their religious beliefs were independent of the wishes of the government. To this end they published in Welsh a number of expositions of the Catholic religion—Morris Clynnog's book was one, Gruffydd Robert's another. Both of these were designed to present the Catholic point of view in simple terms for the uneducated majority. The latter, incidentally, was the first Welsh book to be printed in Wales. Aimed at a smaller public were the translations into Welsh of the works of the great Catholic theologians, books like Hugh Owen's *Dilyniad Crist*, a translation of Thomas à Kempis's *Imitatio Chrisit*, and Rhosier Smyth's translations of the works of Canisius and of *Theater du Mond*, under the title *Gorsedd y Byd* in 1615.

The Jesuits did have some supporters among the Welsh Catholics. One of the most prominent was John Salusbury of Rug who published *A Comprehensive Exposition*, a translation of another standard exposition of Catholic theology, in 1618. But the fundamental disagreement which found expression in the controversy over the English College at Rome was a significant factor in the neglect of Wales by the Catholic missions. The Jesuits won the day—they gained control over the College and other seminaries on the Continent, and as a result of the regulations which they imposed the number of Welsh students at the Catholic seminaries of Europe declined.

This was, however, only one among many of the reasons why the Roman Catholic Church failed to exert anything more than a marginal impact upon Wales during the late sixteenth and early seventeenth centuries. Its leaders appear to have miscalculated badly the strength of Welsh Catholicism—a report from Douay in 1602 suggested that recusancy was very strong in Wales, so strong that no royal official dared apprehend the recusants. This led them to neglect Wales in order to concentrate their efforts upon areas where missionary activity appeared to be more necessary. They may well have been encouraged in this view by the comparative insignificance of Wales, and discouraged by the problems involved in the task of reconversion in Wales. The very conditions which made the work of the leaders of the established Church so difficult also placed obstacles in the path of any would-be campaign for reconversion. The small number of suitably qualified priests had little chance of success against the massive ignorance and the high degree of illiteracy which existed among the Welsh people. Then there were those factors which made for a quiet acceptance of the established order of things. There was the emotional loyalty of the Welsh people to the Tudor family, which was supported by a growing sense of political responsibility among the Welsh gentry. The dictates of self-interest also bore particularly strongly upon the leaders of Welsh society, many of whom had acquired a vested interest in the Protestant Reformation. Not surprisingly, sympathy for the old Church remained dormant among the majority of the people and in course of time disappeared completely.

The Puritans

From the outset there were many among the clergy and laity who were aware of the shortcomings of the established Church and doubtful of any prospect of success in the face of the enormous difficulties which faced it in Wales. They were, too, deeply concerned at the generally low level of religious and moral standards among the Welsh people. The only hope of consolidating the Reformation, as they saw it, was positive action by an efficient Protestant Church which could command the loyalty of the people. But, in addition to being faced by the threat posed by the forces of Catholicism, the Church found its effectiveness was substantially reduced by its own inefficiency. This last was in large measure the result of two factors—the Church's poverty and the measure of control exercised upon it by laymen. They accounted, in part, for the serious manpower shortage, for the pluralism and consequent absenteeism, for the inadequacies of many among its clergy—all of which reduced to a minimum its impact upon large sections of the laity. This was responsible for the slow progress achieved by Protestantism and the low moral standards among a laity which had little respect for the Church.

It was to remedy this state of affairs that some men were inspired to action—to remove the abuses of the contemporary Church and to propose measures which would supplement its efforts. At first there was no criticism of the organization of the Church or of its teachings; but the failure of the Church and the authorities to respond to the efforts of the critics drove some of them on to more extreme paths. The most significant of these was John Penry. His initial concern was the spiritual welfare of the Welsh people whose salvation he wished to guarantee by giving them that necessary 'saving knowledge' of God. To achieve this, ignorance and superstition had to be eradicated, profanity and immorality removed, and it was to this end that he addressed himself in 1587 and 1588 to Parliament and the government. When his appeals proved of no avail he launched an attack upon the episcopacy and the complexity of the church services and finally challenged the right of the civil authority to determine the religious beliefs of the individual. Disillusionment at the failure of his advocacy of reform had driven Penry to occupy a position outside the established Church: in this he found little sympathy and no support in the Wales of his day.

This is not to say that there were none who shared his concern for the deficiencies of the Church, for the absence of the Scriptures, and for the conduct and moral standards of the laity. These were the men responsible for the publication of a number of the devotional works in Welsh during the late sixteenth and early seventeenth centuries. Some were clergymen, others laymen living in Wales, yet others were London Welshmen. Some of the clergy were making positive efforts to raise standards in other ways. Outstanding among these was Rees Prichard of Llandovery whose sermons in verse are now his chief claim to fame, but who was also an able and conscientious minister. He was outspoken in his condemnation of the low moral standards which characterized all sections of his fellow countrymen and uncompromising in his attacks upon feebler colleagues in the Church. His eloquence attracted such huge congregations that he had to preach in the churchyard— a practice frowned upon by the more conventional. He urged his listeners to practise family devotions, to read the Bible, and to observe the sanctity of the Sabbath. All this would have found favour with the Puritans. It helps to explain why his songs were first published under the title *Canwyll y Cymry* (The Welshman's Candle) by that most vigorous Welsh Puritan of the seventeenth century, Stephen Hughes, and accounts for his being numbered among the Puritans by later writers. But he was a true churchman, approved by Laud himself who, when the crisis between king and Parliament was reached, proved his loyalty to Charles by the financial support which he gave the royalist cause.

The need for a preaching ministry led to the establishment of the lecture system whereby unbeneficed men were permitted to 'teach, preach, and catechise'—in the market towns for the most part. This system operated from 1620 to 1636, but with only the grudging approval of the government which placed specific limits upon its efficacy. There were strict rules concerning the issue of these licences; lecturers were permitted to preach only upon some part of the Catechism or on some text taken from the Creed, the Ten Commandments, or the Lord's Prayer; and in 1633 they were allowed to catechise only in the afternoon and to read divine service according to the liturgy. These restrictions were the result in part of the Puritan sympathies displayed by a number of the lecturers, many of whom had come under the influence of those English Puritans who had gathered together in the trading towns of the west of England, especially Bristol.

Despite the efforts of the authorities, evidence of Puritan activity in Wales increased during the 1630s. In 1634 the Bishop of St. David's suspended a lecturer for 'Inconformity' and dismissed a few others for the same reason in the following year. In 1636 he reported Marmaduke Matthews, vicar of Penmaen, for preaching against the observance of holy days, and in 1638 he reported that 'some had been meddling with things forbidden'. Meanwhile in the diocese of Llandaff William Erbury, his curate Walter Cradock, and William Wroth of Llanfaches had been preaching 'very dangerously and schismatically' and had led 'away many simple people'. Wroth and Erbury were brought to the notice of the Court of High Commission and in 1636 they both resigned their livings. Craddock was ejected, to become a curate to Robert Lloyd at Wrexham. The Bishop of St. Asaph, who in 1634 was able to declare that his diocese was free from nonconformity, reported the arrest in 1640 of 'a conventicle of mean persons'. This was probably in the Wrexham district where Walter Craddock was active, and where there was a congregation of Puritans. The Bishop of Hereford in 1639 also complained of Puritan activity on the border of his diocese. 'Brownists', he declared, 'in that part of the diocese adjoining to Wales preach dangerous errors, and stir up the people to follow them. And when they hear of an inquiry they slip over the border to another diocese.' This may well be connected with the Puritan activity in the area where the counties of Brecon, Radnor, and Hereford join, out of which grew the Baptist cause at Olchon. The same year had also seen the establishment of the church at Llanfaches in Monmouthshire by Erbury and Wroth. This was organized according to the 'New England pattern' which, despite important differences, preserved a number of the features of the Church of England and probably maintained connections with the Church. But the Laudian Canons of 1640 permitted no compromise. They insisted upon the acceptance of the doctrines, ceremonies, and government of the Church and instructed all to attend their parish churches to receive Holy Communion. Authority had now called a halt to any form of Puritan activity.

The Civil War

When the conflict between Crown and Parliament began, the vast majority of the clergy remained loyal to the king, and the leading Welsh Puritans dispersed to England. Vavasor Powell took himself to London, the members of Llanfaches retired, for the most part, to Bristol. This was the time of the 'desolation of the Welsh Saints'. But Parliament soon began a positive campaign to raise religious standards and to establish Puritanism in Wales. The Committee for Scandalous Ministers was founded to investigate the matter of the scarcity of preaching ministers, to remove scandalous ministers, and to find replacements for them. Members of Parliament were given the responsibility of informing the House concerning the adequacy of preaching ministers in their respective counties. Parishioners were entitled to maintain a minister at their own charge to preach. Later the direction of the Puritan campaign passed into the hands of the Committee for Plundered Ministers, which was empowered to sequester the livings of scandalous ministers and to replace them with suitable men. County Parliamentary Committees were created to examine charges against scandalous and delinquent ministers and to forward petitions from parishes asking for preaching ministers. A number of Anglican incumbents fulfilled the requirements of the Committee and were allowed to retain their livings or were appointed to others. Humphrey Lloyd, for instance, who succeeded his father as vicar of Ruabon, had been rector of Erbistock since 1626, while Lodowick Lewis had been for nearly thirty years rector of Cosheston in Pembrokeshire before being given the living of Llandyssul in 1646. But there were very many ejections, more so in South Wales than in the North.

In Glamorgan alone thirty-five clergy were removed from their livings, while eighteen suffered the same fate in Monmouthshire.

Parliament was careful not to make the same mistakes as the established Church had committed in Wales. A Committee of the House of Commons was set up in June 1644 to provide Welsh-speaking ministers to accompany Sir Thomas Myddelton on his campaign in the Severn Valley. County committees were instructed to ensure that there should be preaching in Welsh as well as in English in their districts, and this matter must have been an important consideration for the special committee which was established 'to consider the ministers for Wales'. Again, Parliament showed its concern that these ministers should be well provided for—generous payments were made to 'approved' ministers. In 1645 a sum of £300 was set aside from the lands of the see of Llandaff to reward the services of Henry Walter, Walter Cradock, and Richard Symonds, the three itinerant ministers for South Wales, while in June 1648 the Committee for Plundered Ministers ordered the payment of £120 to Morgan Llwyd and £100 each to Vavasor Powell and Ambrose Mostyn, their North Wales counterparts. In return for this the Committee demanded high standards of learning and conduct from its appointees as well as strict obedience to its instructions.

During the 1640s Wales was subjected to Puritan propaganda which, despite some weaknesses, was more effective than had been the efforts of the established Church during the early decades of the century. Sympathy and support had been rallied for Puritanism among a section of the landowners, especially in the south-eastern counties. Churches had been founded, again on the border and in the south-east for the most part. Ministers accompanying the Parliamentary armies had won converts among soldiers and civilians. Too much, perhaps, should not be made of Walter Cradock's claim in 1646 that 'The Gospel has run over the mountains between Breconshire and Monmouthshire as the fire in the thatch'; but the stage had been set for the next part of the Puritan offensive in Wales during the 1650s.

Among the few Welshmen who emigrated to North America before the outbreak of the Civil War were a small number of

Puritans. Some of these accompanied Robert Blinman of Gloucester probably late in 1638 or very early in the following year. One of their number was Marmaduke Matthews, former vicar of Penmaen in Gower, who became pastor of the church at Yarmouth, Massachusetts. At about the same time Griffith Bowen and his family crossed the Atlantic and became members of the church at Boston. Some of these emigrants returned to Wales after the victory of Parliament and the passing of the Propagation Act. They played their part in spreading Puritanism in Wales, and their contribution is an interesting one. The rigid orthodoxy of New England Puritanism had failed to satisfy them and their teaching, when they returned to Wales, contained a mystical, emotional appeal which was lacking in the older, more academic Puritan propagators. This accounted for the very real impression which they were able to create upon their listeners in certain parts of Wales and which, in turn, contributed to the success achieved by the Quakers during the 1650s and the Baptists in West Wales after the Restoration.

SUGGESTED READING

Ven. D. R. Thomas: *The Life and Work of Bishop Davies and William Salesbury*. Oswestry, 1902.

Garfield H. Hughes (ed.): *Rhagymadroddion 1547–1659*. Caerdydd, 1951.

Emyr Gwynne Jones: *Cymru a'r hen ffydd*. Caerdydd, 1951.

O. Aneurin Thomas: *The Welsh Elizabethan Catholic Martyrs*, Cardiff, 1971.

David Williams (ed.): John Penry: *Three Treatises concerning Wales*. Cardiff, 1960.

Thomas Richards: *The Puritan Movement in Wales 1639–1653*. London, 1920.

Articles:

Glanmor Williams: 'Richard Davies, Bishop of St. David's, 1561–81', *Trans. Cymmr.*, 1948.

—— 'The Elizabethan Settlement of Religion in Wales and the Marches', *Jnl. Hist. Soc. Church in Wales*, 11, 1950.

—— 'Wales and the Reformation', *Trans. Cymmr.*, 1966.

J. M. Cleary: 'The Catholic Resistance in Wales, 1568–1678', *Blackfriars*, March 1951.

F. H. Pugh: 'Glamorgan Recusants, 1577–1611', *S. Wales and Mon. Rec. Soc. Pubns.*, 111, 1954.

—— 'Monmouthshire Recusants in the Reigns of Elizabeth and James I', ibid. lv, 1957.

Thomas Richards: 'Eglwys Llanfaches', *Trans. Cymmr.*, 1941.

A. H. Dodd: 'New England Influences in Early Welsh Puritanism' *B.B.C.S.*, xvl, 1954.

I

8. Economic Growth

Changes in agriculture

THE Middle Ages had been a time when the area of land put to productive use had been extended steadily. True, this process had been checked during the fourteenth century as a result of a decline in the population, and the disorders which followed had delayed its resumption, but the return of a more settled state had encouraged another assault upon the waste and woodland. This continued throughout our period and family papers are dotted with references to the enclosure of common, waste, and woodland, and the disputes which were prompted by the apportionment of the newly won land. Not only was more land being exploited, it was also being cultivated more intensively. In those parts inhabited by Englishmen long established in the country some form of three-field system had been in operation, but this was being substantially modified and, as a result of exchange and purchase, consolidated farms were emerging. The tempo of change varied from place to place and there was little uniformity in the pattern of development—these were determined in large measure by the local conditions. In those parts inhabited by the Welsh the system of land usage differed substantially. Here crops were usually raised for a succession of years on the same land by farmers who followed a type of infield–outfield system whereby the land nearest to the farmstead or hamlet was heavily manured and continuously cropped, while beyond it there was a much larger area of land, the greater part of which was used for grazing.

Each farmer tried to be as self-sufficient as possible. While this had the advantage of protecting him in a period of rising prices it did slow down specialization. Even in those areas where stock-rearing was making important strides forward arable farming still remained significant. In the more favoured regions corn was produced on a scale large enough to be exported in substantial quantities—from south-west Wales to Ireland, for instance. The most popular crops were wheat and oats with barley a fairly close third. Rye was much less important and was frequently sown on land which had been won from the waste during the Middle Ages, although in some parts it was the autumn sowing on land which had lain fallow for a year. Enclosure and consolidation of strips had increased the sowing of winter wheat, while beans and peas were sown in small quantities—often in the stubble of former crops after a single ploughing. In addition to these, there were the garden-sized plots for hemp and flax to provide the raw material for spinning, and hops for beer brewing. Occasionally crops were sown together, especially barley and oats, to provide feeding stuff for the animals. One survey of 369½ customary acres in Gower, a part of the country reputed to be 'full of corn', shows that 108½ acres were devoted to wheat, 68½ to winter wheat, 122¾ to oats and 67¾ to barley while three only were used to grow beans and peas.

Welsh farmers tended to cultivate their land more intensively than their English counterparts. This intensive cultivation made necessary the extensive use of fertilizers—of which lime was the most popular. Where limestone outcropped it was quarried and burnt and the lime was mixed with earth to make marl. Of Landimore in Gower it was recorded in 1639 'there be Quarries of Limestones where Tenants time out of mind have used to burn their Lime for the composting of their lands'. In areas near the coast seaweed was used as manure, especially for wheat and barley, and sand was mixed with the soil to make it lighter. According to George Owen 'a man doth sand for himself, lime for his son, and marle for his grandchild'.[1] Other practices were also in use to restore goodness to the soil. In some areas farmers beat and burnt their land—the practice known as denshiring or devonshiring. Many would keep their cattle in movable folds on their arable land except in midwinter; these would be moved from one part of the land to another in order to ensure fairly consistent manuring.

A significant feature was the increasing attention which was

---

[1] A most interesting account of various aspects of the economic life of sixteenth-century Wales is to be found in George Owen's *The Description of Pembrokeshire*, Part 1, published in the Cymmrodorion Record Series, London, 1892.

paid to the rearing of livestock. There was some specialization in parts of the country but generally it was the practice to keep dual-purpose cattle rather than concentrate exclusively on beef animals, while in some areas the 'milk kine' were the most popular. Beef cattle were sold at the summer fairs to middlemen and drovers; there was also a substantial trade in dairy produce, especially across the Bristol Channel. Butter exports from the ports of the Vale of Glamorgan to the West Country, to Ireland and France were valued at £12,000 a year at the time of James I. The rearing of livestock was nothing new in Wales—English writers were in the habit of drawing their own conclusions about the Welsh character in their observations upon this aspect of the rural economy of Wales. Leland, for instance, recorded that the 'Welshmen in times past, as they do almost yet, did study more to Pasturage than Tilling, as Favorers of their consuete Idleness'. Thomas Churchyard too, writing in 1587, implies that it was this deficiency in the Welsh character that accounted for the attention paid to pastoral farming, though he does admit that

> They have begun, of late to lime their land,
> And plowe the ground, where sturdy oaks did stand.

George Owen was, perhaps, nearer the mark when he suggested that cattle rearing 'yields profit with less charge to the owner', although he deplored its social consequences in that 'it procures depopulation and maintains less people at work'.

The attention given to sheep-rearing was only slightly less than that devoted to stock-raising. The vast majority of the Welsh farmers had their flocks—even the small men. The wool produced, which varied considerably in quality, was intended partly for the local markets, but was for the greater part sold to English buyers, or was made into 'white clothes' which were bought by the Shrewsbury drapers. Oxen were also reared— as draught animals or beef stock, while horse-breeding was becoming increasingly important as horses became the mainstay of farm work and were used for carrying, coal especially. There was a busy market for horses in Pembrokeshire, Radnorshire, and West Gower. The inventory of farm animals is completed by the goats, pigs, geese, ducks, and chickens that were reared in varying numbers on almost all farms.

The location of the farms dictated the effect of stock-rearing on the organization of the farms. Those which were conveniently near common land made heavy use of the common for grazing; this meant that the land of the farms was available for arable farming. The more remote of the farms had to apportion less land to the plough and more to pasture. Local conditions also determined variations in common practice, like that of the slaughtering of animals. There is no evidence to suggest that in the more favoured areas there was a large-scale slaughtering of livestock for the winter. In those parts cattle were kept during the winter months on the commons or, more frequently, on fogged pastures near the farm building from which straw, crushed furze, or reeds could be fed to them in bad weather.

Trade in agricultural produce

The most important marketing commodities of Welsh farms were the products of livestock-rearing. Much of Wales is, after all, better suited by its climate, soil, and terrain to pastoral farming and throughout the Middle Ages cattle had been an essential feature of the rural economy. This is reflected in the frequent references to the rearing of cattle in the old Welsh laws and, by the early sixteenth century, the growing number of lawsuits concerning cattle theft and rights of pasture is evidence of the increasing attention being paid to this aspect of farming. Occasionally the inhabitants of a part of the country leave one in no doubt on this score. In 1525 the people of the lordship of Brecon complained to the king that they were 'in right great poverty and necessity' and this they explained by the fact that they could 'have but little sale or utterance of beasts and cattle, which is the chief commodity of those parts'.

The chief centre of cattle-rearing in South Wales was Glamorgan where dairy farming was carried on in the Vale and beef cattle raised in the uplands. In Pembrokeshire, too, it was an important item in the economy, second only to corn in 1603, according to George Owen. The major areas for cattle in North Wales were the counties of Anglesey, Caernarvon, Montgomery, and west Denbigh, although increasing attention was paid to stock-rearing in other parts of Wales during the period. Welsh cattle had been sold in England certainly as far back as the fourteenth century—the Bishop of Winchester was ordering the purchase of fat cattle in North Wales in 1317, while Welsh cattle were bought to provision English troops during the French wars.

The trade in cattle was heavy among the farmers, middlemen, and drovers at the summer fairs. Cattle would be brought to these fairs from a wide area and sold to buyers who had frequently come from even further afield. The buyers were farmers, butchers, and merchants whose main concern was the hides, and the drovers. Of the cattle brought from the counties of Cardigan and Merioneth as well as other parts of Montgomery to the Machynlleth fairs in 1632 a very substantial number were sold to men from Denbigh, Brecon, Flint, and Shropshire—men like Thomas Cadwgan of the parish of Llanfihangel-bryn-Pabuan in Breconshire who for £8. 16s. 2d. and the payment of 12d. toll bought five black cows and a pied cow; or Thomas Price of the neighbouring parish of Llanafan Fawr who for £21. 0s. 5d. and the same toll bought nine cows, all black. To the important fairs at Eglwyswrw in north Pembrokeshire drovers brought cattle from far away Llanelltyd in Merioneth, from Bodferin in Caernarvonshire and from various parts of Montgomeryshire as well as from the south-west counties. In 1599 Ellis ap Lewis of Llanelltyd sold eighteen steers and heifers, while Hopkin John of Llanddarog sold a total of thirty-three animals. Welsh cattle were sold, too, in the market towns of the border counties—in 1575 the sale is recorded at Shrewsbury of two 'great fat oxen' for £9. 6s. 8d., destined for Kenilworth as a present for the earl of Leicester. Some cattle were transported by sea—from ports like Tenby or the small creeks of Glamorgan to Bridgwater, Watchet, and Minehead. More frequently they were driven overland, following established routes to the various marketing centres in England. Of these many were destined for the Midlands, most were driven to the south-east—to Essex, Kent, and Sussex where they were sold at the fairs held at Brentwood or Maidstone or at the Bush and Bartholomew fairs of the metropolis. Then they would be fattened before making the final journey to Smithfield to satisfy the growing demand of the ever-increasing London populace.

The family correspondence of the time reflects the interest in and the importance of the cattle trade in the Welsh economy.

Sir John Wynn excused himself to the Privy Council in 1613 for not having paid the purchase money for his baronetcy on the grounds that the unseasonable weather had hindered the sale of his tenants' cattle, their only means of livelihood, and so made them backward in paying their rents. In another letter on the same subject he informed a friend that he could not pay until the drovers returned from Kent in the latter part of the Michaelmas term. The letters which he received from his son Owen in London contained frequent references to cattle and the market in them. One reports that a new buyer has been found for Sir John's cattle, another gives news of current trends in the market, 'all lean cattle are very dear in Kent and all hereabouts'. Nor were the Wynns alone in the concern which they showed about the trade; it is the subject of much of the letter-writing of the time.

Naturally enough, the men who were responsible for the conduct of the trade, the drovers, were in a position to make the most of the situation. Not only were they indispensable to the economic well-being of these families, they were also a much-used means of communication with relatives, friends, and business associates in London and the other commercial centres of England. Henry Wynn complains to his father in 1624 of the inadequacy of the allowance which he has received by the drover David Lloyd. The drovers had the opportunities, which some of them were not slow to exploit, to establish themselves as business men or as landed proprietors. Some of them penetrated the ranks of the lesser gentry and a few occupied the highest of the local offices in the government of the Welsh counties.

The wool and cloth trade

Wool from Monmouthshire and Pembrokeshire was certainly being sold in English fairs by the fourteenth century and some was being exported to Flanders, Spain, Portugal, and Brittany. There was too a growing cloth industry of sufficient size to merit some regulation—in 1326 Shrewsbury had joined Carmarthen and Cardiff as a staple town for Welsh wool and cloth. During the sixteenth century two significant changes occurred in the cloth industry. There was first a shift in its location from South Wales to mid and North Wales—to the counties of Denbigh,

Montgomery, and Merioneth. This may well have been the result of an attempt on the part of the industry to free itself from the regulations of the towns and the old centres; it may also have been a reaction to the development of coal-mining in South Wales. Secondly, there was during the second half of the century a very considerable expansion in the industry—the inevitable result of the closer trade connections with England, of the growth of large landed estates, of the better state of internal order, and of the exemption of Welsh cloth from state regulation after 1557.

Governmental control of the trade passed through distinct phases. During the earlier decades of the sixteenth century Welsh cloths were exempted from state control because of their coarseness. Then in 1541 a measure was passed stipulating that Welsh cloths should be folded and not rolled in order to make inspection easier. In the following year a much more detailed Act was passed which laid down precise regulations concerning the weight, length, breadth, and quality of Welsh cottons and friezes, and a supervisory system, the alnage, was established to ensure that the regulations were observed. The appointment of supervisors and searchers was in 1550 made the responsibility of the justices of the peace and regulations as to the length and breadth of Welsh cottons and friezes were included in the general Act of 1552. Then in 1557 this control was relaxed and Welsh cloth was virtually freed from control until 1601 when many of the regulations were revived. But the industry continued to enjoy a substantial measure of freedom and was given legal protection against the monopoly established by the Shrewsbury drapers. An Act of 1604 allowed a wide variation in respect of the length, breadth, and weight of Welsh cottons, another of the following year made a Content Seal unnecessary, and in 1624 was passed an Act for the free trade of Welsh cottons.

Welsh cloth was coarse and poorly made—according to Camden it was 'thin'—and it was expensive; nevertheless there was a steady growth in its sale. The local outlets were the fairs of which there were some 233, and which were attended by English traders who bought the cloth in considerable quantities. At Newport fair in 1594 they bought 365 pieces of Welsh cloth and they were engaged in considerable purchases at Abergavenny, Caerleon, and Usk at the same time. In North and mid

Wales, the area which witnessed the expansion of the industry, the most important marketing centre was Oswestry, of which Leland observed as early as 1539 that it 'stands mostly by sale of cloth made in Wales'. Its cloth markets were held on Mondays, and there were three big fairs, in May, August, and November, at which the most prominent groups of the traders were the drapers of Coventry, Shrewsbury, and Whitchurch as well as those of Oswestry itself. The most important of these were the Shrewsbury drapers whose company, founded in 1462, was employing during Elizabeth's reign 600 shearmen to improve the quality of the Welsh cloth which it purchased.

Contacts between Shrewsbury and Oswestry were close despite the dangers of the journey which were involved. One of the drapers of the former place provided in his will for special prayers to be read at St. Alkmund's Church on Monday mornings, 'before the drapers set out for Oswestry market'. As late as the 1580s precautions had to be taken against attacks —the drapers undertaking the journey were to 'wear their weapons all the way, and go in company—not to go over the Welsh bridge before the bell toll six'. As Shrewsbury absorbed an increasing proportion of Welsh cloth, its drapers stepped up their agitation for a monopoly of the trade and were eventually able to overcome the objections of Oswestry whose inherent weaknesses as a centre had been becoming increasingly apparent. By the late sixteenth century all Welsh cloth was bought and sold in the Drapers' Hall at Shrewsbury and from here it was dispatched to London and Bristol, much of it to be exported.

The export trade in Welsh cloth was expanding steadily. As early as 1560 the Merchant Adventurers reported the sale of Welsh cottons in France, Italy, Spain, and even in the Low Countries, and by the last quarter of the century it had reached a respectable volume. From London it was exported to the French ports, to Rouen in particular which by 1576 was absorbing over 90 per cent of the Welsh cottons shipped out of the capital. From Bristol it was dispatched to the ports of the west coast of France, to Ireland, St. Jean de Luz, and far-away Leghorn. The importance of the trade to the Welsh economy was emphasized in the preamble to the Act of 1624 which freed it from the control of Shrewsbury. This Act which was the result of a Welsh pressure group in Parliament claimed that the trade was responsible for much prosperity in Wales and that by it Welshmen had grown 'to such Wealth and Means of Living as they were thereby enabled to pay and Discharge all Duties Mizes Charges Subsidies and Taxations which were upon them imposed'.

Minerals and metals

The mineral resources of the country had been exploited from very early times, but it was during the sixteenth century that a determined effort was made in this sphere of industrial enterprise. As a result of the union the prerogative of the Crown over mines royal was extended to the whole of Wales, and this proved a decisive factor in the development of the mining industry.

Coal-mining

Coal had long been mined in Wales. Certainly by the Middle Ages coal-mines were operating in different parts of the country—near Roch and in Coedrath Forest in Pembrokeshire during the thirteenth century, at Ewloe, Mostyn, and Hope in Flintshire soon after. The monks of Margam were mining coal on the Abbey's estates in the fourteenth century, and coal was being produced at Kilvey near Swansea before 1340—by the turn of the century the annual output of the Kilvey workings was some 300 lasts (that is, *c*. 4,000 tons). But there was no rapid expansion of coal-mining in Wales—industry made little demand, transport was difficult, and there was much prejudice against its use as a domestic fuel. Progress was most rapid, therefore, in areas like south Pembrokeshire where timber was scarce, or like the Swansea district which was near the coast and so convenient for export. During the sixteenth century, however, concern for the preservation of timber and the demands of an expanding iron industry gave a boost to coal production.

In the north-east coalfield mines were worked in the Wrexham area—at Holt, Brymbo, Esclusham, Eglwysegle, Coedpoeth, Gresford, and Ruabon. Elsewhere in Flintshire and Denbighshire coal was mined at Holywell, Whitford, and near St. Asaph, while old mines were developed and new ones

O Coal mining   Δ Lead mining   Ⅱ Iron mining and manufacture   C Copper mining / smelting

MAP 4. Industries in Wales

(Based on maps (pages 73, 83, 129, 277) in William Rees, *Industry before the Industrial Revolution*, vol. i, by kind permission of the author.)

opened at Ewloe, Hawarden, Mold, Northop, Aston, and Flint. Coal was also mined at Chirk and in the northern part of the lordship of Oswestry. In the south the most important centres of the industry were in the Neath and Gower districts. In the former there was extensive mining at Cadoxton, on the common lands of the borough, and in the districts to the north and east of the town. In the latter the old mines at Kilvey were developed, and coal was mined to the north of Swansea and at a number of places in Gower. East of Neath the old mines of Margam Abbey were being worked, in the Ffrwdwyllt Valley especially. In the uplands fringing the Vale of Glamorgan—at Brynmenin, Llanharan, Llanharry, and Pentyrch—there were coal-workings. Further north—at Hirwaun, Rhigos, and Dowlais, on the outskirts of Aberdare, in Glyn Rhondda, and the Cynon Valley, at Senghenydd and in the area north of Cardiff there were flourishing enterprises. In the west—around Kidwelly and Llanelli and in the Gwendraeth Valley—coal was mined. Leland in the 1530s noted the difference between the anthracite coal of the Gwendraeth and the bituminous coal of the coastal districts. Finally, in Pembrokeshire there were coal-pits near Lamphey and Tenby and workings at Steynton, Picton, Johnston, Kingston, Jeffreston, Begelly, and elsewhere.

Much of the coal which was raised was exported—despite efforts made to impose statutory restrictions on its export—usually to Ireland and France. Some was sold to other parts of the country—to Anglesey from the north-east, to the West Country and the border counties from the south. Some was used to meet the demands of nearby ironworks. Transport was difficult, and so as much use as possible was made of the coastal sea routes and the navigable rivers. Coal was shipped from the port of Mostyn to Beaumaris and from Swansea up the Severn. Altogether there was quite a considerable trade in the shipping of coal—during the early sixteenth century some 120 to 150 lasts were being sent annually by sea from Swansea. This dropped to 34 by the middle of the century, but picked up again and by 1607 76 cargoes carrying a total of 874 weighs were sent by sea from Swansea. From Chester and its creeks 7,709 chaldrons of coal were shipped to Ireland in the year 1638–9. There were other outlets for coal. At a time when increasing attention was being paid to fertilizers, some of it was used for lime burning. In Chirk some of the coal mined in the seventeenth century was coked for use in drying malt on the Myddelton estate.

The increasing opportunities offered by coal mining encouraged capital investment on a fairly considerable scale. The leasing of mining rights began to figure prominently in business transactions—in 1526 Sir Mathew Cradock of Swansea leased mines at Kilvey and in Gower, in 1566 William Hopkins obtained a ninety-nine-year lease from Richard Cromwell on the grange of Cwrt y Bettws near Neath with the right to dig coal. Despite the risks involved profits were attractive—in the Neath area 800 weighs of coal were produced in the year 1653–4 at a cost of £173. 14s. 9d. and sold for £518. 7s. 3d. But the risks were considerable and increased as the scale of working became larger. Surface seams were worked to a depth of 24 feet by a drift or slope, but by the early seventeenth century pits seven-foot square were sunk to a depth of 12, 16, or 20 fathoms. The deeper the workings the more the dangers multiplied—from the fall of rock, from flood-water, and from gas. Explosions, caused by fire damp, occurred at Upfylton near Flint and at Baglan, and a particularly serious one at the Mostyn collieries in 1673. Some of these were, in a superstitious age, attributed to the evil working of supernatural agencies— among the miners there was a widespread belief in demons.

Despite the expansion taking place, it must be remembered that the scale of production was, by modern standards, very small. A substantial pit might employ some sixteen persons— 3 diggers, 7 bearers, 1 filler, 4 winders and 2 riddlers—and would produce some 80 to 100 barrels of coal a day. To achieve this the men worked from 6 a.m. to 6 p.m. with an hour's break at noon. In addition to their wages, they were entitled to an eating and drinking allowance—a daily $\frac{1}{2}d$. worth of bread and drink worth 4d. for every twelve men. Their conditions of work were appalling, and their calling, together with the influence it had on their conduct, made them a race apart in the eyes of those who gained a livelihood in other ways. Small wonder that they availed themselves of every opportunity to absent themselves from their work—it was generally accepted, for instance, that they observed all holy days.

The iron industry

The iron industry had a long history before Lewis Glyn Cothi, writing in the mid-fifteenth century, mentioned the Englishmen who had settled in Flint and built furnaces there. The Mwynddu mines near Llantrisant in Glamorgan were being worked in Leland's time and their ore smelted near by. A certain Sion ap Howel Gwyn seems to have been busy in the Aberdare district at much the same time erecting a furnace at Llwydcoed and other places. But the greater opportunity offered by Union for the investment of English capital in Wales really marked the beginning of substantial developments. English ironmasters were not slow to avail themselves of this opportunity. Sir William Sidney obtained haematite ores in Glamorgan for his Sussex ironworks and in 1564 his son Sir Henry with partners opened a forge and furnace near Cardiff which worked in close co-operation with their Sussex works. Iron plates were manufactured which were transported to Robertsbridge in Sussex to be converted into steel—in 1565 he paid one bill of £33 for the freight of 21 tons of plate from Cardiff to Rye. But the decline of the works at Robertsbridge after 1570 had unfortunate results for their works in Glamorgan.

The county attracted other investors. William Relfe, had, with William Darrell and Ievan ap Howell, opened a forge at Pontygwaith and a furnace at Duffryn near Mountain Ash. Anthony Morley in 1586 acquired a controlling interest in this undertaking and at this time the output at Duffryn amounted to some 8 tons of pig iron a week. Morley extended the scope of his activities—he built forges near Castellau and at Merthyr, but he over-reached himself and became bankrupt. His place was taken by Thomas Mynyffee who continued to extend the industry in the district. An ironworks was operating at Merthyr during the second half of the sixteenth century, probably near Abercanaid. Iron ore was being mined at this time at the headwaters of the Rhymney and on the mountain wastes near Llangynidr. At Rhigos, too, there was fairly extensive mining of iron ore to supply the furnace at Cwmhendre Fawr, and to be carried on the backs of mules to Llantrisant and Melincwrt.

The Mathew family of Radyr acquired a lease to work the haematite ores at Pentyrch and a furnace was built here in 1565.

One of Sir Henry Sidney's partners, Edmund Roberts, was busy in the area developing the local high-grade ores for the works at Robertsbridge; later, in 1576, he set up a gun foundry at Abercarn. Other Englishmen were manufacturing iron at Radyr, among them Thomas Mynyffee who had already established an interest further north. Sir William Mathew's interest in the industry was carried on by his heir Edmund who controlled works at Radyr for the manufacture of ordnance. In 1602 he was charged by the Privy Council with exporting about 150 tons of ordnance between 1582 and 1600 in defiance of the embargo placed upon its export. By the early decades of the seventeenth century the Cardiff district had earned a very considerable reputation for the quality of its ordnance. Further north iron was being manufactured in the lordship of Senghenydd during the sixteenth century although the first positive evidence of it dates from 1625. This was the furnace at Tongwynlais owned by Thomas Hackett who also had an iron mill or forge at Rhyd y Gwern in Machen, a works which had been in operation since 1569.

The continuing success of the wireworks and foundry established at Tintern by the Society of the Mineral and Battery works provided an impetus to the iron industry in south-east Wales. Established in the 1560s the wireworks and foundry had been farmed out to Richard Hanbury and two partners in 1571 at an annual rent of £150. The growing demand for cards for carding wool and the protection given by the government ensured their success and during the seventeenth century they were employing some four hundred men. To meet the demand for iron from Tintern works were established at Monkswood, Trevethin, Pontymoel, Abercarn, Machen, and Blaina by Richard Hanbury in the late sixteenth century.

Further west, in the lordship of Coity, too, the iron-ore resources of the district were being exploited. Robert Sidney acquired the estate of Coity after his marriage in 1584 to Barbara, heiress of Sir William Gamage. In 1589 he granted to John Cross and John Thornton the right to build a blast furnace and forge at Coity. They prospered for a while but ran into difficulties late in the century and by 1600 Willard and Bullen were in possession. Iron was also being worked early in the seventeenth century at near by Varteg Isaf, on the land of the Stradling family at Pont Ynys Afan and at Baglan. There were, too, iron centres at Cilybebyll in the lordship of Neath, at Kidwelly and Whitland in Carmarthenshire, and at Llanbedr in Pembrokeshire—though these were much smaller.

In North Wales the most important iron-producing district was around Chirk. An iron furnace and forge were in operation during the early seventeenth century at Weston Rhyn; there were forges also at Old Mill in the lordship of Whittington and at Maesbury in the lordship of Oswestry. During the years preceding the Civil War Sir Thomas Myddelton had an ironworks at Pont y Blew on his Chirk estate. Further west, in Merioneth, attempts to work iron ended in failure. In 1588 two English speculators, John Smith and William Dale, leased land at Ganllwyd from Hugh Nanney Hen of Nannau to build an ironworks. They ran into difficulties, one of which was the unsuitability of the wood they bought for smelting. Smith tried again in 1596, renting an ironworks owned by Hugh Nanney in the township of Nannau. He converted them into a blast furnace with forges to supply iron for the forges of William Grosvenor at Chester. This too failed and the works were closed in 1604.

The growth of the iron industry before 1640 was the result of a number of factors. There were the iron resources of the country and the opportunities afforded for exploiting them after the union; there was a plentiful supply of timber for making charcoal and the water power necessary to work the bellows which produced the blast. The long struggle against Spain boosted the demand for ordnance, and there were the restrictions which were imposed upon the manufacture of iron in the neighbourhood of London. On the whole, however, the iron industry during this period consisted of isolated furnaces or forges owned by individuals or families and operating on a small scale. It suffered a severe set-back as a result of the Civil War, one from which it did not recover until our period ends.

The non-ferrous metals

Lead was being mined at Llantrisant during the Middle Ages, and the Craig y Mwyn in the Ystwyth Valley of Cardiganshire was being worked by 1504. In 1538 Leland noted that 'There has been in times past a great mine digging for lead in Cwm

Ystwyth a vi miles from Strata Florida, where is a grange
belonging to Strata Florida. But some men suppose that it
ceased, because the wood is sore wasted.' It was not until the
second half of the century that the more intensive exploitation
of the non-ferrous metal resources of Wales began. In 1564
Elizabeth granted the right to search for copper and other
precious metals in Wales and parts of England to Thomas
Thurland and the German Daniel Hochstetter. Four years
later their enterprise was formally incorporated as a joint stock
company, the Society of Mines Royal. In the meantime, the
Society of the Mineral and Battery Works had been established
with the sole right of making brass and wire. As early as 1566
experiments were being conducted in the manufacture of brass
at Tintern. The enterprise was not successful and the brass
manufacture ceased in 1582. During the 1580s a subsidiary of
the Mines Royal turned its attention to Neath where it built a
copper-smelting house. The German Ulrich Frosse was in
charge and it was certainly operating by 1584. Its success,
however, was short lived, for it was dependent upon Cornwall
for its supplies of ore and when these became inadequate the
works came to a stop. It was never very large—at no time did it
employ more than thirty men—and it was certainly closed
before 1602.

Meanwhile, the Mines Royal Society had begun to exploit
the lead-ore resources of the country. During the 1580s Thomas
Smith acquired a lease of the Society's mines in Devon, Cornwall, and Cardiganshire for a rent of £300 a year. His agent in
the Welsh county, Charles Evans, concentrated his efforts on
the Cwmsymlog area—opening shafts, levels, and drifts, but
without much success. Unsuccessful, too, was the venture of
Sir Thomas Cannon and his father-in-law John Voyle who
leased mines for silver in the parish of St. Alwys in Pembrokeshire. The success story of the Cardiganshire mines really starts
with Hugh Myddelton who took out a lease on them in 1617
at a rent of £400 a year. Within a few years he was reputed to be
doing very well—reports suggested that he was making a clear
£2,000 a month from Cwmsymlog and the neighbouring mines.
His success inspired others and an increasing volume of English
capital was ploughed into lead mining. In 1617 a twenty-one-
year lease of the mines at Craig-y-Mwyn in the Briwnant

J

district was granted to William Winckfield and Mathew de Quester; ten years later the lease was renewed at a rent of £25 to Mathew and Josse de Quester, and in 1631 was transferred to William Collins and Edward Fenn of London. In North Wales, lead was mined near Caerwys, at Halkyn and Holywell and in the hundreds of Coleshill and Rhuddlan during the last quarter of the sixteenth century. By the early seventeenth century there were mines in operation at Minera and Eryris in Denbighshire and at Halcetor in the lordship of Montgomery.

The most successful of the lead-mining pioneers of the time was Thomas Bushell. In partnership with Sir F. Godolphin he leased the Myddelton mines from Sir Hugh's widow. Godolphin soon died but Bushell carried on alone, receiving a confirmation of the lease in 1637, despite the very considerable difficulties with which he was faced. There was much flooding in the mines as a result of the shaft-sinking techniques of Myddelton and his predecessors; he had to face strong local opposition, and there was his quarrel with Lady Myddelton whose men, Bushell alleged, pulled up the pumps, threw rubbish into the mines, and did their best to destroy them. But he persevered, concentrating on the mines at Darren Fawr, Tal-y-bont, Brynllwyd, Goginan, and Cwmerfyn. He adopted the technique of driving adits and introduced the German ventilating device. Finally, after four years of persistent effort he got through at Talybont into the thirty-eight-fathom shaft of the old flooded works. He had at last won through—his weekly production of silver was estimated at £100 and of lead at £50. In 1637 he was authorized to set up a mint at Aberystwyth for the coining of the silver extracted from the mines of Wales. This concession and the favour which he was shown by Charles I was to be repaid during the Civil War when Bushell supplied clothes to the king's army, loaned the king £40,000, and raised and maintained a regiment of his miners to fight for the king. By the 1640s he was employing some 260 miners at his Cardiganshire mines, together with three 'moniers', nine smelters, and the same number of washers. The war brought him its troubles from both business rivals and the king's enemies. But with the end of the fighting he was able to re-establish his good fortune, and he continued his success story during the Protectorate.

The maritime trade

The maritime activity of the period reflected the changes taking place elsewhere in the economic field—the general expansion of industrial activity, the changes that were taking place in emphasis, the shifts in the geographical location, and the effects of governmental policy. The volume of sea traffic increased substantially during the period and this applies to both branches of the trade—foreign and coastal. The policy of the government had much to do with this. The defences of the Welsh coast were improved as was their administration; piracy was suppressed with growing efficiency; careful surveys were made of all ports, creeks, and landing-places; the supervision of local trading activity was improved as was the machinery for the administration of the revenue. More significant, how-ever, were the developments which were taking place in the economic activity of the country.

During the Middle Ages the greater part of Welsh overseas trade had been with France. French wines and salt had been imported into Wales which returned fleeces and hides, and the carrying of the goods had been done almost exclusively in French ships. This continued to be true of the early decades of the sixteenth century except that increasingly Welsh shipping began to play a more active part in the trade. As the century wore on coal displaced wool as the outstanding export com-modity and, almost inevitably, the coal exporting ports became the chief markets for the French trade—only occasionally did French ships make contact with the ports of Cardigan Bay and North Wales. This is reflected in the number of ships which left Swansea and Neath and in the shipments of coal which, in the case of Swansea, rose from 159 weys in 1579–80 to 657 weys in 1594–5. There was a marked drop in the exports of coal during the last year of the sixteenth century but it picked up again and stood at 302 weys in 1602–3. This, however, did not last long for the Swansea coal trade was hard hit by the heavy taxes on coal imposed by the early Stuarts and especially by the measures of 1636 which prohibited the export of coal to foreign countries.

With Spain and Portugal trade during the Middle Ages was mainly in wines, salt, sugar, and iron, in return for which Welsh cloth was exported. This trade continued fairly steadily during the first three-quarters of the sixteenth century despite the growing tension in the relations between the two countries. After 1580, however, there are records of only few direct trading contacts, although this does not mean that the trade was discontinued completely for cargoes of Spanish goods were imported in Dutch and Scottish ships.

The trade with Ireland was centred in large measure upon Beaumaris and its associated creeks, at Milford Haven and the ports of north Pembrokeshire and south Cardiganshire. Welsh ships took part in the carrying-trade from Bristol and there was a substantial increase in the export of coal and culm from South Wales and Flintshire, and in slates and minerals from the north-west. The later years of Elizabeth's reign saw an appreciable increase in the volume of corn exports. Before 1593 few ships carried goods from Ireland, and their cargoes were usually salt, herrings, Irish wool, flax, cloth, and occasionally foreign wines and iron. After this year there was a considerable expansion in the trade, especially in the import of livestock, timber, and timber wares. The volume of the trade with Scotland was never very significant, although Scottish hides did constitute a fairly considerable part of the carrying-trade with Spain and Portugal. This accounts for the cargoes of corn, oil, linen cloth, and Gascony wines brought to Beaumaris from Glasgow—outgoing cargoes to Scotland were mainly cloth, friezes, and coal. There was, too, some traffic between the North Wales ports and the Isle of Man in Welsh slates and Manx corn.

This formed the bulk of the overseas trade, although there are occasional records of more distant contacts. From Newfoundland, for instance, were carried a few cargoes of fish and train oil. A Dutch ship brought a load of tobacco into Swansea and another of cloves into Milford, while Welsh iron was exported to Flushing and Welsh wheat to Venice.

The coastal trade expanded very considerably during the period. This was the result of a number of factors. There was, first, the more intensive exploitation of the mineral resources of the country, especially in the case of coal, iron, and lead. Expanding industries also made their contribution—more English iron was carried to Wales as the industry developed, and the progress made by the West of England cloth industry increased the demand for Welsh wool which was shipped across the Bristol Channel. English imports rose substantially and many of these imported goods came to Wales via England. The national economic policy fostered trade especially in foodstuffs from surplus areas—this is reflected in the growth of grain imports from the creeks of the English side of the Severn estuary. Finally, the investment of English capital in Wales gave an impetus to industrial growth, especially in iron and lead, which became significant items in the coastal trade.

The most important export commodity in the coastal trade of South Wales was coal. From Swansea and Neath especially, but also from Llanelli, Carmarthen, and some of the Pembrokeshire ports, it was transported to Bristol, Bideford, and London. The ports of Carmarthenshire and Pembrokeshire also did a considerable trade in Welsh cloth, although from the last twenty years of the sixteenth century there was a substantial increase in the export of wool and a corresponding drop in that of cloth. Corn too figured prominently as did dairy produce in the cross-channel trade from Pembrokeshire and the small harbours of the Vale of Glamorgan and Gower to Devon, Somerset, and Gloucester. In return cargoes of malt and barley were imported from the Severn ports. The most important centre of the North Wales coastal trade was Beaumaris, dealing mainly with Liverpool and the ports of Cheshire and Lancashire. Outgoing commodities from Beaumaris consisted for the most part of dairy produce, hides, tanned leather, and slates, but the balance of trade was very much against the Welsh port, for the imports —of pitch, tar, brass, pewter, prints, wines, salt, and iron were considerably greater in volume than the exports. The small ports along the coast of Cardigan Bay dealt largely in herrings and traded with English ports like Bristol as well as with the North Wales ports.

The Welsh traders were drawn from a number of very different social spheres. The majority were merchant seamen and sea rovers, but among the shipowners there were yeomen, members of the gentry class, and, in one case, a bishop. The trade was not large enough for elaborate companies, so that the commercial unit was either the individual who owned his own ship or simple partnerships. The ships themselves were usually very small—in 1577 there were three ships only of over a hundred tons and twenty-seven of between forty and a hundred tons involved in the trade.

It is interesting to follow the fortunes of one of these ships. The *Le Mychell* of Laugharne under her master David Allen was busily involved in the Bristol Channel trade during the twelve months following Michaelmas 1566. On 11 November she arrived in Carmarthen from Bristol carrying 1 butt of malmsey, 17 barrels of honey, 2 barrels of black soap, ½ cwt. of white soap, 4 fardels of canvas, 1½ cwt. of madder, 4 cwt. of hops, 2 chests, 2 hampers of worked pewter, 40 teasle staves, 1 t. of iron, 5 cwt. of brass, 1 dry vat of divers goods, 1 piece of grapes, and 1 cwt. of alum. On the 25th of the same month she left Carmarthen for Bristol carrying 40 packs of frieze for the merchant Richard Roger of Laugharne.

On 5 January 1567 she docked in Laugharne from Bristol with 1 t.l.p. of iron, 8 barrels of honey, 1 hogshead, and 2 ferkins, 2 hampers of dry wares, 1 butt of malmsey, 1 millstone, 12 pieces of raisins, 1 packwood. She was leaving Carmarthen for Bristol on the 19th of the month with seven packs of frieze for Gruffydd ap Eynon. The 5th of February saw her back in Carmarthen from Bristol carrying a cargo of 14 packs, 6 barrels, 6 chests of dry wares, 5 fardels of linen, 6 cwt. of white soap, 4 cwt. of hops, 6 t. of iron, 1 butt of sack, 1 hogshead of vinegar, and 2 barrels of black soap for one Oliver Hodges. It was not until 12 May that she is next recorded as leaving Carmarthen for Bristol, this time carrying 46 packs of frieze for John Palmer, Renold White, Richard Roger, and David Palmer.

There is no record of her return to Wales on this occasion but on 25 June she again left Carmarthen, carrying 34 packs of Welsh frieze for Richard Roger and David Wilcocke of Laugharne. It was to Laugharne that she returned on 4 July with 20 cwt. of brass and pewter, 1 pack, 1 fardel of linen, 1 t. gaid'de Insulis, 4 cwt. of white soap, 2 cwt. of hops, and 1 cwt. of iron for David ap Ievan of Carmarthen. On the 17th of the month she was putting out of Carmarthen and carrying 50 packs of frieze on William Webb of Laugharne's behalf.

The final crossing for the twelve months as recorded was her return to Laugharne on 25 July, this time carrying 1 t. of oil, 1 barrel of honey, 3 t. of brass, 2 cwt. of cheese, 4 packs of linen, 8 chests, 4 cobbardes, 1 cwt. of crocke brass, 100 dozen pan brass, 2 hampers of dry wares, 2 cwt. of black soap, and ½ cwt. of alum for John Palmer of that place. There a discreet curtain of official silence is drawn upon the to-ing and fro-ing of the *Mychell* for the year. Her business was not identical in every detail with that of other ships concerned in the cross-Channel trade, but it is sufficiently typical to give us a good general picture of the trade.

SUGGESTED READING

E. A. Lewis (ed.): *The Welsh Port Books, 1550–1603*. London, 1927.

William Rees: *Industry before the Industrial Revolution*. Cardiff, 1968.

T. C. Mendenhall: *The Shrewsbury Drapers and the Welsh Wool Trade in the XVI and XVII centuries*. Oxford, 1953.

Joan Thirsk (ed.): *The Agrarian History of England and Wales, IV, 1500–1640*. Cambridge, 1967.

W. J. Lewis: *Lead Mining in Wales*. Cardiff, 1967.

Articles:

C. A. J. Skeel: 'The Welsh Woollen Industry in the Sixteenth and Seventeenth Centuries', *Arch. Camb.*, 1922.

—— 'The Cattle Trade between England and Wales from the Fifteenth to the Nineteenth Centuries', *Trans. R. Hist. S.* 4th series, lx, 1926.

B. E. Howells: 'Pembrokeshire Farming', *N.L.W. Jnl.*, lx, 1956.

F. V. Emery: 'West Glamorgan Farming circa 1580–1620', ibid., ix and x, 1955–7.

E. A. Lewis: 'The Toll Books of some North Pembrokeshire fairs, 1509–1603', *B.B.C.S.*, vll, 1934.

—— 'The Port Books of the Port of Cardigan in Elizabethan and Stuart Times', *Trans. Cards. Antiq. Soc.* vll, 1930.

M. C. S. Evans: 'Carmarthen and the Welsh Port Books, 1550–1603', *Carm. Antiq.* 111, 1960.

9. The Social Order

THE profound changes in the organization of Welsh society which took place during the sixteenth and seventeenth centuries were the product of a number of very different causes. There were those developments which had long been under way and which were now maturing; there was the impact of the union and of the closer contact with England which followed; there were the opportunities for economic exploitation afforded by the land which was brought on to the market by the religious changes of the time. Other more general factors—the rise in prices and the increasing emphasis on pastoral farming to mention but two—also made their own contribution to the growth of a new social order in the Wales of our period.

The population of the country

In spite of the absence of detailed population statistics before 1801, the careful estimates which have been made on the basis of the available information reflect the nature of these social changes. The century which followed the accession of Elizabeth saw a substantial increase in the population of Wales—an increase of some 120,000, from an estimated 225,826 in 1545/1563 to an estimated 341,674 in 1670. This was not, however, evenly distributed over the country—there was a much greater growth in North Wales than in the south. This difference was in large measure the result of the influx into the north-eastern counties of numbers of English families during the second half of the sixteenth and throughout the seventeenth centuries. It has been estimated that between 1550 and 1670 some 700 English families moved into the county of Flint, 680 families into that of Denbigh, and 580 into that of Montgomery. These immigrants produced a chain reaction, in that many families of the north-east moved west to the counties of Caernarvon, Merioneth, and Anglesey. The result was that, with only slight exceptions, there was a considerable over-all increase in the north. Anglesey was the county least affected by this migration factor, but even here growth was well above the average for the country as a whole.

In South Wales the increase was nowhere near so impressive, nor was it so uniform. In the south-west, for instance, the population of some parts of Pembrokeshire increased significantly, Cemais and Cilgerran in particular; otherwise it was an area of little growth—although the true picture may not have emerged since it seems very likely that the figures for Carmarthenshire are unreliable. In Radnorshire too the population did not expand to any appreciable extent, while that of Breconshire was very little better. Glamorgan was the county of most significant population growth in South Wales, and here the increase was much more substantial in the eastern half than the western. This lack of uniformity in those areas least affected by the pressure of immigration is, of course, quite natural and is a useful pointer to the extent to which the economic resources of particular districts were being exploited.

Interesting also is the growth in the number of town-dwellers. Again, the most significant increase was in the towns of North Wales—120 per cent in the case of Caernarvon, 112 per cent in that of Wrexham. But the ports of South Wales and market towns in other parts of the country also expanded considerably. The population of Cardiff, Swansea, and Pembroke increased by 75 per cent or more, Montgomery which in the mid sixteenth century had a population of 308 had more than doubled its numbers by 1670. There seems to have been little correlation between the increase in the numbers of town-dwellers and that of the population of the surrounding countryside. The number of the inhabitants of the county of Cardigan increased during the period by a mere 15 per cent while the population of the town of Cardigan rose by 69 per cent. Even more significant is the case of Llanidloes in Montgomeryshire. The population of the hundred rose by a mere 8 per cent, while that of the town increased by some 150 per cent, from 324 to 814. The towns, it would appear, were attracting many of their new inhabitants from their own immediate environs.

Population figures alone, especially when they are approximations, are not in themselves sufficient basis for positive conclusions. Certain features, however, do emerge which are indicative of the changes taking place in the Wales of the period. The expansion of the population, although substantial, was not altogether remarkable, especially when much of it was the result of immigration. The implication of this is that, while there was economic progress, it was achieved on a narrow front—in pastoral farming where the demand for labour would not of necessity correspond with the expansion of the industry, or on a limited scale—in coal-mining and iron manufacture where the size of the industrial unit was relatively small. Despite the growth of these industries in the north-east and south-east, the vast majority of the inhabitants of Wales made their living from the land.

The landowners

One of the outstanding features of the social life of the sixteenth and seventeenth centuries was the development of the landowning gentry class. This was a process which had begun long before the battle at Bosworth but the events and general climate of the sixteenth century gave it a tremendous impetus which continued throughout the century that followed. Wealth in land was the basis of this group's social pre-eminence and the acquisition of land the prime concern of its members whose ingenuity is reflected in the variety of the methods by which they accumulated their large estates. Some estates, for instance, were the result of steady accumulation and consolidation by succeeding generations—the purchase of a holding here, the lease of some Crown lands there. The hard core of others were the former monastic lands which came on to the market after the dissolution of the monasteries, later to be added to by purchase and lease. Some were the rewards of loyal service to the government; others were existing estates bought and added to by individuals who had made their fortunes in the professions and the commercial world.

This can best be appreciated if we examine the story of some of these estates. The Maurices of Clenennau were one of the outstanding North Wales families of the late sixteenth and early seventeenth centuries, the Barlows of Slebech were one of the leading Pembrokeshire families. The economic foundations of the former's pre-eminence were laid by a certain Morris ap John ap Meredydd. He had obtained a gift of land from his foster father, a small freeholder, and had probably taken up residence at the original house at Clenennau some time before 1487. He acquired on the principle of *pridwerth* in this year all the lands at Clenennau of a certain Madoc ap Hugh ap Meredudd. Twenty years later he bought a portion of the Cesail Gyfarch lands in the hamlet, and in 1509 he bought from his brother, Evan of Brynkir, a tenement there, Tyddyn Ievan ap Einion ap Gawys. His elder son, William Llwyd, had moved to Rhiwaedog, and Morris was succeeded at Clenennau by his second son Eliza. The latter continued on the lines laid down by his father with the purchase in 1529 of a parcel of lands of Ievan ap Owen and in 1533 of lands belonging to David ap Madoc ap Inko. Then in 1545 he bought a 101-year lease upon the lands of Humphrey ap Meredudd of Gesail Gyfarch. By 1551 father and son had established a substantial estate with property in the hamlet of Clenennau, in the township of Penyfed and in Pennant which included the demesne farm of Clenennau together with thirteen other tenements and scattered fragments of land.

This was not the end of the story. The Clenennau family had, like its neighbours, encroached upon the Crown estate of Tregest which had been lying waste and unpopulated during the late fifteenth century. Eliza Morris had regularized the family's position in this respect when in 1531 he secured a Crown lease upon Tregest for twenty-one years, a lease which was renewed in 1546 and again in 1567. The maximum use was made of this situation and by 1575, when William Maurice became Crown farmer of Tregest, no less than twenty new holdings had been created by ditching and enclosing. This was not the only contribution made by William to the growth of the estate. He bought lands in Harlech, lands which were extended as a result of the enclosure of Harlech marsh, and he acquired property in Caernarvon, Pwllheli, and Cricieth.

Very different were the foundations on which the Barlows of Slebech built their local influence. Sometime before 1540 Roger Barlow, who had made a fortune in trade, followed his brother William into Pembrokeshire. He did not miss the opportunity offered by the dissolution of the monasteries—his first move was to obtain a lease of the estate of the Hospitallers of St. John at Slebech. Then in 1546 he and his brother Thomas bought the site of the preceptory of Slebech, the lordship and the manor there together with lands in the parish; they also bought the lordship and manor of Minwear, the site and lands of the priory of Pill, and at Haverfordwest they acquired the monastery, with Cresswell Chapel and the house of the Black Friars. At the same time Roger was busy buying other lands in the district, and then in 1553 he bought out his brother and became the sole owner of the Slebech estate. In the years that followed he obtained a lease of part of the property of the hospital of St. John at Tenby and lands in the manor of Rhosmarket. He was followed by his son George who added to the estate by the purchase of the lordship, manor, castle, and forest of Narberth. By the early decades of the seventeenth century these, and families like them, dominated the social scene in every county in Wales.

Their estates were not established without disputes, fierce and protracted in some cases, nor indeed without some sharp practice. One major difficulty was the persistence of certain features of the old clan organization. Before the union the accumulation of holdings was complicated by the hereditary rights enjoyed by proprietors in the pasture and waste which the community controlled (*cytir*); while areas of wood and pasture could only be acquired by meeting those claims upon them which were bound to the individual arable holdings of the clanland. Such land could, therefore, only be obtained piecemeal, frequently in very small portions, and this, of necessity was a slow process. There were frustrations, too, in the notion of the indestructibility of hereditary rights to land. This had been overcome by the *prid*—a mortgage on land which could be renewed every four years, and to which an absolute title could be obtained if the *prid* were not redeemed after sixteen years. But this again was a slow and frustrating business. Another factor which gave rise to much confusion and irritation was the difference which persisted in the organization of common rights in various parts of the country. In some, usually the lowlands, unappropriate waste land remained undivided and individual members of the community exercised their acknowledged rights to it; in others, usually upland townships, the waste had been divided into sections and allocated to individuals for pasture.

The Act of 1542 solved these legal problems, but there was still room for conflict and resentment among the land hungry and those determined to safeguard their rights. William Maurice, for instance, as Crown farmer of Tregest, had difficulties with occupiers whose claims to the lands they held were based on the inheritance of fictitious freeholds. Some of these he bought out; with one family, the Ellises of Ystumllyn, he conducted a struggle which continued for over forty years. George Barlow's lawsuit over the lordship and manors of Narbeth was equally bitter but with an opponent of very much greater eminence—none other than Charles, Prince of Wales. There is also evidence of conflict between the Crown farmers and the free tenants concerning manorial rights, especially in the case of commons and wastes. The Crown farmers were accused of infringing old-established rights of the tenants to common of pasture, of enclosing waste land and forest and parts of the common land and converting them into meadow and arable land, of extending manorial rights of commons over unenclosed lands, of restricting the free tenants' rights of common and of extending the payment of heriot.

In the manor of Uwchmynydd in Radnorshire the tenants claimed that John Lewis, one of the Crown farmers, had during the reign of Elizabeth built a mansion in the forest and limited rights of common of pasture to the winter months only. The tenants could ill afford these restrictions upon their common rights and expressed their disapproval that 'the said lords of this manor do keep the said forest in several yearly between the feast of the purification of our Lady the Virgin and the feast of St. Michael the Archangel which forest heretofore time out of mind was used and enjoyed by the said tenants and borderers as a common of pasture for all manner of cattle sans number *at all times* and *seasons in the year till about three and thirty years last past*'. Although in Wales the friction provoked by enclosures did not assume the proportions which it did in parts of England, there is evidence that members of gentry families enclosed both pastoral and arable land. At Ffinnant in Breconshire hedges were destroyed and their planters tied to the tails of horses in 1560. In 1582 a bill of complaint was submitted to the Court of Exchequer by the householders of the town and lordship of Rhosmarket complaining of the enclosures of a certain Morris

Walter who had converted arable land into pasture 'and daily threateneth to convert all the rest of the arable ground into pasture'. There were frequent instances of intrusion upon royal lands, common and waste, by neighbouring landowners. In 1639 Roger Lort of Stackpool admitted that he had caused depopulation in north Pembrokeshire by such practices.

But for the greater part of Wales where a pastoral economy supported a sparse population, where many of the commons were so large that allotments to individuals gave satisfaction, it was possible to enclose land with a fair measure of amity. And so, some estate building was achieved without friction— much of it was accomplished by peaceful exchange and enclosure initiated by the landowners who bought out the tenants of these enclosed lands at a satisfactory price.

The landowners drew their strength not only from their properties. They monopolized the local administration of the country—as sheriffs, justices of the peace, and holders of other offices. This did more than give them power at local level, for they were able to exploit their authority to line their own pockets. Much has already been written about the conduct of the Welsh local officials during the period and, although the most severe strictures should be treated with care, there is no doubt that local government office afforded the landowner with opportunities to establish himself in an unassailable position in the Welsh countryside.

Another important feature was that of marriage alliances. A prudent marriage could bring a man additions to his estates and consolidate his position at the head of local society. In the case of the more prominent families these marriages established ties of a much more than local significance, and the correspondence of the time reveals the care and attention to detail which were lavished upon matches. The leading families of Wales were linked together by a virtual web of matrimonial alliances—the Wynns of Gwydir, for instance, were joined in this way to the Maurices of Clenennau, the Bulkeleys of Baron Hill, the Caermilwr Salesburys, and the Griffiths family of Penrhyn. In the south, too, the future prosperity of the Morgans family of Tredegar and the Vaughans of Trawscoed, to name but two, owed much to the care bestowed by their predecessors on the marriage of their children.

These were the means by which the gentry families established themselves at the head of the social structure of Wales. Both Rowland Lee and George Owen may have been guilty of some overstatement when the former in 1536 claimed that north of Breconshire there was hardly one Welshman who owned land to the value of £10 a year, while the latter at the end of the century boasted of the numbers who enjoyed an income of £500, £300, and £100 from the same source. But there is sufficient truth in the contrast to offer some yardstick with which to measure the progress achieved by these families. A Sir Richard Bulkeley, with estates in Anglesey, Caernarvonshire, and Cheshire worth £4,300, and 'having always a great store of ready money lying in his chest', had no equal in the Wales of the early seventeenth century. There were very few who enjoyed an income of £1,000 a year and not many more who could boast £500—it was easier in 1636 to find fifty gentlemen with an income of £100 a year than five with £500. The annual income of the more substantial landowners was usually between £300 and £400, but the majority—'the mountain squires' especially—fell far short of this. In terms of wealth, these compared with the reasonably substantial yeomen of England.

Within this section of society there were then wide differences in many respects—in wealth, prestige, local influence, and contacts with the wider world. It is, however, possible to discern features which were characteristic of these families. There was, for instance, their land hunger—official records and family papers both testify to the tremendous interest which they had in the acquisition of land. Then there was the pride which members of the class felt in their families. Sir John Wynn of Gwydir was not the only one to consider it a great heart's ease to discover that he was well descended. This was typical of the *nouveaux riches* desire to establish oneself socially, but it also reflects the tremendous part which kinship had for centuries played in Welsh life not only in general terms but more specifically in determining rights in land. It must also be remembered that theirs was a period of transition in which the family remained the social unit with which the individual could best identify himself. A more aggravating characteristic was their litigiousness—they were for ever taking one another to court.

This was no doubt the result in part of the very busy market in land, but it also reveals the very real respect they had for the outward forms of law and their appreciation of the results achieved by the new laws and the courts which administered them. Finally, there was the welcome which many of them gave to anglicizing influences. This was not new, nor should we exaggerate its extent, for many of the gentry remained thoroughly Welsh throughout our period. At the same time, it cannot be denied that the English language, English attitudes, and English family connections were becoming increasingly characteristic of the gentry families.

Among the more permanent of the memorials to their growing prosperity are the houses which they built for themselves and their families. Their desire to create an impression upon their neighbours coupled with the increasing prosperity which rising prices brought them led many of the gentry to give more attention to their domestic comfort. Insignificant as is the size of many of their houses by later standards, the period witnessed important developments in the domestic architecture of the countryside. Some of the great magnates continued to live in their castles, though they altered them substantially, paying less attention to their defences and more to the comfort of the occupants. The most common type of house for much of the sixteenth century was the 'hall house'. Originally a single room occupying the full height of the building it developed into a three-unit house—there was the open hall and entrance passage, below the passage was the service room and beyond the hall a retiring-room. Its walls were made of stone or were timber framed with the panels filled with wattle and daub. The roof was of stone, slate, or thatch, and was supported by a cruck truss. Windows were usually unglazed and consisted of closely spaced wooden mullions, with sometimes a thin, horn-like sheet stretched across the mullions, and they had shutters. The hall was heated by an open hearth in the middle of the floor, and there was no chimney.

After 1550 particularly there were marked changes in house building—houses of two storeys became general, with fireplaces, chimneys, and permanent staircases. At first these were no more than the old hall-house with the hall floored over and a permanent stair and fireplace added. Gradually, however, the cruck-truss gave way to the 'box-frame' structure. These houses varied substantially in the details of construction, especially in respect of the place of entry and the siting of the fireplace.

(a) House with lateral entry and inside cross passage.
(Joan Thirsk: *The Agrarian History of England and Wales*, Fig. 40, p. 794)

These variations reflected certain social differences and the influence exerted by the regions of England. In North Wales houses with an inside cross passage and chimneys on the outside walls were common (*a*) whereas in South Wales the more usual point of entry was at the end of the house (*b*). The new houses of mid Wales were different in that the chimney was sited in the centre (*c*).

K

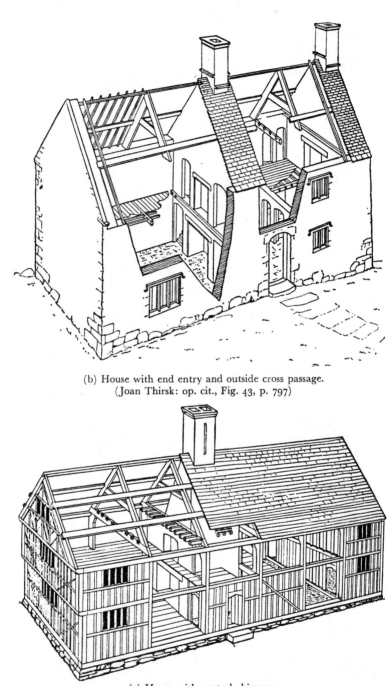

(b) House with end entry and outside cross passage.
(Joan Thirsk: op. cit., Fig. 43, p. 797)

(c) House with central chimney.
(Joan Thirsk: ibid., Fig. 46, p. 800)

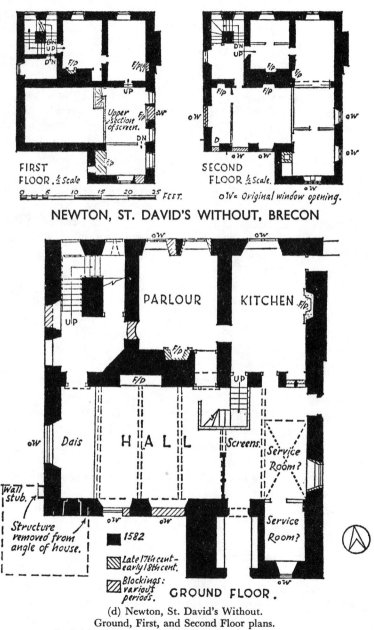

NEWTON, ST. DAVID'S WITHOUT, BRECON

(d) Newton, St. David's Without.
Ground, First, and Second Floor plans.
Brycheiniog, Vol. xl, 1965 (ed. D. J. Davies, Fig. 6, p. 27).

The late sixteenth century saw the appearance of houses which bore the influence of the Renaissance. These were built for wealthy men of the world and imitated the style of the Court. They were compact, centrally planned and compartmentalized, completely different from the traditional, long, open-type house. The staircase was sited in a central position near the entrance to provide easy access to all parts of the house. There was much more emphasis on the appearance of the house: the porch was often storeyed, the use of glass allowed more freedom for the siting of windows, chimneys were ornamented, as were the doorways and interior woodwork (*d*). Impressive these houses may have been, but they were by no means typical, for few houses only before 1640 show any considerable Renaissance influence. At the close of our period the vast majority of Welsh houses were still built according to the traditional plans of their own neighbourhoods.

The occupants of the houses

It would be as unwise to generalize about life in these houses as about the houses themselves. There were in the Wales of the time many gentry families, but very few of them had the means to live on a scale at all comparable with that of the majority of their English counterparts. While the houses of these few were imposing and well furnished, it should not be forgotten that they lacked many of the domestic amenities which are considered essential in any modern house. As for the majority of the houses, they were little better than larger farmhouses of a later age, with few of the material comforts of life. The standard of living of their occupants was modest and the horizons of their daily round limited. Much more is known of the daily life of the minority, for the bulk of the family papers which have survived were those of the wealthier Welsh gentry. Fascinating as is the picture which they give of the lives of these families, we should not be misled into thinking that they reflect the life of any but the wealthiest among the Welsh gentry.

The master of the house had enough to occupy his time. There were the affairs of the estate which involved him in a multitude of activities—supervising the farming, marketing the produce, attending to leases, collecting rents, seeing to improvements, and, of course, acquiring more land whenever the opportunity arose. Many a Welsh gentleman had broadened the scope of his interests and was involved in mining enterprises —for coal, iron, or lead—quarried the stone on his land, had engaged in maritime trade or even in fishing. Then there were his responsibilities as an official in local government: administering justice, seeing to the performance of the ever-increasing number of obligations with which local administrators were saddled by the central government—supervising the relief of the poor, issuing licences of various kinds, hunting out recusants, organizing the militia, and recruiting soldiers.

There were, too, his duties to his family. Arrangements had to be made for the education of his children—schools and university places had to be found for his sons, tutors for his daughters. Sons had to be settled in a profession or trade, marriages had to be arranged for sons and daughters alike. All these were matters which he took very seriously and to which he devoted much care and attention. Nor were the members of his immediate family alone in making their demands upon him. Relatives and friends importuned his assistance in a host of different ways. Some merely wanted a buck or a piece of venison from his deer park; others pleaded for his support to obtain church livings, household positions, or desirable marriages for their children or charges; yet others begged his intervention in legal matters, family feuds, domestic squabbles, or business transactions.

His position in society required that he participate in the business of the county, especially in that increasingly important matter of electing members of Parliament for the county and county town. He was expected to play his part in the hunting, hawking, fowling, and fishing of the district. It was incumbent, on him to entertain—lavishly if there were a visiting notability —from time to time.

All these responsibilities he accepted—albeit grudgingly in the case of some. For many a Welsh gentleman they were sufficient in themselves; others, however, pursued their own particular interests. They collected books, patronized poets, supported scholars, studied astronomy, or experimented with fruits and flowers in their gardens.

Finally, from time to time, his business interests or public responsibilities took him away from home. Sometimes it was merely to visit the near-by county town for a day or two; sometimes to the more distant Ludlow, the seat of the Council of Wales and the Marches, or to London itself. These latter visits involved weary days on horseback over treacherous roads and possible attacks by thieves and robbers. His family took advantage of these visits of his—they commissioned him to obtain for them the clothes, furnishings, and other articles which they required.

The lady of the house was drawn from the same social circle as her husband and had, more often than not, been married at an early age. She was kept equally busy, though her activities may not have been so varied nor so interesting as her husband's. For the most part, she organized the household, took charge of the children, appointed the servants and supervised their training. She had been less exposed to the prevailing influences of the time than her husband, and it was from her usually that the children learnt to speak the Welsh language. There were occasions when she set aside her mere household duties to concern herself in her husband's affairs. In some respects, she enjoyed a greater measure of independence and exercised a wider degree of influence over the affairs of the family than did her counterpart in England. Certainly she enjoyed more protection—in customs which had their origins in the old Welsh laws.

Families were usually large by present-day standards. The practice of early marriage helped to compensate for the frequent deaths at childbirth or in early infancy. Few equalled the nineteen children of Roger Vaughan of Cathedine in Breconshire, but families of six or more children were by no means uncommon. Sir Thomas Stradling of St. Donat's in Glamorgan had six children; his son, Sir Edward, had eleven. Maurice Wynn of Gwydir had seven children; his son, Sir John, had twelve. Small wonder that the rearing, training, and settling of their children caused the parents no little concern and involved them in no inconsiderable expense.

The farmers

Below the gentry Welsh rural society was graded from the yeomen farmers to the landless labourers, though there were no rigid demarcation lines between the different grades. A person's status depended in large measure upon his personal wealth and the impression he created by his way of living. One consideration was the nature of a person's tenure of the land which he farmed. There were, for instance, the freeholders who, despite the name, did owe some obligations. They were liable to pay relief, they owed suit of court, and had to grind their corn at the lord's mill; they might also be summoned to perform various tasks like guarding the church when wrongdoers had taken refuge within its walls, protecting wrecks along the coast, and following the lord in time of war. These freeholders were to be found most frequently in the Welsh parts: in the anglicized districts their place was taken by the customary tenants. These paid their rents in money and dues and in the performance of certain services. In 1610 on the earl of Pembroke's manor of Caegurwen in Glamorgan customary tenants, in addition to their money rents, had to pay a heriot of the best beast they owned, or five shillings if they owned no beast, and a fine of five shillings to alienate any lands. In addition, they had to grind their corn at the lord's mill for which they had to pay the miller an agreed portion of their corn; they had to 'scoure and cleanse the mill ditch water courses that runneth to turn the same' and to thatch the mill house. They had to attend the two Leet courts which were held annually and the monthly Manor Court and to take their turn in performing the office of beadle. There were, too, the socage tenants, holders of small units of land, who in addition to their rents made token payments of a gillyflower or a pound of pepper for their holdings. Finally, there were the leaseholders, men who held land relet by freehold or customary tenants for varying periods—for life or a term of lives or a period of years.

The yeomen were often business men as well as farmers. They frequently accumulated land and manorial rights; the wealthier among them often invested money in trade—in the local market towns or as part-owners of boats engaged in the carrying trade or in fishing. Some took advantage of the need for ready capital to lend money to neighbouring farmers, others became substantial cattle traders. There were those who hired livestock to less wealthy neighbours or let land with stock in return for rent—which they often specified should be paid in kind, in order to avoid depreciation through rising prices.

The more successful among them were able to make the most of their opportunities and climb into the ranks of the squire-archy.

The smaller farmers lived close to subsistence level—even among the better-to-do reserve capital was practically non-existent. A poor harvest or an outbreak of murrain might well spell the doom of a number of the financially weaker farmers. It is dangerous to generalize, but a personal estate of £50 could well command for its possessor a place among the yeomen. The majority of the farmers would have considerably less—under £30—while there were a substantial number with a personal estate of under £10. In terms of acreage, a farm of 30 acres or so would be considered a substantial one; much more numerous were units of some 12 acres. It is not surprising, there-fore, that rights of common were jealously guarded for these were very important to people operating on so small a scale. In fact, the use which could be made of the common often determined the organization of the farm—the proportion of arable to pastoral was frequently dictated by the farm's proximity to the common land. In the case of the adjacent farms some two-thirds or even three-quarters of the land might be under the plough, the more remote would obviously have to forgo some of their crops in order to pasture their animals.

The farmer's year was dictated by the seasons and controlled by custom. The general pattern varied from one region to another, but generally the busiest time of the year was between Midsummer and Michaelmas, the end of the old farming year. By All Hallows Day the winter corn was to be sown and the cattle driven into the byres for the cold months. At Candlemas tillage was resumed after the winter and the cattle driven from the spring corn field which was generally under seed by Lady Day. The cattle were put out to pasture by May Day and the sheep dipped between then and Midsummer Day—the tradi-tional start of the hay harvest. Thereafter, the farming year built up to its climax with the corn harvest, followed by the slaughtering of cattle for the winter, except in those more favoured areas where they could be kept through the winter months.

The landless

Day labourers, artificers, and masterless servants constituted the lowest ranks of rural society. The majority of these were the landless labourers whose days were spent in 'continual labour in tilling of the land, burning of lime, digging of coals and other slaveries and extreme toils'[1] from dawn to dusk. True they were allowed a respite of an hour or so at noon, and in some Welsh parts of the country there was the custom whereby between May Day and the corn harvest they were allowed a two-hour siesta between noon and two o'clock. Nor must it be forgotten that, in addition to Sundays, there were quite frequent holy days on which they were not required to work. Altogether these numbered between twenty-five and thirty in the year by the end of the sixteenth century. There was no month in the year without at least one of them, in most there were at least two and there was a veritable rash of five in the latter part of December. No doubt it was on these days that they tended their garden patches on which they grew their vegetables—leeks, cabbage, onions, peas, and beans.

Their staple foodstuffs, however, they had to buy and it is in relation to these that we are able to hazard some estimate of their living standards. The general picture in this respect is not one of increasing affluence—quite the contrary. By the end of the sixteenth century a day labourer might earn 6*d.* a day, with an additional penny at harvest time; this represented a substantial drop in real earnings as compared with those of his counterpart in the early fourteenth century. The first twenty years of the seventeenth century saw a further deterioration in the labourer's economic condition for this was a period of rapidly increasing prices. George Owen estimated that a farm worker at the end of the sixteenth century consumed annually about six and a half bushels of oats, one bushel of oat malt for ale, three-quarters of a Cardigan stone of cheese, one and a half gallons of butter, and half a quarter of meat. At the 1615 level of prices this would cost about £2 a year, the equivalent of eighty days' wages, and this was not the peak of the price rise. Somewhat different was the position of the single labourers, the *qweision*, who agreed terms for the year at the hiring fairs which

---

[1] George Owen: *The Description of Pembrokeshire*, Part 1, op. cit., pp. 42–3.

were usually held in October, and generally lived with the farmer's family.

Regulation of labour was an integral part of governmental economic and social policy. Wages were fixed by the justices of the peace to accord with prices and the high constables convoked annual 'sessions of labourers' whose functions were to consider cases of the payment of excessive wages, of complaints brought by masters against servants, or of those who wished to hire or retain servants for the following year. Juries of twenty-four substantial freeholders were convened to discover whether the terms of the Statute of Artificers had been observed. Fugitive servants were hunted down and the mobility of labour was restricted as much as possible. These were the precautions which were taken to keep the landless labourers in order, and they became increasingly repressive as the poverty among the lower ranks of rural society became more acute. This last was the outcome of the growing population, the concentration of landholding, and the increasing popularity of livestock farming —all of which were, in large measure, outside the control of the local officials.

The towns

The vast majority of the eighty-seven towns of medieval Wales had been established as English plantations during the two hundred and fifty years that followed 1066. Their founders had, for the most part, been English marcher lords and English kings, though a few towns owed their existence to the initiative of native Welsh princes and Welsh landowners. Many of them had attracted a considerable number of burgesses despite the dangers involved in living in a recently conquered and frequently hostile area. They varied very considerably in size— from Cardiff with its 421 burgage plots in 1296 to Old Dynevor with its 11 in 1301. Between these two extremes a number topped the three hundred burgages—Haverfordwest, for instance, had 360 in 1324; more contained between two and three hundred—Newport (Monmouthshire) had 256 in 1296; a substantial number had between one and two hundred— Conway had 124 in 1312; and there were many with fewer than a hundred—Llanidloes had 66 in 1309, Bala 53 in 1311, and Cefnllys 20 in 1332.

The function of many of the towns was to serve the castles under the shadow of whose walls they had developed, so that their location was determined by strategic considerations. These castles had been built to consolidate English penetration into Wales—on the border between England and Wales, on the frontiers of marcher lordships, and on the fringes of conquered territory far into Wales. Other towns were sited at important communication points which were defended by castles—fifteen of them were seaports, eight estuarine ports, and nine inland river ports. The high density of towns in medieval Wales is, in part, explained by the fact that so many were intended to serve the castles which proliferated in Wales because of the nature of the terrain and of the means by which English penetration was accomplished. But it has been suggested that it was also the result of economic factors—the difficulties of transport and communication in Wales and the marketing needs of a primarily pastoral as opposed to an arable economy.

Inevitably some of the planted towns were failures—and the reasons for their failure are to be found in local and particular conditions. But after 1330 there was a general contraction in town life throughout Europe, not least in Wales. Basically this was a response to a slowing down in the rate of increase of population and in the colonizing of new land. Not surprisingly, therefore, there is at the opening of our period abundant evidence of urban decay.

Leland, writing in the 1530s, observed some of this—Mold had so declined that 'in all be scant forty houses'; Criccieth was 'now clean decayed'; Hay 'within the walls is wonderfully decayed'; and Llandovery 'hath but one street, and that poorly built of thatched houses'. One of the most unfortunate of the towns had been Kidwelly in Carmarthenshire. The old town around the castle walls had declined steadily and was 'near all desolated', but a new town three times as large as the old had grown up on the other side of the river, the Gwendraeth Fechan. But when the haven became unsafe for shipping as a result of the silting of the river, the town received a blow from which it did not recover.

In addition to the general contraction in urban life already referred to there had been the ravages of the Black Death which decimated the population and whose effects were particularly felt in the congested and insanitary towns. In Wales, too, the revolt of Owain Glyn Dŵr and the disorders of the fifteenth century were calamities from which some towns took a long time to recover. Leland reported that the ruin of Hay was 'ascribed to Owain Glyn Dŵr' and Sir John Wynn informed his readers that grass grew in the market place at Llanrwst in the opening years of the Tudor period. Nor was Harlech the only town which suffered during the Wars of the Roses. But wars and infectious diseases were not the only forces making for change. Many of the town buildings were of wood so that they were particularly vulnerable to fire—102 burgages in Trellech (Monmouthshire) had been destroyed by fire in 1296. In many cases towns had outgrown their original subservience to the castles, a number of which had been allowed to fall into decay. The towns which had been established around them were thus deprived of the *raison d'être* of their existence; certainly the original pattern imposed upon them by the role which had brought them into existence was unsuited to the new functions which they were called upon to perform.

Some towns had met the challenge by modifying the original sites. In the case of Denbigh, for instance, there were, by Leland's time, a bare eighty householders within the walls of the old town whereas outside the old walls a new town had developed much more conveniently situated in respect of transport and water supply. Leland confessed himself to be at a loss to explain the changes which had taken place at Denbigh— 'whether it were by fire or for lack of water, whereof there is little or none, or for lack of good carriage into the town standing somewhat high and on rocky ground'. Other towns were more fortunate—they had fewer problems to overcome, they had suffered less damage or were so situated that they could respond more easily to the changing times. Tenby, for instance, was prospering, and this was reflected in the overspilling of the urban community beyond the old walls—a pleasant suburb was growing outside the gate leading to Carmarthen. Carmarthen itself had profited by Kidwelly's misfortune and had grown considerably. Brecon was bursting at the seams and a suburb was beginning to grow outside one of its gates.

Urban growth was a characteristic feature of the social life of the sixteenth and seventeenth centuries. Almost without exception the expansion of the towns outstripped the general growth in population, and this is especially noticeable in the areas of slow population growth. In the middle decades of the sixteenth century there were a few towns, like Carmarthen and Brecon, with an estimated population of near or just over 2,000; others, like Wrexham and the ports of Cardiff, Swansea, and Haverfordwest were near or above 1,000; and there were about thirty small market towns whose population varied from two to four hundred. Estimates of population in 1670 show a significant increase in the size of almost all towns in Wales. In North Wales, Wrexham's estimated 1,515 of 1545/1563 had increased to 3,225, Caernarvon's 800 to 1,755; in mid Wales Montgomery's 308 had grown to 678, Knighton's 400 to 495; while in South Wales Swansea's 960 had increased to 1,733, and Pembroke's 632 to 1,202.

The growing congestion within the old towns drove many of the more prosperous inhabitants to the less busy suburbs, in much the same way as later generations were to retreat from the factories and iron works. There was, too, the incentive for many of escaping from the restrictions imposed by the town regulations upon trade and industry. Before the end of our period this process was well advanced—Brecon in the mid seventeenth century had some four hundred families, of which only 152 lived inside the walls. Nor was it in mere numbers that there had been important changes. The towns had been the exclusive preserves of English settlers, but contraction and depopulation had created a situation where Welshmen were first permitted and later encouraged to settle in them. At Bala there were Welsh inhabitants as early as 1346, while of Brecon's four hundred families at the end of our period only thirty were of English name and descent.

The bonds between the towns and their environs had always been close, they were to become even stronger as a result of the changes which were taking place. Townsmen who had prospered were investing money in land and laying the foundations of the county families of the future; wealthier landowners found it both politic and convenient to establish bases for themselves in the local shire towns and so bought or built town houses. The yeomen who had capital to spare ventured into the world of commerce which was centred upon the towns; dispossessed farmers drifted into the towns to find a home for themselves and their families. Townspeople became increasingly dependent upon the produce of the countryside, the inhabitants of the latter ever more involved in the marketing facilities of the towns. As government made itself increasingly felt at local level, so the towns—its natural bases of operation—became the administrative as well as the economic centres of their districts. The larger of them became provincial capitals exerting an influence upon an area wider than their immediate neighbourhood.

The inhabitants

At the top of the social scale were the outsiders—the families of the great who owned town houses and occasionally visited the different parts of their widely scattered estates. They exercised a very considerable influence over the destinies of the towns, despite their prolonged absences, through their stewards and officials. Next to them were the local gentry families who had residences within the town, from whose ranks were frequently drawn the borough members of Parliament and not infrequently the chief officers of the borough. Relations between these and the townspeople were not always friendly—conflicts often occurred as a result of the town's wish to free itself from their control. The commercial activity of the town was controlled by the tradesmen and craftsmen, the shopkeepers, and the yeomen engaged in trade. Some of these were wealthier than the gentry who resided in the towns, but they occupied a lower position in the social structure and their way of life created less of an impression in an age of ostentation. Below them there were the manual workers and labourers employed on a daily wage. At the bottom of the social ladder were the poor—the aged and infirm, those who would or could not obtain a means of earning their livelihood.

Of the inhabitants of the borough the significant section was that of the freemen. These were the individuals who possessed the full rights of the townsmen. They attended the Court Leet of the borough, monopolized the trade within its boundaries, enjoyed the right of pasturage on the commons of the borough, and elected the member of Parliament, and from their numbers were drawn the officials of the town and the council members.

What proportion they constituted of the total population is impossible to say for there were substantial variations as between one borough and another. Qualifications for entry into this privileged group also varied—in some boroughs freedom was achieved by a successful completion of apprenticeship, subject to the approval of the principal officer and the body of freemen; in others some could claim the right by birth and there were yet others where it was gained by election at the Court Leet. The conditions to be fulfilled also varied—in some towns it was necessary to be resident within the borough and freedom could be lost by a continuous absence of a year and a day; in others this residence qualification did not apply—and this opened the door to a number of malpractices, especially at parliamentary elections.

They were also members of their respective trade or craft guilds. True, gilds were in decline at this time, but every one entitled to membership was expected to join his particular guild, and the period witnessed deliberate attempts to breathe new life into these organizations. They had their officers, duly elected and formally sworn in; they might have their chapel in the local church to which they paraded with due ceremony on their patron saint's day; they made their corporate contributions to the social activities of the town. But they were essentially organizations of traders and craftsmen who had bought the privileges enjoyed by their members. There were, for instance, the corvisers of Ruthin who had obtained in 1496 from George Grey, earl of Kent and lord of Ruthin, a virtual monopoly on the sale of footwear in the town in return for the payment of twenty shillings and an annual four shillings. Unfortunately this had been ignored and circumvented and they had later to pay a further £5 and an annual twenty-five shillings to obtain confirmation of the original grant. They had their own charter and the usual officials; they also had their articles for the control of the craft within the town. These regulated terms of entry into the trade, stipulated the conditions on which individuals were to participate, and defined the responsibilities of individual members to the guild and its officers.

SUGGESTED READING

Calendars of family papers in the National Library of Wales; especially:

Calendar of Wynn (of Gwydir) Papers, 1515–1690 (ed. Ballinger). Aberystwyth, 1926.

Clenennau Letters and Papers in the Brogyntyn Collection. Part 1 (ed. T. Jones Pierce). Aberystwyth, 1947.

Calendar of Salusbury Correspondence, 1553–c. 1700 (ed. W. J. Smith). Cardiff, 1954.

G. Dyfnallt Owen: *Elizabethan Wales: the Social Scene*. Cardiff, 1962.

H. A. Lloyd: *The Gentry of South-west Wales 1540–1640*. Cardiff, 1968.

Articles:

David Williams: 'A Note on the Population of Wales, 1536–1801', *B.B.C.S.*, viii, 1935–7.

Leonard Owen: 'The Population of Wales in the Sixteenth and Seventeenth Centuries', *Trans. Cymmr.*, 1959.

W. Ogwen Williams: 'The Social Order in Tudor Wales', ibid., 1968.

E. D. Jones: 'The Register of the Corvisers of Ruthin, 1520–1671', ibid., I, 1940.

10. The New Learning

THE general changes of the sixteenth and seventeenth centuries were, on the one hand, reflected in, and, on the other, themselves determined to a considerable extent the developments which took place in the cultural life of Wales. The closer ties with England, the increasing social pressures—English in origin or by adoption, the influence of an education which was classical and English, and of printed books published overwhelmingly in the English language—all were powerful forces making for change. Ambition, avarice, and snobbery combined with other, less unworthy, motives to promote English and things English among the able, the well-to-do, and the worldly of Wales. Nor was this left to the mere operation of chance, for the English government and some of the leading Welsh exponents of the New Learning were anxious to encourage a knowledge of the English language among the Welsh people. The inevitable anglicization of the gentry which followed caused many of them to pay scant regard to their mother tongue and to neglect their responsibilities as patrons of the bards. Their negligence in this respect was partly responsible for the serious deterioration which occurred in the traditional literary activity of the country during the later sixteenth century and was to become increasingly apparent during the century that followed. All this must, obviously, weigh heavily in any balance account to be drawn of the profit and loss which accrued to Wales during these years.

The language

While there is no denying the unfortunate consequences of the period upon the Welsh language, there are certain points worthy of consideration. First, it must be remembered that the Welsh language, alone among the Celtic languages of the British Isles, was able to withstand with any measure of success the English challenge of these years. Secondly, those individuals

L

who succumbed to anglicization before the time of rapid industrial growth constituted only a small proportion numerically of
the population. It is true, however, that this was the socially
significant section of the Welsh people, whose members
determined for two centuries after the union the religious,
political, and economic destinies of their fellow countrymen.
But, again, it was not the union, nor yet the victory at Bosworth, which set in motion those forces which changed the
linguistic loyalties of the leaders of Welsh society. Finally, the
transformation was not accomplished until after the close of our
period and this was, in part, the result of a radical change in the
nature and composition of the gentry class in Wales. It has been
suggested that up to 1558 the gentry were more Welsh than
English in their language, that during the years 1558 and 1650
they became more English than Welsh, and that after 1650 they
were thoroughly English. But we must remember that during the
seventeenth century, especially from its middle decades, the
number of the gentry families fell considerably as individual
families acquired, through purchase or marriage, ever wider
estates. Demotion to the yeoman class was the price paid by some
for the increasing prosperity of others. It seems, therefore, that
in the context of the language we again face a paradox in the
Wales of our period. There were in operation those forces which
intensified the threat to the Welsh language, and others which
favoured its preservation, or at least put a brake on its decline.

The contacts which existed between Welshmen and English
have already been considered. In various walks of life—
administration and commerce, the law and education, social
habits and family relationships—these contacts were close and
frequent. The Welshmen concerned acquired, to differing
degrees, a competence in the English language which became
more apparent with the passage of each succeeding generation.
This reached a climax during the hundred years that followed
the union, partly because of the broadening of the fronts on
which the existing contacts were made, partly too because of
the growing strength of the English language and the operation
of other factors which were new and powerful.

The victory of Henry Tudor at Bosworth and the union of the
two countries had obviously increased the traffic over the
Severn—of Englishmen bound for Wales in search of heiresses

and a wider scope for their enterprise, as well as Welshmen seeking fame and fortune in England. English had always possessed the advantage of being the language of the larger, more powerful, and economically more advanced community. But earlier this had been discounted to some extent by the fact that in polite society it had only since the fourteenth century ousted French as the accepted medium of polite speech and because Latin was until very much later the language of the Church and of scholarship. During the sixteenth century, however, English gained strength by becoming the linguistic symbol of the new unity which England acquired in State and Church, and through its promotion in the Celtic fringe by a central government anxious to impose a stamp of uniformity upon the various parts of its realm. Finally, the circulation of English books among Welshmen educated according to the English pattern must have exercised an influence upon the literate of Wales less apparent, certainly, but not unlike that of the mass media of communication and entertainment of the present day.

Nevertheless, there were circumstances which favoured the continuance of the Welsh language. The nature of Welsh society, based on an agrarian—and much of that a pastoral— economy, involved few concentrations of population of any appreciable size, poor communications, and little mobility among the mass of the people. This limited contacts outside the immediate neighbourhoods and predisposed the inhabitants to cling to the accustomed and the familiar habits—and of these the most obvious was the use of their mother tongue. That the vast majority of the people remained monoglot Welsh was a fact of life with which government and gentleman had to come to terms. The language clauses of the Act of 1536 simply could not be implemented, the hopes of the government could not be realized. Available evidence suggests that more Welsh was used in the lower courts than English and that much Welsh was spoken too in the Quarter Sessions and the Great Sessions; that minor officials in the local government had to be recruited from the ranks of Welsh-speaking Welshmen, and that a knowledge of Welsh was considered necessary by many among the gentry for the management of their estates and the conduct of public business.

The religious changes of the time also made their contribution. The need to propagate Protestant beliefs and teaching could only be effectively met through the medium of the Welsh language. The translation of the Bible and the Book of Common Prayer made it possible to conduct services in Welsh. The tactics of the Welsh Protestant propagandists could not but engender a certain loyalty to their language among the mass of the people. The continuance of the Welsh language was part of the price which had to be paid for the success of the established Church—and the government was aware of this. Not that it had shown any positive hostility to the language; its approach had been rather to encourage a knowledge of English among the Welsh people.

Especially significant in the persistence of the language in the households of the gentry families was the influence of the women. Since education was the prerogative of the other sex, they were not exposed to the same degree to anglicizing influences. Moreover, they were in more frequent contact with their Welsh-speaking servants—a knowledge of Welsh was necessary for the efficiency of their household management since most of their domestic servants were drawn from monoglot Welsh men and women. Fathers saw to it that their daughters acquired some facility in the language, husbands who had married English wives did likewise. It would not be surprising that they transmitted some of their knowledge to their children. Sir Peter Mytton, for instance, enjoyed a distinguished career at the bar, became a member of Parliament and of the Council of Wales and the Marches, and was appointed a judge. He was nearly forty years of age when he married an orphan, and the letter in which he explained to his mother the terms of the marriage settlement was written in Welsh. The more distinguished earl of Pembroke was praised for his loyalty to his mother's language—'yr hwn na phlychiai arno ag ny 'mattaliai 'mysc goreugwyr y Deyrnas adrodh iaith ei vam' (he who would not refrain from speaking his mother's language in the company of the greatest in the kingdom). True, this would not be the language of the bards or of learning, but the practice would help to slow down the disappearance of Welsh in this section of society.

A lowering of linguistic standards in some respects there may well have been, a marked deterioration in literary achievement undoubtedly took place, among the well-to-do and the educated the language all but disappeared. But these were not the results of a determined policy to destroy the language, nor was the picture one of unrelieved gloom. James Howell, educated at Hereford and Oxford, and employed thereafter exclusively outside Wales, could claim a fair competence in the Welsh language, 'for the cask flavours still of the liquor it first took in'. Judge David Jenkins, after a long and illustrious career at the bar and on the bench, spent his declining years at his home at Hensol in Glamorgan, where he patronized the bards and presided at the eisteddfod held at Ystradowen. Moreover, there was positive achievement in intellectual and cultural activities. Translators provided a body of religious literature in Welsh; collectors safeguarded much of the poetry of Wales; grammarians and lexicographers made Welsh a fit medium of scholarship. The tragedy for Wales was that these men failed to exert any decisive influence upon the traditional bardic culture of the country—a failure which is to be explained partly in terms of the alien forces which the humanists represented and partly in the very nature of the bardic tradition.

Cultural activity

A growing awareness of the need for and the opportunities provided by education took many young Welshmen to Oxford and Cambridge. The widening scope of governmental activity offered lucrative offices to ambitious young men who possessed the necessary qualifications; the efficient management of the growing family estates required education and training; the host of lawsuits which accompanied the dealings in land were an incentive to many to become learned in the law. Added to this was the encouragement given by a government anxious to recruit educated officials in both secular and ecclesiastical administration. At the universities and Inns of Courts these young men were exposed to the New Learning, to a classical education—whose ethos was considered especially relevant to the training of enlightened administrators. But one of the most significant features of the New Learning in England was the study of the Scriptures and it found its most positive expression in the spheres of religious thought and practice.

It was not unnatural, therefore, in the circumstances of the sixteenth century that the immediately visible effect of the New Learning in Wales was to be seen in the sphere of religion and morality. The Welsh humanists attempted to combine the classical and Christian literatures in order to produce purified versions of the Scriptures and restore the old virtues taught by the philosophers and poets of ancient Greece and Rome. The impact which they created would depend very much upon their ability to propagate these among the people at large, and for this the one available medium was the Welsh language. Of course their efforts would receive added support from the existence of an educated body among the laity to whose members the English products of the New Learning were available. That they appreciated this is made clear in the first three books to be printed in Welsh. Sir John Price's *Yn y llyfr hwn* contained translations of those portions of the Scriptures which were in regular use; William Salesbury's *Oll Synnwyr Pen* was a collection of old Welsh proverbs designed as a preliminary to the translation of the Scriptures, and his Dictionary, based on a bardic word list, was intended to assist Welshmen to learn English.

This combination of the religious propagandist and the humanist is the first and most noteworthy feature of the New Learning in Wales. Since the Welsh language was to be the vehicle for the spread of religious teaching and humanist ideals it had to win popular esteem; it had also to be adapted in form and content to make it suitable for the printed book and the conveying of new concepts. It was this which on the one hand accounts for the constant reference to the antiquity of the language, for the arguments that it was a fit medium of learning—as good if not better than other European languages, and for the assumption that its very survival in the face of so many difficulties was proof that God had a special mission for it to perform. On the other hand, it was to equip the language to fulfil its allotted task that determined efforts were made to enrich its vocabulary and standardize its written form. This it was which lay behind the collections which were made of old Welsh literature; it was in part responsible for Salesbury's controversial orthography, and it explains the work of the grammarians like Gruffydd Robert, Siôn Dafydd Rhys and Dr. John Davies, Mallwyd. They were attempting to preserve as much of the old as possible while at the same time borrowing words from other languages and making them acceptable to their fellow countrymen.

The greatest achievement of the humanists was the translation of the Scriptures into a Welsh which, though not spoken, was understood and constituted a standard language superior to any dialect. The project begun by Salesbury and Richard Davies, accomplished by William Morgan and perfected by Dr. John Davies, has made an inestimable contribution to the religious, cultural, and linguistic life of Wales. These men did not labour alone. Thomas Huet made his contribution to the translation of the New Testament, and among the many whose assistance William Morgan acknowledged was Edmwnd Prys, the scholarly poet-priest, humanist, and master of the bardic craft, whose metrical version of the Psalms in Welsh was widely used in the church services.

The religious motive predominated, too, in the translations into Welsh of religious works from English and Latin, but, subsidiary though it might be, the concern for learning was very obvious in them as was the desire to safeguard the Welsh language. This was characteristic of the work of both Protestant and Catholic propagandists, and it is interesting to note that differences of religion did not prevent admiration of one another's work. Some of these publications were intended for the educated few, like Morris Kyffin's translation of Jewel's *Apologia Ecclesiae Anglicanae*, or Rhosier Smyth's Welsh version of *Theater du Mond*; others were intended for use by the parish priests, like Edward James's Book of Homilies; a few were simple books designed for the ordinary people, like Gruffydd Robert's *Y Drych Cristionogawl*. As the religious controversy became more acute during the seventeenth century the emphasis on learning receded in the face of mounting religious propaganda, but in the earlier publications especially the humanist element is clearly apparent in the prose style, in the content and in the objectives which the writers set themselves.

The religious motive is subsidiary to that of the humanist in the attention given to the work of collecting Welsh literature and copying poems, and in the researches into pedigrees and antiquities. The library of Robert Vaughan of Hengwrt was the most important of its kind, but there were other members of the Welsh gentry who were active in this field—men like Sir John Price and Sir Edward Stradling, Humphrey Llwyd and David Powel. The transcribing of manuscripts was a pastime for enlightened gentlemen and clerics, a means to an end for scholars like Dr. John Davies and a professional occupation for copyists like Gruffudd Dwn of Ystrad Meurig, Llywelyn Siôn of Glamorgan, and John Jones of Ysgeifiog, Flintshire. Their work in this field had a direct utilitarian value for the scholars and translators of the time, but it also preserved for future generations a vast body of early Welsh literature which would otherwise have been lost.

Closely connected with this was the interest shown in other aspects of the Welsh past. The defence of Geoffrey of Monmouth's interpretation of Welsh history was the object of an unpublished work by Siôn Dafydd Rhys, as it was of Sir John Price in writing his *Historiae Britannicae Defensio*. It was this refutation of Polydore Virgil's attack upon the old Welsh traditions that Humphrey Llwyd 'augmented and made perfect', and which David Powel, having 'corrected, augmented and continued', published under the title *Historie of Cambria* in 1584. His object was to record 'the whole doings and government of the Britains the first inhabitants of the land, who continued their rule longer than any other nation', and to disprove those slanders against his fellow countrymen 'which do most commonly not only elevate or dissemble all the injuries and wrongs offered and done to the Welshmen, but also conceal or deface all the acts worthy of commendation achieved by them'. Others were concerned less with the past of Wales than with that of their own families or with the genealogies of local families, but their objective was not dissimilar. Was it not 'a great temporal blessing . . . and a great heart's ease to a man to find that he is well descended?'

There were yet others whose primary interest was the past of their own neighbourhoods. For some of these the incentive was the light which their researches would throw upon local precedents, customs, and claims of overlordship. Less utilitarian was the intention of men like Rice Meyrick of Cottrel in Glamorgan whose *A Book of Glamorganshire's Antiquities* was written to afford 'not only necessary and pleasant remembrance . . . but also good examples to the Amendment of life'. The best known, perhaps, of this group was George Owen of Henllys—historian, antiquarian, and genealogist. The centre of a circle of Pembrokeshire writers, a patron of Welsh poets, he was on friendly terms with a host of fellow antiquarians, English as well as Welsh. He was familiar with their writings, corresponded with them, and aided them in their researches. His chief claim to fame is his *The Description of Pembrokeshire* which contained a history of the county and a fascinating portrait of the life, customs, and practices of its people in his own day. He also wrote a number of essays on the lordship of Cemais, inspired no doubt by the lawsuits in which he was involved concerning his claims to manorial franchises there, and made extensive investigations into the genealogies of local families. In addition to all this, he wrote *A Dialogue of the present Government of Wales, A Treatise of Lordships marchers in Wales*, and *The Description of Wales*—works which bear witness to his industry and insight into the Wales of his time.

The impact of all this effort depended in large measure upon two factors: the accessibility of the books themselves and the degree of literacy among the people. In neither of these is it at all possible to be very specific, but it is certain that both presented enormous difficulties. In England the printing press had been established since the late fifteenth century, but there were still risks involved in printing. In Wales, where there was neither a press nor the capital available for establishing one, the risks were, therefore, enormous. The monopoly enjoyed by the Stationers and the difficulties of printing in the Welsh language in London were hurdles high enough in themselves. But in addition, the social conditions in Wales were such as to limit the market even without the added complication of the fact that the printed word was not a suitable medium for Welsh poetry. Patrons, too, were few and far between, even though Sir Edward Stradling financed the publication of Siôn Dafydd Rhys's grammar in 1592 and London Welshmen, like Sir Thomas Myddelton and Rowland Heilyn, met the expense of publishing the first cheap edition of the Welsh Bible in 1630. Small wonder that Ieuan ab William ap Dafydd ab Einws of Powys declared that many of the works he copied were available in print in England, but had to be handwritten in Wales.

The degree of literacy may have been rather greater than has been thought. The probability is that it was almost universal among the gentry and clergy, substantial among the business men and yeomen, and not completely absent among the heads of the other households in Wales. The competence of members of the last group to follow the arguments and appreciate the learning contained in the books is doubtful; certainly the expenditure necessary for their purchase must have proved a stumbling-block. There was, it appears, very little hope of a wide Welsh-reading public; there was too the difficulty that a knowledge of the English language—in which much reading material was available—was confined to relatively few. It was partly to remedy this that so much interest was shown in the establishment of schools.

Education

During the Middle Ages the Church was responsible for providing what education was available to the children of the laity. Some parish and chantry priests taught the young of their parishes in their churches, while song schools were maintained at cathedrals, at collegiate and at some parish churches. There were grammar schools, too, supported by cathedrals and collegiate churches and also by some parish churches and guild priests. At Penllech in Caernarvonshire, at Wrexham, and at Haverfordwest the parish churches maintained grammar schools and at Montgomery another was kept by the guild priest—and it is probable that Montgomery was not alone among the old market towns of Wales in this respect. The contribution of the monasteries to education is a more vexed question. While there is no direct evidence that any of the Welsh monasteries kept a free school, some parish schools continued to exist when their parishes had been appropriated by a monastery. It is likely, too, that monasteries offered some training in the social graces to children of well-to-do families in their neighbourhoods, and that they made some kind of provision for the training of their own novices. We must, however, be careful not to exaggerate their commitments because Welsh monasteries were, most of them, small and in the later Middle Ages seriously undermanned. Inadequate and haphazard as the provision of formal education undoubtedly was in medieval

Wales, that opportunities did exist is testified by the not inconsiderable body of Welshmen among the students at the Universities of Oxford and Cambridge.

From the middle decades of the sixteenth century a number of factors operated in favour of the establishment of schools in Wales. Fathers anxious that their sons should be equipped to take advantage of the opportunities that were coming their way; a government eager for a body of educated men from whom it could recruit the officials it required; committed Protestants hoping to create a literate public in Wales; scholars and enlightened individuals desirous of spreading the New Learning and its ideals; wealthy individuals with a social conscience wishing to offer opportunities of intellectual and moral training to the young of their native districts—all these combined to create a demand for schools and to provide the means whereby this demand might be satisfied.

The first move came from the government. The royal licence for the foundation of Christ College, Brecon, in 1541, to which reference has already been made, expressed concern at the low level of education in the area. It also gave an insight into the Tudor government's objectives for the new schools in Wales— that they should, above all, produce good Christians and loyal subjects, and to this end that they should teach the English language. The school was sited at the house of the Friars Preachers in Brecon and was provided with endowments to pay the salaries of the schoolmaster and usher, a reader of divinity and a preacher whose responsibilities were 'to give instruction in letters, and to expound the gospel purely and freely'. No fees were to be required from the scholars or their parents. The leaders of the new church followed the lead of their master. In 1561 Bishop Thomas Davies of St. Asaph announced that 'the teaching of children is very necessary' and enjoined that 'all good Christians in my diocese to pay such their stipend, accustomed to be paid to the Lady priest, to such schoolmaster as shall be thought meet by me'. There already existed one grammar school in the diocese, though not in Wales, at Oswestry, founded early in the fifteenth century; but it was not until 1595 that another was established—at Ruthin by Gabriel Goodman, Dean of Westminster.

Wealthy laymen also made their contribution. Geoffrey

Glynn, advocate of the court of Arches, provided for the free grammar school at Bangor which was founded in 1557. Sir Edward Stradling in 1608 founded his grammar school at Cowbridge that the young of the district might be trained in the rudiments of grammar and so be the more easily furnished with a good character, and thereby 'might the more felicitously imbibe the sacred precepts of religion'. Nor was Stradling alone—Sir Rice Mansell had made provision for a grammar school at Margam and Sir John Wynn was to establish one at Llanrwst. They were joined by men who had made their fortunes in trade and the professions. John Beddowes, a clothier of Presteign, endowed a grammar school there in 1565 to teach the youth of the town 'virtue and learning'. David Hughes, a native of Llantrisaint in Anglesey, who became steward of the manor of Woodrising in Norfolk, established the grammar school at Beaumaris in 1602 and gave it further endowments in 1609. In 1603 a grammar school was established at Wrexham through the generosity of Valentine Broughton, an alderman of Chester. Monarch and merchant, cleric and gentleman, lawyer and scholar—they provided schools or contributed to the education of the young in many of the larger towns of Wales during the second half of our period. In some cases, they made provision for the maintenance of a schoolmaster, in others they founded schools whose lives were of comparatively short duration. But a number of the schools which were established have continued to educate the young of their districts to the present time.

The schools, frequently modelled on older English schools, were intended to bring the young of Wales into contact with the products of the New Learning and to ground them firmly in the new Protestant faith. The regulations of Friars School, Bangor, for instance, were drawn up by Dr. Alexander Nowell, Dean of St. Paul's. The principal subjects in the curriculum were Latin and Greek, though English was taught in the lower forms of many schools, and provision was made for religious education. A 'short material Catechism' was prepared for the school at Llanrwst in which the pupils were to be instructed on Friday afternoons; the bishop frequently visited the school at St. Asaph to examine the children. The schools offered no instruction in Welsh, and the pupils were discouraged from its use even at play. Dr. Henry Rowlands instructed that the master of his school at Bottwnog had to be an Englishman, while at Ruthin pupils caught speaking Welsh 'shall be deemed faulty and an Imposition shall be given'. Though virtue and learning were the keynotes of the schools, one catches an occasional glimpse of less austere activities—Sir Roger Mostyn, after commending the excellent teaching of English at Hawarden, observes that 'there, if you please, they may learn to dance a musician being in the town' and Sir John Wynn provided a field at Llanrwst 'for a place of recreation and easement for the scholars'.

By modern standards the schools were very small. At Christ College there was provision for twenty 'poor scholars', at Cowbridge the number of free pupils was limited to about fifteen—though the numbers were increased by fee-paying scholars. When, however, it is remembered that some of the wealthiest families employed private tutors, that many sent their sons to be educated in English schools—Shrewsbury and Hereford, but also Westminster, St. Paul's, Eton, and Winchester, one need not be unduly surprised that some thousand Welsh students enrolled at the universities between 1571 and 1621. Humphrey Llwyd's assertion that 'There is no man so poor but for some space he setteth forth his children to School' may have little basis in fact, but it is certainly true that these schools offered opportunities which many young Welshmen seized and, thereby, advanced themselves in wealth and social position as well as learning and piety.

For those who required more than the grammar schools could offer in the way of education and training there were the universities of Oxford and Cambridge. In 1571 Jesus College, Oxford, was founded on the initiative of Dr. Hugh Price of Brecon to cater for the needs of his fellow countrymen—but, though Jesus became the 'Welsh' college, it enjoyed no monopoly of Welsh students. At Cambridge, too, though it did not recruit as many students from Wales as did Oxford, there was a growing Welsh element. Many Welshmen became fellows of colleges at one or other of the universities; some gained considerable distinction as academics and occupied the highest positions in the university teaching hierarchy; others became heads of colleges—and not of Jesus only. Yet others taught in the grammar schools of England and, in some cases, became the headmasters of the most famous schools in the country. The popularity of a career in the law guaranteed a regular supply of Welsh students at the Inns of Court, Lincoln's Inn and Grays Inn especially, some of whose senior members were themselves Welshmen. Finally, there were those who went further afield in search of knowledge—they studied at the centres of learning on the Continent, some of them to gain considerable reputations for their scholarship outside their native Wales.

SUGGESTED READING

R. Brinley Jones: *The Old British Tongue*. Cardiff, 1970.

Thomas Kendrick: *British antiquity*. London, 1950.

Thomas Parry: *Hanes llenyddiaeth Gymraeg hyd 1900*. Cardiff, 1944. English translation: H. I. Bell: *A History of Welsh Literature*. Oxford, 1955.

Articles:

I. M. Williams: 'Ysgolheictod hanesyddol yn yr unfed ganrif ar bymtheg'. *Llên Cymru*, 11, 1952–3.

Glanmor Williams: *Dadeni, Diwygiad, a Diwylliant Cymru*. Caerdydd, 1964.

W. Ogwen Williams: 'The Survival of the Welsh Language after the Union of England and Wales: The First Phase, 1536–1642', *W.H.R.*, vol. 2, No. 1, 1964.

11. Wales in the Early Seventeenth Century

The Scottish succession

IT has been suggested that the dividing line between Tudor and Stuart Wales was drawn by two events which took place in 1601. The first of these was the death of the second earl of Pembroke, for it marked the end of that period during which the President of Wales and the Marches had enjoyed real prestige. The Council had been the Tudor Government's prime instrument in the administration of Wales and its President the royal representative in the country. Already by the later years of Elizabeth's reign the conditions for which it had been designed had changed radically, and so at the turn of the century the Council entered upon a new era in its history which was reflected in the changed stature of its President in Wales. Pembroke's death also marked a change in the nature of the family's contacts with Wales. True, his son held offices under the Crown in Wales and exercised considerable influence over Welsh members of Parliament, but his relationship with Wales was altogether more remote and sustained through intermediaries rather than by direct personal contact. Whereas the father was described as 'the eye of all Wales', the son had become a 'pillar of the kingdom'. The second event was the Essex Rising. The earl's estates in Wales and the influence which he exercised, as the Queen's favourite and the commander of those military expeditions in which many Welshmen were involved, had drawn many of the Welsh gentry into his intrigue. Its disastrous failure marked the end of that period when ambitious Welshmen had pushed their fortunes under his patronage and coincided with a slackening of that control by which the great aristocratic houses had directed the destinies of Welshmen.

The significance of these events should not be misunderstood, for they did not so much inaugurate a new process but rather occasioned a change within a pattern of development already established. Forces which had really been let loose during the sixteenth century were approaching maturity. Welshmen were progressively coming to terms with the practical realities of union and identifying themselves more closely with the concept of the unity of the two countries. This was not a uniform process and inevitably the inhabitants of those parts of the country which were most accessible to the influences of the day advanced more rapidly than their countrymen in the more remote areas. Welsh acceptance of the implications of the new material order is seen in the eagerness with which Welshmen exploited the opportunities which it offered them. It can also be seen in their reaction to the new religious order. At the turn of the century there were few Puritans in Wales but many champions of the new Church of England. This was, in part, the result of the translation of the Scriptures into Welsh and the use of the vernacular in religious services and acts of divine worship, in part, of the development of what might be called political Protestantism to which Welshmen were becoming increasingly committed. Even among the Welsh Catholics few became involved in the plots against the old queen, and the vast majority accepted James as her heir.

All this is important to an understanding of Welsh reaction to the Stuart succession. Early in his reign James I had occasion to remark that Welsh 'Loyalty, Faith and Obedience' were well known to him. Nor was this conclusion founded merely on the conventional addresses of loyalty which he received from various quarters of Wales. The Catholics were the most likely source of opposition to James's succession, and indeed there were Welshmen who were involved in Catholic intrigues against the government. The organizers of the Watson Plot of 1603 were so confident of Welsh support that consideration was given to instigating it in Wales. A very few Welshmen seem to have been involved in pro-Spanish intrigues against James, and certainly on the Continent there were Welsh Catholics, chief among whom was Hugh Owen, who were committed to the cause of a Spanish Catholic Crusade against the heretic king. But the majority of the Welsh Catholics accepted James as king, preferring to hope for some relaxation of the laws against themselves than the prospect of a Spanish ruler on the throne of

England. In this they were encouraged by the fact that James's queen was a convert to their religion as well as by the general undertakings that James himself had given. When the Watson intrigue did come out into the open—in London—support from Wales was negligible.

The reasons for the favourable reaction among the Welsh to the accession of James I are not far to seek. There was the family loyalty which he inherited—James was after all the great-grandson of the victor at Bosworth, and this was without doubt a factor of considerable importance in his favour Elizabeth had recognized him as her heir and so had added her blessing to his succession. James had prepared the ground well by his intrigues with the powerful among Elizabeth's subjects— with Cecil, for instance, and with Essex who wielded so much influence among the gentry of South Wales. The long struggle against Spain identified the Protestant succession in the popular mind with national independence. This would be felt particularly in those areas of south-west Wales which were vulnerable to a Spanish Catholic invasion from the Continent and Ireland. There were those Welshmen whose loyalty was the product of their hopes for rewards at the hands of the new king—and they were not disappointed. Welshmen received their share, and more, of preferment in the Church, within the legal hierarchy and even at Court during James's reign. But more important, perhaps, than any other single consideration was the fact that James's succession threatened least to the new order which many Welshmen had learned to welcome and in which many more had acquiesced.

Horizons widen

Welshmen of the sixteenth and seventeenth centuries welcomed the opportunities offered them by the union and its aftermath. In every walk of life, the professions, scholarship, trade, public office, and the armed forces, Welshmen pressed their fortunes—some with marked success. The vast majority conformed to the established order and benefited thereby, though there were a few rebels, and even the most eminent proved that they were not mere time-servers. We can perhaps best appreciate this widening of horizons if we follow the careers

M

of a few of those Welshmen who seized their opportunities and remember that they were exceptional in the eminence which they achieved rather than in the paths which they trod.

The Church was a much-favoured avenue for advancement, and as the years passed Welshmen certainly received their fair share of ecclesiastical preferment. Welsh bishoprics were increasingly occupied by Welshmen while English sees, royal chaplainships, and high office in the Church hierarchy fell to the lot of a number of them. *Thomas Young*, born at Hodgeston in Pembrokeshire, had held a number of livings in south-west Wales before he became Precentor of St. David's in 1542. Despite his opposition to Ferrar he was a committed Protestant and spent the years of Mary's reign in exile. He returned to Wales to become in 1559 one of the royal investigators of the Welsh bishoprics and, later in the year, the Bishop of St. David's. Then, in January 1561, he was promoted to the archbishopric of York. This, together with his appointment as president of the Council of the North, of necessity made him an important agent in establishing the Elizabethan settlement in the north of England. *Richard Vaughan* of Dyffryn in Llŷn entered the Church during the 1570s. He did not have to wait long for preferment—appointed chaplain to the Bishop of London, he soon became Canon of St. Paul's and then Archdeacon of Middlesex. In 1595 he was promoted Bishop of Bangor and two years later transferred to Chester; then in 1604 he became Bishop of London. His brilliant career was transcended by that of another Caernarvonshire man—*John Williams*. Born at Conway and related to some of the most prominent families of the north-west, educated at the grammar school at Ruthin and St. John's College, Cambridge, his promotion was rapid. Private chaplain to the Lord Chancellor Ellesmere by the time he was thirty, Dean of Westminster eight years later, he was appointed Lord Keeper of the Great Seal and Bishop of Lincoln before he was forty. After a period of frustration and turbulent quarrels during which he lost the favour of Charles I and Laud, he became Archbishop of York in 1641. His last years were an anti-climax, but he had wielded considerable power and had accumulated a large fortune. Then there were the *Goodmans*— *Gabriel* and his nephew *Godfrey*. The former, though denied the highest rank in the Church, became Dean of Westminster and exercised very considerable influence over government policy in Wales during Elizabeth's reign. The latter doubtless owed much to his uncle's connections, for his promotion was again rapid and by 1625 he was Bishop of Gloucester. Thereafter his career was clouded by his leanings towards Roman Catholicism and he suffered much during the Civil War. *Thomas Howell*, of Llangammarch in Breconshire, had to exercise more patience but he too trod the path of clerical preferment and enjoyed the distinction of being the last bishop to be consecrated for sixteen years when he became Bishop of Bristol in 1644.

So popular was a career in the law that one scholar has claimed that the Inns of Court were a positive force in the process of the assimilation of Wales with England. Among the prisoners taken at Hereford by the Parliamentary forces in December 1645 were *Marmaduke Lloyd, David Jenkins*, and *Walter Rumsey*—all judges of the Great Sessions in Wales. Lloyd, the senior judge, was the son of Thomas Lloyd, Precentor and Treasurer of St. David's Cathedral. His career had been a glittering one. Called to the bar in 1609 he was appointed King's Attorney in Wales and the Marches 'for life' in 1614 and made a member of the Council of the Marches in the same year. He had become Recorder of Brecon in 1617, Puisne Justice of Chester in 1622, and his progress had been crowned in 1636 when he was made Chief Justice of the Brecknock circuit. His colleague in this last post was Rumsey who, though descended from an old Hampshire family, had been born at Llanover, Monmouthshire, in 1584. He was called to the bar a year before Lloyd and, with David Jenkins, was made joint Attorney-General in the counties of Carmarthen, Cardigan, Pembroke, Brecon, and Radnor in 1613. He made a substantial fortune and acquired considerable repute at the bar, where his ability earned for him the nickname of 'Picklock of the Law', before being appointed Second Justice of the Brecknock circuit in 1631. *David Jenkins* of Hensol in Glamorgan had a more chequered career. Called to the bar in 1609 and appointed, with Rumsey, Attorney-General in South Wales, he too made a fortune out of the law. During the 1630s he ran foul of the bishops for his opposition to the influence they exercised in political affairs and of the king for his criticisms of the methods adopted by Charles to obtain money. Eventually he became Justice of the Carmarthen circuit in 1643. After his capture at Hereford he became a fearless defender of the king's position and a daring critic of the Parliament.

The most glittering of the earlier success stories which featured those Welshmen who made their fortunes in the business world was that of *Sir Richard Clough*. A younger son of a Denbigh glover, he made his way to London where he found employment in the service of Sir Thomas Gresham. Much of his adult life was spent on the Continent, where he acted as Gresham's agent at Antwerp. He is credited with having been the one who proposed to Gresham the idea of establishing in London an Exchange on the model of that operating at Antwerp. He accumulated a very large fortune, invested in land on a considerable scale, built extensively—and became the second of Katheryn of Berain's four husbands. Outstanding, also, were the careers of the *Myddelton* brothers, *Thomas* and *Hugh*. Thomas, the elder, was apprenticed to a London grocer, and in course of time was granted the freedom of the Grocers' Company. He was appointed Surveyor of the Outposts about 1580, became one of the original shareholders in the East India Company and an important partner in much of the maritime activity of the Elizabethan sea-dogs. He branched out further, became a banker and money lender, invested money in land, was associated with the Virginia Company and supported the New River scheme. His knowledge of commercial affairs was recognized by the government which frequently sought his advice in this sphere. In 1603 he became an alderman and sheriff of London and in 1613 Lord Mayor of the city. His brother, Hugh, was apprenticed to a goldsmith, and it was in this business that he laid the foundations of his wealth. One of his early ventures, as a coal operator, was not a success, but his lease on the lead mines of the Mines Royal Company in Cardiganshire was very profitable. He is best remembered for his ambitious New River scheme whose purpose was to ensure a regular supply of water for the inhabitants of London—'the most serviceable and wholesomest Benefit that ever she received'.[1] *William Jones*, born in Newland, Gloucestershire, grew up in poor circumstances in the town of Monmouth. He migrated to London and from a shop boy became a partner in

---

[1] James Howell to Robert Brown in *The Familiar Letters of James Howell* (ed. Joseph Jacobs). London, 1890, p. 80.

a flourishing haberdashery business. He acquired a large fortune and made a number of benefactions to the town in which he had spent his early days.

No Welsh family reached greater heights through its service to the state than the *Herberts, earls of Pembroke* of the second creation. From the 1540s succeeding earls played a dominant role in Welsh affairs and exercised no inconsiderable influence at the centre of government. William, the first of his line, climbed, through the patronage of the earl of Worcester, into royal favour. Under Henry VIII, his son and daughters, he occupied positions of very considerable importance at court and in the administrative hierarchy. Honours, lands, and offices were showered upon him until he made the mistake of supporting the marriage of Mary, Queen of Scots, and the duke of Norfolk. His son Henry followed in his father's footsteps and, though honours were not bestowed upon him with the same abundance as upon his father, his, too, was a distinguished public career. In turn, he was succeeded by his son William, patron of letters and favourite of James I. He occupied high office and exercised considerable influence until his star waned under Charles I. His brother Philip continued to enjoy royal favour until the Bishops' Wars. Thereafter, he sided with Parliament in its opposition to the king, though he tried more than once to achieve a settlement of the quarrel.

Sir Robert Mansel of Oxwich owed much to the favour of the Pembroke family. He served under the earl of Essex at the siege of Cadiz in 1596 and acquitted himself so well that he was rewarded with a knighthood, first from Essex and then from the queen herself. In the following year he was again engaged in fighting against the Spaniards and 1599 saw him in command of a squadron of three ships off the coast of Ireland. In 1601 he was on duty in the English Channel, responsible for intercepting Spanish ships bound for Dunkirk, Nieuport, and Sluys. Three years later he was made treasurer of the Navy for life and headed a royal commission on the reform of the Navy. Further royal service followed—in 1612 he was involved in a project to discover the North-West Passage. Then in 1613 came a temporary set-back when he was imprisoned for a short period, but this did not last for long and in 1617 he was appointed Vice-Admiral of England. His was a remarkable career—despite his failings as a naval administrator. He was, too, involved in various business ventures, especially those which followed the grant to him and his associates of a monopoly for the manufacture of glass with sea and pit coal. He had factories at London and Newcastle which prospered for a while, despite the attacks upon monopolies by the House of Commons in 1624. Active, too, in politics, he represented a number of constituencies in Wales and England from 1601 to 1628.

The entourage of Prince Charles in Madrid in 1623 contained at least three Welshmen—*Sir John Vaughan*, his son *Richard*, and *James Howell*. Sir John had married the daughter of Sir Gelly Meyrick, the Welsh agent of the earl of Essex, and had fought in Ireland under the earl in 1599. He had extended the family estates in Carmarthenshire and had represented the county at Westminster. Knighted by the king in 1617 he was in the same year appointed Comptroller of the Household of the Prince of Wales. It was in this capacity that he attended Charles on the ill-fated mission to Spain. In 1621 he was created Baron Vaughan of Mullingar and in 1628 the earl of Carbery. His son Richard succeeded him in 1634, played an important part in the Civil War in south-west Wales, survived the interregnum and, after the restoration of Charles II, had honours and positions showered upon him, chief of which was the Presidency of the revived Council of Wales and the Marches. Very different was the story of James Howell. The son of a curate of Llangammarch, educated at Hereford and Oxford, he earned a living first as an employee in Mansel's glass-making venture, during which he travelled extensively on the Continent, then as a private tutor. He was employed on a government mission when Charles visited Madrid and was in close contact with the prince's party. He later held minor government posts and was employed as a government agent. But his claim to fame rests upon his writings. From 1640 a spate of works of all kinds and on a wide variety of subjects flowed from his pen, though he is best remembered for his letters, the first collection of which appeared in print in 1645 under the title *Epistolae Ho-elianae*. Imprisoned by Parliament during the Civil War, he made a living by his pen during the 1650s and in 1661 was appointed Historiographer Royal. Riches and high office did not fall to his lot, but he won for himself a safe place in the history of literature as a pioneer of a literary form in English which has been used by many since.

Among those who played their parts in the maritime and colonial activities of the time, there were two Welshmen whose contributions were particularly interesting. *William Vaughan*, of Torycoed, brother of the earl of Carbery, tried to establish a Welsh settlement in Newfoundland. As early as 1600 he had published his views on estate management and in 1616 he purchased land in Newfoundland which had been granted by the king for colonization. In the years that followed he paid the passage of settlers and in 1622 he himself may have joined them. His settlement was named *Cambriol* and Welsh names were given to various parts of the settled area. The venture was not successful, but during his stay he wrote three books which were published soon after his return in 1625 part of whose intention was 'to stir up our Islanders' minds to assist and support the Newfound Isle'. Though his colonizing venture was his chief claim to fame, William Vaughan wrote a number of books on religious and philosophical subjects. Very different was the career of *Sir Thomas Button*. He saw service at sea and in Ireland during the late years of Elizabeth's reign. A member of the 'Incorporated discoverers of the North-West Passage', he was commissioned by the merchants of London in 1612 to investigate further the recent discoveries of Henry Hudson and to search for a North-West Passage. He sailed along Hudson's Straits as far as Digges' Isle, then from Southampton Island he sailed into Hudson Bay to the mouth of the Nelson River. Here he wintered and early in the following spring he explored the mouth of the river, the names Button Bay and New Wales bear witness to his endeavour. Then he sailed north to continue his search, but he failed to discover the passage, though he was convinced of its existence. He returned to England in the autumn of 1613. Soon after his return he was appointed 'Admiral of the King's ships on the coast of Ireland', an office in which he won considerable repute. In 1620 he took part in the expedition against Algiers and the Algerine pirates which was commanded by Sir Robert Mansel. Kept busy by the pirates who infested the west coast and the Irish Sea, his later career was clouded by the disfavour of the duke of Buckingham.

These men, and others like them, won fame and fortune

outside their native Wales by identifying themselves with the forces that came into operation after the union and by exploiting the opportunities which they offered. To do this they spent most of their adult years in England; many of them married the daughters of English houses, bought English estates, and founded English county families. Their children and grandchildren became progressively more English even when their homes were in Wales. But very many of those with whom we are concerned did not forget their roots or dissociate themselves from their obligations as Welshmen. Richard Vaughan, it is said, gave support to William Morgan in his work of translating the Bible into Welsh; Gabriel Goodman too helped William Morgan and also established Christ's Hospital, Ruthin, and the grammar school which was attached to it in 1595. David Jenkins, when he retired from active life, patronized Welsh bards and the eisteddfodau in and around his native Pendoylan. Thomas Myddelton helped to finance the first cheap edition of the Welsh Bible in 1630, and John Williams, the goldsmith, was well informed in the history and literature of Wales. James Howell permitted no doubt about his origins and was anxious at all times to give his readers lessons in things Welsh.

There were those among them for whom self-advancement and self-preservation were the mainsprings of action. But, on the whole, they did not sell themselves cheaply in order to win preferment. True they were loyal to the establishment, but they did voice their criticism of those aspects with which they did not agree. John Williams, the Lord Keeper, made his stand against Laud, Thomas Howell was suspected of overmuch sympathy with the Puritans. David Jenkins got into hot water for his attacks upon royal policy during the 1630s. Sir Robert Mansel stood up to Buckingham when the latter was at the height of his influence with Charles I. And these were men who, when the crisis broke in 1642, sided with the king.

The regime criticized

There were a number of issues on which Welsh voices were raised to criticize the established order. The early decades of the century witnessed a sustained attack upon the Council of Wales and the Marches. The instigators of this attack were the Westminster lawyers and the gentry of the English border counties, though it is probable that they had the sympathy of many among the gentry of the eastern counties of Wales. They were, of course, concerned with their particular selfish interests—the lawyers to increase their fees and the gentry to free themselves from the Council's control, and it was not until the renewed energy shown by the Council during the reign of Charles I that deeper issues became involved. Some of the charges which they advanced were unjust, others were exaggerated; but there was much truth in many of the complaints. After 1602 the President was more often than not an absentee; a number of key positions in the Council were held by a single individual; offices were held by absentee courtiers who showed no concern for their responsibilities; there was a very substantial increase in the number of the Council's officials—more than was warranted by the volume of business conducted or by the level of efficiency attained. Moreover, these offices were bought and their holders, therefore, were anxious to recoup themselves, and so kept the court as busy as possible while at the same time increasing its fees. This reflected itself in the lattitude allowed informers, the increasing number of fines imposed in the absence of the defendants, and of fines imposed for non-prosecution. All this was responsible for many of the injustices of which the court was guilty, especially during the 1630s when it was very much more active than during the earlier years of the century. It contributed also to the significant increase in the number of civil cases which were brought before the court. On the one hand, the complainants were correct to deplore this as a very real departure from the original function of the court, which was to try and determine breaches of law and order. At the same time, it should be remembered that it reflected the changed conditions which had been achieved in Wales by the early seventeenth century. And this was in part the measure of the success of the Council's endeavours. But, true though this may have been, there were Welshmen who welcomed the Act of 1641 abolishing the Council of Wales and the Marches.

There was, too, criticism of certain aspects of royal policy, though this was neither consistent nor did it mature into serious opposition. Thus, there was a small group of committed Protestants among the Welsh members of Parliament for whom too close a friendship with Spain was seen as a threat to the

Anglican Church, whereas there were those among whom the end of the peace policy with Spain caused alarm. Numbers of Welshmen had been deeply involved in the struggle against Spain—at sea and on the expeditions to the Continent. Others were alive to the dangers of the vulnerable Welsh coastline and of the possible threat posed by Ireland. The first Parliament of Charles's reign was much exercised by this problem. Buckingham's pro-French policy provoked marked hostility in the Commons, and though Sir Robert Mansel tried to calm the government's critics he was forced to admit that he had serious misgivings concerning an attack upon Spain. Gradually he was forced more and more into opposition to Buckingham's policy, despite his being Vice-Admiral and a member of the Council of War. He had, as a result, to suffer the king's displeasure and was removed from the commission of the peace for his criticism of Buckingham. Another Welsh casualty of these years was John Williams, later Archbishop of York, who was deprived of the Great Seal soon after the fighting against Spain had started. Prominent also among Buckingham's opponents was the earl of Pembroke who controlled the activities of a number of Welsh members of the House of Commons.

Nor was it only at Westminster that Welshmen were apprehensive of Buckingham's policy. In Wales the poor response to the king's requests for a loan and a 'free gift' of money reflected the general reaction. His demands for men to take part in the expeditions could not fail to irritate Welshmen who were all too aware of a possible invasion and the inadequacies of the coastal defence system at a time when there was a real fear of a Roman Catholic crusade directed against England. This was particularly acute after 1627 when the French turned against England and revived fears of a French, Spanish, papal *entente*. But positive Welsh opposition was directed against Buckingham not the king, and it disappeared when the earl of Pembroke and John Williams made peace with the king's favourite. The immediate involvement of Welsh members in the events of 1628 at Westminster was not significant—although a few were aligned with the parliamentary opposition. But the immediate threat of invasion seemed to be over by then; within a year Buckingham was dead: Welsh fears receded and what opposition there had been from Welshmen disappeared.

There was criticism, too, of the financial demands of the early Stuarts in Wales, and this became particularly apparent during the period of Charles's personal rule. The duty on the import of wines seems to have aroused some opposition and it seems that Welshmen were preparing a case against the payment of a tax on wines. The basis of their argument was that the mises paid by the Welsh were in consideration of their ancient customs which included exemption from the imposition on wine. The benevolence which had been required in 1622 to assist James's son-in-law, Frederick, provoked opposition, as did Charles's forced loan of 1626. Prominent Welshmen, like David Jenkins of Hensol, raised their voices against the financial expedients of the 1630s, and the response in Wales to the repeated demands for Ship Money showed quite clearly that their views were shared by many. Whereas only two counties defaulted in respect of the 1635 writ, the number increased with each succeeding writ until in 1639 all the counties defaulted to a greater or less extent. Then, the government demands for men and money for Ireland and the Bishops' Wars met with little sympathy in Wales, and there were instances of refusal to comply with the demands.

The ecclesiastical policy of the government also provoked resentment in Wales. Welshmen criticized the activities of the Court of High Commission and the interference of the bishops in matters of state. The burden of a speech made by William Thomas, member for Caernarvon in the Long Parliament, was 'how unlawful it was for them to intermeddle in temporal affairs, to use civil power, or to sit as Judges in any Court, much less in the Court of Parliament'. And Thomas was no admirer of Presbyterianism. The government's endeavours to improve standards in the Church aroused hostility, especially when they involved recovering for the Crown the patronage of livings and limiting the freedom of action of bishops in respect of granting leases of Church property. Laudian High Anglicanism and the apparent sympathy shown at Court for the Catholic Church would do little to assuage the fears in Wales of Roman Catholic attempts to restore the old faith by force. The accounts of secret preparations for an armed rising at the castles of Raglan and Powys may well have been inspired; they were certainly exaggerated. But they reflected the same hysteria which was expressed in the Monmouthshire petition of May 1642 in which the petitioners declared that 'we in Wales of all others, and in Monmouthshire above the rest, cannot but be most sensible and suspicious of our own imminent destruction, as being compassed about with Papists, more in number, and stronger in power, Arms, Horse and Ammunition than any other Country (as we conceive) in the Kingdom besides'.

The interest shown in the elections for the parliaments of 1640 may well have been the result of something more than local rivalries. Certainly there were criticisms of the Court from Welsh members in the Short Parliament and the first session of its successor. Some of these criticisms were met by the legislation of 1640–1, others were silenced by the turn which events were taking. As the time of crisis approached many of the politically conscious among the Welsh could not, despite their hostility to certain features of the existing regime, 'without trembling entertain a thought of change'; many declared their willingness to hazard their lives and fortunes in defence of the king's person and prerogative. But the royalism with which the Welsh have been credited during the Civil War was not a blind royalism. It was not, among the politically conscious, the product of an uncritical loyalty to the powers-that-be—for criticism there certainly had been.

SUGGESTED READING

A. H. Dodd: *Studies in Stuart Wales*. Cardiff, 1952.

Thomas Richards: *Cymru a'r Uchel Gomisiwn, 1633–40*. Liverpool, 1930.

Articles:

David Mathew: 'Wales and England in the Early Seventeenth Century', *Trans. Cymmr.*, 1955.

A. H. Dodd: 'The Pattern of Politics in Stuart Wales', ibid., 1948.

—— 'North Wales in the Essex revolt of 1601', *E.H.R.*, lx, 1944.

—— 'Wales and the Scottish Succession', *Trans. Cymmr.*, 1937.

—— 'A spy's report, 1604', *B.B.C.S.*, lx, 1937–9.

—— 'Wales in the Parliaments of Charles I', *Trans. Cymmr.*, 1945, 1946–7.

Penry Williams: 'The Attack on the Council in the Marches, 1603–1642', ibid., 1961.

12. Wales and the Civil War

Welsh opinion

REACTIONS in Wales to the struggle between Crown and Parliament were confused and complicated. True, the factors which produced opposition to the king either did not exist or existed only on a very small scale in the greater part of Wales. Naturally enough, therefore, the majority of the Welsh people were royalist. It is also true that, where conditions approached those in the economically more advanced parts of England, support for Parliament was more apparent. But it is difficult to define areas where support was exclusively for one side or the other and almost impossible to reach a satisfactory conclusion as to nature of the loyalty given to Charles by his Welsh supporters. These two problems have been met by the explanation that choice of sides in Wales was in large measure determined by such local issues as family alliances and feuds, and the patronage and persuasions of powerful individuals.

This argument would seem to rationalize the situation in Wales during the 1640s. Wales was, despite the developments of the preceding century, economically backward; to be compared rather with the north and west of England than with the south and east. Few only of the influential families were in a position to become involved in the rivalry of the 'ins' and 'outs'; there were few towns of any size; the commercial section was relatively small; Puritanism was a much tenderer plant than in England and had established roots only in those areas near the border; Wales was remote from the centre of things; and the language barrier created a propaganda blockage which the king's opponents were unable to penetrate. Under such circumstances Parliament could hardly be expected to find ready support. In those areas where these features were less marked, support for Parliament was more in evidence. In Pembrokeshire, for instance, whose ports were in constant touch with Bristol and where there were significant numbers of traders and of English-speaking inhabitants, the influence exerted by the earl of Essex, the parliamentary general, could arouse sympathy for his cause. In Denbighshire, some of whose landed families were in touch with the commercial world of London and where, in the Wrexham area, Puritanism had established firm roots, there was support for Parliament.

But to consider Wales as being royalist for the most part, with the odd pocket of parliamentary support, is to oversimplify the situation. Most Welsh counties produced some prominent adherents of the parliamentary cause. Pembrokeshire, of course, had its Laugharne, Poyer, Rice Powell, and Hugh Owen; Denbigh its Myddelton brothers—Thomas and William, the Thelwalls, and Sir John Trevor of Trevalun; Merioneth had its Colonel John Jones and Robert Owen of Dolserau; Cardigan its John Lewis of Glasgrug who put the case for Parliament in his *Contemplations upon These Times*; Brecon its William Lewis, William Watkins, and Henry Williams of Caebalfa; Glamorgan its Philip Herbert, Philip Jones, and Rowland Dawkins; Monmouth its Henry Herbert of Coldbrook. There were those, like Sir Trevor Williams of Llangibby in Monmouth, who changed their allegiance, and others who, though parliamentary sympathizers, conformed to the majority opinion of their districts—but with little enthusiasm, men like Thomas Glynne, John Bodwrda, and William Lloyd of Caernarvonshire.

The pressures that dictated the conduct of men like these were many. Puritanism certainly led some into the ranks of parliamentary supporters; many more followed the lead given or responded to the pressure exerted by some of the great families, like the Devereux and the Herberts. Some saw in the war an opportunity to continue local feuds, others to recover lost family property. Some were soldiers of fortune, others members of the lesser landowning families who saw a chance of obtaining land or local power. Then, as the war progressed, there were those who objected to the conduct of the war by the royalist commanders. Colonel John Jones, the Regicide, for example, was the younger son of a small Merionethshire squire, brought up in the household of the Myddeltons in London and Essex, who had come very much under the influence of Morgan Llwyd. Henry Herbert of Coldbrook had close links with London, and was determined to recover Herbert lands which had been acquired by the Raglan family. Laugharne had been a page in the Devereux household, and Sir Trevor Williams, who fought bravely for the king at first, objected to the alliance between Charles and the Catholics and supported the Pembroke Herberts against the Somersets of Raglan.

Similar pressures operated among the Welsh royalists. Support for the king was the outcome of the respect and affection which many felt for Charles himself, and of the conviction that the king was in the right and that any challenge to his authority was a blow aimed at the rule of law which was the guarantee of the freedom of the subject. On the king's side, too, were those who wished to maintain the existing system and preserve their own peace, prosperity, and security. Then there were staunch Anglicans, determined to safeguard the Church in whose articles of faith they believed and of whose order of service they approved. There were those whose support for the king was the outcome of their conviction that Parliament was responsible for the war and, more heinous still, for exposing them to the war's attendant horrors.

These are the reasons which men gave at the time for the support which they gave the king. But if we are to understand their conduct we must examine what lay behind these reasons. One factor undoubtedly was conservatism, the outcome of their respect for the old order and a determination to preserve it. On a few it was the superficial aspects of the past, its pomp and pageantry, that weighed heavily, but for many there was much more. They and their families had, after all, done very well out of the system which had been established during the sixteenth century. They saw in the war a threat to that 'rare conjuncture of Peace, Security, Honour and Plenty' which had served them so well. James Howell would have found many among his fellow countrymen to agree with him that 'Innovations are of dangerous consequence in all things, specially in a settled well temper'd State', for they might 'shake the whole frame of Government, and introduce a change; and changes in Government are commonly fatal, for seldom comes a better'.[1]

This last was, too, a lawyer's point of view, and there is no doubt that for many Welsh royalists it was the legal not the

[1] James Howell: *Parables Reflecting upon the Times*, 1644

political question that was uppermost. A substantial number of them had undergone a period of legal training and had been responsible for the administration of the law at local level. They had naturally a healthy respect for the law as it stood and for its role as the framework of the social order. The close connection between the maintenance of stability and the administration of the law, together with their role as local partners of the central government was apparent to them. They had no desire to see the system disrupted. Moreover, they enjoyed a considerable measure of freedom in the exercise of their local functions—a freedom which they had put to good use in promoting their own interests and those of their families and friends. Here was one feature of the established order of which they approved, and for the preservation of which they were prepared to fight.

Another feature of the old order which they were determined to defend was the established Church. It was the guardian of the true faith whose moderation and respectability, the beauty and simplicity of whose services they found so much to their liking.

> Ti a fuost gyfannedd, yn cynnal trefn santedd,
> Ac athro'r gwirionedd, cysonedd i sain.[1]

More important, perhaps, was the co-terminality of Church and State which made the former a powerful unifying force. Erastianism was one of the foundation stones of the old order, one which would be lost if freedom of worship were permitted. For the king to lose the loyalty due to him from his subjects as the head of the Church would be a severe blow to his prerogative. At local level too there existed this close interdependence between the clergy and the gentry, one from which the latter derived much benefit. Former Church lands and revenues were an important factor in the prosperity of the gentry families; the patronage over Church livings which many of them enjoyed was significant in itself and important in that it gave them control over the most effective means of propaganda for the maintenance of their local pre-eminence. For many of their members, too, the Church offered an avenue of promotion which could bring wealth and prestige. To remove the mono-

---

[1] *Thou wast a dwelling place, maintaining a holy order; and the teacher of the truth, constant in its intonation* (from Huw Morus: *Yr Hen Eglwys Loeger*).

poly over the religious life of the country which the Church exercised might well endanger all this. Hence the bitter hostility shown to the Puritans by many of the Welsh gentry. They took exception to the lack of respect shown by the Puritans to the Church, to the confusion which they caused by their differing religious teachings and, more especially, to the disregard they showed for the proprieties of corporate worship. There were many who echoed James Howell's sentiments when he wrote 'if I hate any, 'tis these schismaticks that puzzle the sweet peace of our Church, so that I could be content to see an Anabaptist go to Hell on a Brownist's back'.[1]

On the other hand, there had been resentment at various aspects of royal policy. Some Welshmen and their representatives at Westminster had criticized the Court, royal administration, conciliar government, and even the Church. The Council of Wales and the Marches had been charged with oppression, injustice, corruption, and partiality. 'A man', it was claimed could do nothing, 'but he shall be subject to be questioned wrongfully, before the Council and fined to as much as he is worth and more'. The Court of High Commission too had come under attack from some quarters as had Star Chamber, and there would have been sympathy for John Bodvel's sentiments when he reported to Owen Wynn of Gwydir that 'The Bills abolishing the Star Chamber and Court of High Commission are passed, a blessing which should encourage men to pay poll-money more cheerfully'.[2] The financial expedients adopted by Charles during the 1630s were condemned and the general reaction to them is shown by the progressively increasing number of counties which defaulted in the collection of the succeeding writs of Ship Money. Loud objections had been raised among the gentry to Laud's attempt to set limits to their exploitation of the Church, to the bishops' intermeddling in temporal affairs, and to 'the Tyranny of Episcopal government'.

Moreover, there were the lessons to be learnt from contemporary Europe and the Wales of earlier centuries. James Howell was not the only seventeenth-century Welshman to witness the ravages of the Thirty Years War in Germany, nor was Sir John

[1] In his *The True Informer*, etc., 1642.
[2] For the grievances against the Council, see Skeel, op. cit., p. 140. For Bodvel's letter, dated 6 July 1641, see *Calendar of Wynn Papers*, op. cit., p. 273.

N

Wynn alone among his fellow countrymen in his awareness of
the harsh realities of those bloody and ireful quarrels of the
fifteenth century. Horror of the consequences of war was a
recurring theme of the literature of the time. They appreciated
the dire consequences for the country as a whole—'The whole
Kingdom is, and shall be yet more, by the continuance hereof,
unspeakably impoverished and plunged into all kinds of
miseries', wrote one Welsh Churchman.[1] But their concern for
the well-being of their families and their strong local patriotism
made them more acutely aware of the dangers to themselves
and their hard-won prosperity. One protestation from the
gentry of the south-western counties expressed concern at the
holding of Pembroke by parliamentary forces because it was
'an encouragement to invite foreign and rebellious forces to
enter the said counties and ruin the same'. Those Glamorgan
men who became involved in the 1647 rising advanced the
grievance that members of the County Committee 'having
sequestered the Estates of most of the chief Gentlemen of that
County, have not only enriched themselves thereby, but their
Servants and Retainers who as well as their Masters insult over
the Gentry'.[2] The poets described in gruesome detail the rapine
and plunder, death and destruction of the war. They agreed
with Judge David Jenkins when he appealed to all sections to
settle the war and reach agreement, otherwise there would be
'neither truth nore peace in this land, nor any man secure of
any thing he hath'.[3] Of special significance to them was the
'llosgi a lladd pob cyfriw o radd'[4] that took place in the fighting.

There was too among very many a lack of awareness of the
issues involved in the quarrels which had produced the war.
Among the lower orders the language barrier combined with
communication difficulties and the nature of Welsh society to
create an almost impenetrable propaganda barrier. Many of
their betters had conditioned themselves to an almost exclusive
concern with the affairs of their own immediate localities.
On more than one occasion the Welshman was satirized as
intending to inquire 'wherefore her must fight and for what her

[1] Griffith Williams, Bishop of Ossory. See his *The Discovery of Mysteries.*
[2] *The Heads of the Present Grievances of the County of Glamorgan,* etc., 1 July 1647.
[3] *Some Seeming Objections of Master Prynne's,* 1647.
[4] *The burning and the killing of persons of rank.*

must venture her teare plud, for twas not yet manifest to her mind for what her did fight'.[1]

These were the factors which determined not merely the side to which Welshmen gave their support, but also the nature of this support. King and Parliament found loyal supporters in Wales. There was Sir John Owen of Clenennau who went 'forth and continued with his King in order to protect Wales from injustice and to defend his country and the true faith', or old William Salesbury (Hosannau Gleision) who desired 'not to live longer than I approve myself true to my King and country'. There were the Joneses, John and Philip, who were unswerving in their devotion to Parliament. Most Welshmen, had they been challenged, would have declared for the king— but would have qualified their willingness to become involved in the struggle. Very many accepted royal sovereignty and approved of a strong central government whose partners they were, but their actions were dictated by the sentiment—'God Almighty amend the times, and compose these woful divisions which menace nothing but public ruin'.[2] At best these were moderate royalists, at worst they had to be bullied or cajoled into giving the king their support. Owen Wynn, for instance, owed money to the wife of Doctor Bayley, a debt which had been transferred by her to the Prince Rupert for the king's cause. He had ignored repeated demands for its settlement and in April 1644 he had to be reminded that 'it will be conceived by such delays that you wish too well to the king's enemies, and that you are not so well affected to the cause in hand as your allegiance binds you to be'.[3] The king's generals had little confidence in the steadfastness of the Welsh. One of them wrote of Carmarthen and Cardiganshire, 'Those countries as now they stand, being in general, like to yield themselves to the first danger'.

One marked feature that emerges from the literature of the time is the small measure of positive interest in the struggle among many Welshmen and their apparent indifference to its outcome. The Welshmen, if one is to believe a satirical poem

[1] *The Welshman's Resolution,* 1642.
[2] James Howell to Sir Bevis Thelwall, 1643.
[3] William Erskin to Maurice Wynn, 1644, *Calendar of Wynn Papers,* op. cit., p. 282.

written in 1642, had no wish to fight in earnest; he wanted to avoid any heavy fighting so that he might turn his attention to plundering the English countryside. In a pamphlet written a few months earlier in the same vein the Welshman is made to declare that he would be no deputy because he wished to keep his neck on his shoulders, no bishop because he had no wish to be sent to the Tower, no judge that he might not lose favour with the Parliament and, for much the same reasons, he had no inclination to be a papist or a Roundhead. There is an amusing account of an alleged meeting of the Welsh citizens of Hereford when the city was in danger of capture by a parliamentary force under Waller in 1643. The points to be considered on the agenda were: 'What her thought best to be done for the present to save herself without fighting if it were possible, and, if not, nor noe wayes for her to run away, ten to propound upon what conditions her should yeeld to her enemy.'[1]

This lack of interest was in part the outcome of ignorance: it was too the result of an attitude of non-involvement which is reflected in the cryptic comment of one Welsh landowner, who wrote in 1644 to a friend that all was well, that what he needed was money, peace, and agreement. ('Pob peth yn dda, eisiau arian, heddwch a chytundeb'.)[2] Almost it seems as if some were deliberately opting out of the struggle. Sir John Vaughan, after a long career at the bar, sought advice at the outbreak of the conflict as to what he should do 'to keep even with the world, and to secure himself from trouble, at the same time doing no harm to his king and country, but as much good as he could to both'.[3] Finally, there were those who hedged and trimmed. The Vaughans of Golden Grove thought first of their own fortunes and then of the king's cause, while their neighbours in the south-west pursued a tortuous course in trying to obtain guarantees from both sides. Others were less astute or interested in concealing their real intentions. Edmund Jones of Buckland in Breconshire earned quite a reputation for the ingenuity which he showed in pleasing both sides, while Henry Vaughan of Derwydd in neighbouring Carmarthenshire was

---

[1] *The Welshman's Lamentation at the Loss of Hereford to Parliament*, 1643.

[2] Griffith Carreg to William Caledfrine, *Calendar of Salusbury Correspondence, 1553–c. 1700*, op. cit., p. 161.

[3] J. Gwynn Williams: 'Sir John Vaughan of Trawscoed, 1603–1674', *N.L.W. Jnl.* viii, 1954.

described by a contemporary as 'anything for money, a proselyte and favourite to all the changes of times . . . tyrant in power, mischievous by deceit; his motto, *Qui nescit dissimulare, nescit vivere*'.[1]

Sir Hugh Vaughan might well assure Prince Charles at Raglan that 'In what the true and ancient Britons may serve you, you may command us to our uttermost strength, our lives and fortunes to be ready . . . The common people with hands and hearts are ready to help you in all honourable attempts, and our gentry will show their ancient virtue and valour in your service.'[2] But the royalist officers concerned with the business of fighting the king's war would have been more of the opinion of Captain Thomas Dabridgecourt when he poured out his woes to Prince Rupert—'if your Highness shall be pleased to command me to the Turk, or Jew, or Gentile, I will go on my bare feet to serve you, but from the Welsh, good Lord deliver me . . . And I shall beseech you to send me no more into this country . . . without a strong party to compel them . . . They value neither Sir John Winter, his warrants, nor mine, nor any. Some say they will not come; the rest come not and say nothing.'[3]

Wales and the Civil War

When in the summer of 1642 the king raised his standard at Nottingham the loyal protestations which he had received while at York gave him every reason to feel confident of Welsh support. He marched west to the Welsh border to recruit men for his assault upon London. While he made his headquarters at Shrewsbury, and established a second base at Chester, to enlist men and money, the Prince of Wales was dispatched to Raglan to obtain support for the royalist cause in South Wales. By the early days of October Charles had doubled his strength, and on the twelfth he marched out of Shrewsbury with an army of some 16,000 men, among them a substantial number of Welshmen from the north and south. The earl of Essex with the parliamentary army, which had meanwhile been lying

---

[1] *He who knows not how to dissimulate, does not know how to survive.* Attributed to Owen Price of Gorllwyn, Carmarthenshire. See *N.L.W. Jnl.*, xl, 1959–60.

[2] *A Loving and Loyal Speech Spoken unto the Excellency of our Noble Prince Charles*: By Sir Hugh Vaughan, 1643.

[3] J. R. Phillips: *Memoirs of the Civil War in Wales and the Marches*. London, 1878, vol. 11, p. 139.

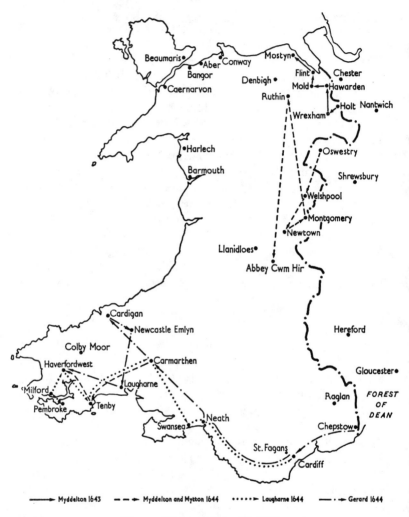

MAP 5. Wales and the Civil War

idle in and around Worcester, was slow to take up the pursuit, but overtook the king's army near Keynton at the base of Edgehill. Here was fought the first battle of the Civil War. The Welsh royalists, ill armed and untrained, played an inglorious part in the battle—many were killed and many more deserted. The indecisive outcome of the battle enabled the king to move on to Oxford and from here he advanced upon London. At Brentford the Welsh under Prince Rupert distinguished themselves in storming the enemy barricades, but a parliamentary show of strength at Turnham Green persuaded Charles to withdraw to Oxford. In the meantime, the marquis of Hertford, to whom the king had given supreme command in the west, had with the aid of the Raglan family recruited another army in South Wales. On 4 November he left Cardiff to join the king at Oxford, but he was overtaken at Tewkesbury by the earl of Stamford, the parliamentary governor of Hereford. In the battle which followed the Welsh royalists were again defeated with very heavy losses. Hertford was able to regroup his forces and take Hereford which had been abandoned by Stamford, so that all was not lost. But the early engagements of the war had offered the Welsh cold comfort indeed.

Wales was important to the royalist cause. It was one of the king's most promising recruiting areas—the response to his early appeals had already shown this. It served to counterbalance the Parliament-controlled east of England and offered him a strategic base for future military operations. Moreover, it offered easy access to Ireland where the king was already conducting negotiations for support in men and money. It was, therefore, vitally important for the king to control the border counties; equally it was to Parliament's advantage to seal Wales off. The struggle for control of the marches was inevitably a theatre of the war of considerable significance. At the outbreak of hostilities there was a fairly equal balance of strength in the region—the royalists with Chester, Shrewsbury, and other strong points controlled the northern part, while Parliament's hold upon Hereford, Gloucester, and Bristol gave them control in the south. Welsh support gave the king the initiative at first, and the occupation of Hereford late in 1642 strengthened this.

In the north Parliament established headquarters at

Nantwich and Wem to contain the royalists of Chester and North Wales. Here there was deadlock during the early months of the war—royalist attacks upon Middlewich and Wem failed, as did a brief parliamentary campaign from Nantwich. Further south Hertford and his Welsh troops joined with Rupert and Maurice in the capture of Cirencester and proceeded to besiege Gloucester. Another Welsh force recruited by Lord Herbert, after a successful skirmish at Colford in the Forest of Dean, joined in the siege of Gloucester. Again, however, the Welsh intervention ended dismally, for Herbert and his troops were trapped at Highnam between Waller's army which, having crossed the Severn, attacked from the west and a party from Gloucester itself. Once more the house of Raglan exerted itself on behalf of the king—it raised another army for a further assault upon Gloucester. The siege began on 10 August, but the city held out for twenty-six days until it was relieved by Essex. For the time being Parliament had successfully isolated South Wales. At Bristol the royalists were more successful, for after a long siege and bitter fighting, in which Welsh troops were involved the city fell on 26 July. This royalist success was to have important repercussions on the situation in south-west Wales.

Meantime, the parliamentary commander in Cheshire, Sir William Brereton, had been consolidating his position. Then, after a raid into Denbighshire by Sir Thomas Myddelton who had been appointed sergeant-major-general for the counties of North Wales, a parliamentary army advanced west from Nantwich. It captured Holt, entered Wrexham, took Hawarden, Mold, and Flint, and pressed as far north as Mostyn before the landing of forces from Ireland occasioned its withdrawal. Although this success had been shortlived, it had effectively destroyed the sense of security which the royalists of North Wales had enjoyed. Parliament had reason to feel fairly satisfied with the situation on the border at the end of 1643. Further west the situation was less satisfactory.

When the war opened the majority of the leaders of the three south-western counties declared for the king, although the conduct of many of them showed no great zeal for his cause. Only in and around the town and castle of Pembroke was there any real measure of parliamentary strength. But this, together with the presence of parliamentary ships patrolling the Bristol

Channel under the command of Captain Swanley, made the gentry of these parts reluctant to leave the area. They feared an attack from Pembroke and at the same time realized the futility of an assault upon the town as long as its defenders could obtain relief from the sea. The capture of Bristol gave the royalists some strength in the Channel, and the royalist commander in the area, the earl of Carbery, having established himself in Carmarthenshire, advanced into Pembrokeshire in the summer of 1643. He received a warm welcome at Tenby and at Haverfordwest, and by September the whole of the area outside Pembroke was under royalist control. All the principal towns were garrisoned by Carbery's troops and many of the country-houses, Carew Castle and Roch Castle, Stackpole Court and Trefloyne, had been converted into royalist strongholds. Late in the year plans were being laid for the capture of Pembroke.

In the north-east too there were preparations for another royalist offensive at the close of 1643. Lord Byron won some minor victories for the king in Cheshire and then laid siege to Nantwich where the parliamentary garrison resisted stubbornly until it was relieved by Brereton and Sir Thomas Fairfax. Then followed a series of important parliamentary successes, the first of which was the capture of Oswestry. Myddelton and Sir Thomas Mytton led a campaign into mid-Wales, defeating royalist forces at Welshpool and at Tarvin. Myddelton advanced west, took Newtown and Montgomery Castle where he inflicted a severe defeat upon the royalists, captured Powys Castle, and then marched north to take the town, but not the castle, of Ruthin. Finally, he turned south through Montgomeryshire into Radnorshire where he captured Abbey Cwm Hir. This remarkable campaign gave Parliament the initiative in North Wales by the summer of 1644.

Meanwhile, the initiative passed from one side to the other with remarkable speed in the south-west. In January 1644 the royalists were making their final preparations for the assault upon Pembroke. Supplies had been collected, royalist garrisons strengthened, and a request sent to Bristol for ships to blockade the town from the sea. Then when all seemed ready, the situation changed dramatically. In mid February the parliamentary ships guarding the south-east coast of Ireland were driven by storms to seek shelter in Milford. When Swanley realized what was happening he began an attack upon Milford Pill, and this gave Rowland Laugharne, the parliamentary commander at Pembroke, his opportunity. He led a force out of the town, captured Stackpole Court and Trefloyne, then turned his attention to Milford. With the aid of the navy he captured the Pill. This achieved, he advanced to Haverfordwest which capitulated with little or no resistance, and pressed on to Tenby which he took after a much stiffer resistance. On 10 March Carew Castle surrendered, and Laugharne had established control over Pembrokeshire. He then mustered his troops on Colby Moor on 11 April and advanced upon Carmarthen which surrendered after a mere formality of resistance. Swansea was called upon to surrender but refused and Laugharne did not press an engagement, but Cardiff was captured from the sea. The king, it seemed, was in danger of losing the whole of South Wales. Gerard was appointed to replace Carbery as commander of the royalists in the area. He advanced rapidly from Chepstow, recovered Cardiff and pushed his way into Carmarthenshire early in June. The county town was taken and by the end of the month royalist control had been reasserted over the whole county. Gerard recaptured Cardigan, defeated a parliamentary force at Newcastle Emlyn and recovered the castles at Laugharne and Roch. On the march to Haverfordwest which he entered on 13 July, he inflicted a heavy defeat on Laugharne. By the midsummer of 1644 royalist control had been re-established in the south-west except for Pembroke.

Early in 1645 parliamentary forces under Brereton were besieging Chester, Beeston, and Hawarden in the north-east. The royalists made desperate efforts to raise these sieges and met with some success. But then in February Mytton captured Shrewsbury and Parliament gained a firm grip on the area. The early summer brought disaster for Charles at Naseby, and immediately he retreated to South Wales in the hope of re-cruiting another army. At Hereford on 19 June Welsh royalists promised him men and arms and he decided to make Raglan his headquarters while the troops were brought together. This proved to be a much more difficult task than had been antici-pated, so instructions were dispatched to the sheriffs to call out all men fit for service. But the troops who were enlisted demanded redress of their grievances before agreeing to any proposals. Charles met the 'Peaceable Army' of Glamorgan at St. Fagans on 29 July, but although he complied with their demands, he soon gave up hope of any assistance from Glamorgan and made his way north.

In the south-west, Gerard's successes in the early summer of 1644 had been followed by a summons to Bristol to join Rupert. Laugharne took advantage of his absence to recover some of what had been lost. Laugharne Castle was recovered and so was Cardigan. This brought Gerard hurrying back from the north. He advanced via Llanidloes to Newcastle Emlyn where he defeated Laugharne on 23 April. Cardigan Castle, deserted by its garrison, was recovered, as were in rapid succession the castles at Picton and Carew. Once more he entered Haverfordwest and re-established royal control in the area. But not for long. He was recalled to England and in his absence Laugharne won a decisive victory over Stradling and Egerton at Colby Moor on 1 August. This victory and the capture of Bristol provided the incentive for the Glamorgan leaders to enter into negotiations with Laugharne. Conditions were agreed, Edward Pritchard of Llancaiach and Philip Jones were made governors of Cardiff and Swansea respectively, and Bussy Mansel was given command of the forces in Glamorgan. The other counties of South Wales—Carmarthen, Cardigan, Brecon, and Radnor followed the lead of Glamorgan and declared for Parliament. By the late summer of 1645 the king had lost control.

Parliament's control and certainly the conduct of its local representatives aroused considerable resentment in some quarters. In Glamorgan there were complaints against the authority wielded by outsiders, objections to the contributions demanded, and the exclusion of the local gentry from the county committee, and exception was taken to the propagating of Puritanism. In February 1646 the sheriff Edward Carne declared for the king, marched to Cardiff, and summoned Edward Pritchard to surrender the castle, while the royalists of Monmouthshire advanced upon Cardiff under the command of Keymes. Again Laugharne served Parliament well and the rising was crushed. Raglan alone now held out for the king, and it was taken on 19 August.

In the north too the months that followed Naseby saw the inevitable defeat of the king. Chester still resisted grimly, but the parliamentary victory at Rowton Heath marked the end of any real hope for the royalist cause in North Wales. A determined effort was made to save Chester. Sir William Vaughan collected troops from garrisons along the marches to relieve the desperate city, but this force was destroyed at Denbigh Green. Chester continued to hold out for the king until 3 February before it capitulated. Then followed Mytton's campaign into North Wales. He swept to the west, capturing one royalist stronghold after another, and by the early summer only a few isolated pockets remained. These held out with great courage but, one by one, they fell and when Harlech was taken on 1 March 1647, resistance was at an end.

The Second Civil War

Parliament had won the Civil War, but the fruits of victory were not sweet. In the country at large there was unrest—men were weary of the fighting, exasperated by the heavy taxation, and uneasy at the continued existence of the army. Within the parliamentary ranks there were disagreements as to the future of the king—some wished his restoration on the basis of the terms of the Newcastle Propositions, others wanted a more radical change. The army was voicing its grievances, especially on the matter of the arrears of pay due to it. The lack of sympathy shown at Westminster to its complaints widened the gulf between the soldiers and the politicians. The negotiations between the army and the king in the early summer of 1647 sparked off a fresh outburst of activity among the defeated royalists. In Glamorgan during the second half of June they collected an armed force which advanced within two miles of Cardiff to demand a redress of the grievances which they held against the County Committee. They wanted guarantees until 'the present unsettledness of supreme affairs be composed', and this they anticipated would be accomplished very soon. The general situation also occasioned a torrent of royalist propaganda. Pamphlet after pamphlet was published by Judge David Jenkins whose intentions were to put Parliament in the wrong, to place on its shoulders the responsibility for the sufferings of the time, and make Charles appear the defender of peace, order, and justice. In Pembrokeshire, moreover, John Poyer quarrelled bitterly with the local gentry, many of whom had fought with him during the war. There were charges and countercharges of lack of loyalty, peculation, and irregularities.

Then, late in December 1647, Parliament decided to disband the army. Soldiers who had enlisted since 6 August 1647 were to be dismissed without pay, the others were to receive two months' pay towards clearing their arrears which were to be finally settled at the discretion of the commissioners. The disbanding was undertaken in February 1648. In the south-west there were violent protests from the soldiers whose cause was taken up by Poyer. A Colonel Fleming was dispatched to Pembroke to supersede Poyer as governor of the castle. The latter refused to submit, troops sent from Bristol to support Fleming were defeated, and Poyer remained in command at Pembroke—of both town and castle. On 10 April he declared for the king, committing himself to the restoration of Charles. He had already been joined by Rice Powell who, after defeating Fleming, advanced east through Carmarthen into Glamorgan, where he seized Swansea and Neath before marching on to Cardiff. He was joined by Laugharne on the outskirts of the town. Meanwhile Horton, who had been dispatched to Wales to supervise the disbanding of the troops, had been marching south to intercept the army from Pembroke. At St. Fagans on 8 May Laugharne, Poyer, and Powell were defeated in what was the largest single engagement in Wales during the war. Thereafter it was merely a matter of mopping up some strongholds which held out for the king.

In North Wales, too, a combination of general grievances, local conflicts, and the efforts of some intransigent royalists created trouble for Parliament. The disbanding of the army caused unrest among the soldiers; the appointment of the deputy governorship of Anglesey sparked off an incident as a result o which Beaumaris Castle was held against Mytton. Lord Byron who was active on the king's behalf in Lancashire was anxious to create a diversion in North Wales, while Sir John Owen was raising forces for the king in Caernarvonshire. Parliament sent Twisleton, the Parliamentary commander of Denbigh Castle, to the area and he defeated a royalist force at Barmouth before proceeding into Caernarvonshire. The royalists attempted to

intercept him between Bangor and Aber, but were defeated at
Y Dalar Hir, near Llandegai. Then the defeat of the Scottish
army at Preston cut short Byron's plans in Lancashire. Despite
Archbishop John Williams's advice to sue for peace, the
royalists now concentrated in Anglesey under the command
of Richard, Lord Bulkeley's son. Mytton crossed the Menai
Straits, overwhelmed the small guard which had been placed
at Cadnant, and destroyed the royalist force in battle in the
Red Hill fields.

After the battle of St. Fagans, Cromwell decided on a show
of strength in South Wales. He advanced through Cardiff and
Swansea upon Pembroke. Tenby was captured on 31 May and
finally Pembroke, after a stubborn resistance, capitulated on
11 July. Organized royalist resistance was now at an end.

The war and the Welsh

The conduct of the Welsh during the war was dictated in
part by the attitudes which have already been noted, in part
by the realities of the fighting and the progress of events. The
war brought its calamities—Welshmen were pressed into the
royalist armies, supplies and money were commandeered by
both sides, towns and homes were plundered by the soldiery—
especially the Irish troops under Gerard—houses and property
were destroyed, trade was dislocated—the cattle and wool
trade particularly. All this created resentment, dampened
enthusiasm, prompted many to concern themselves exclusively
with the safety of their property and their localities, and
fostered hopes of an early end to the fighting. This helps to explain the comparative ease with which many towns and strong-
points were captured, the alacrity shown by many among the
gentry to come to terms with their opponents when an invasion
of their districts was threatened. It explains the readiness with
which the counties of South Wales submitted to Laugharne
in the summer of 1645 and the reluctance of Glamorgan's
'Peaceable Army' to follow the king. The factors which produced
the conflict had for many been remote and almost irrelevant;
its harsh realities urged upon them the pressing need for bringing it to a speedy close.

There were, however, other factors at work. One of the most
powerful of these was the operation of personal and local

considerations. These can best be illustrated by examining the conduct of some prominent Welshmen. Archbishop John Williams who had fled from York at the opening of the war spent much of his personal fortune in fortifying Conway Castle for the king. But he gave the king unwelcome advice and was replaced as governor of Conway by Sir John Owen. The quarrel which this provoked and Williams's concern for the safety of his property in North Wales led him to come to terms with Mytton in 1646 and to take part in the parliamentary attack upon Conway. Rowland Laugharne and John Poyer who had fought loyally for Parliament throughout the first war, declared for the king in 1648. In Laugharne's case this may have been the result of the overtures made to him by the royalists, but it was also the outcome of his disenchantment with Parliament after the death of his patron, the earl of Essex. Poyer's conduct in 1648 was in no small measure determined by his bitter quarrels with those gentry who exercised authority under Parliament in Pembrokeshire when the fighting was over in the south-west. There was also his disagreement with the religious policy of the new order, for it appears that Poyer was a loyal churchman. One of the most interesting personalities was Sir Trevor Williams of Llangibby. He declared for the king in 1642, but his zeal was tempered by the favour shown by Charles to the Somerset family of Raglan. He was, after all, a loyal tenant of the earl of Pembroke and a good Anglican. He expressed his disapproval of the king's commission to the earl of Glamorgan to bring Irish Catholic troops to fight in Wales and hindered the raising of troops for the king in August 1645. He was imprisoned, and after his release took Monmouth Castle which he held against the king and assisted the attack against Raglan Castle in 1646. But in 1648 he turned against Parliament. His defection is explained in part by the grant made by the House of Commons to Cromwell of the estates of the Somerset family in Glamorgan and Monmouthshire, for these included the estates in the Chepstow area of which Williams himself had been hoping to take possession.

Finally, the Welsh leaders did not want too radical a change in the existing order. Sir Thomas Myddelton had distinguished himself in the fighting, but he opposed the trial of the king and, like his son, was ejected from Parliament by Pride's Purge in

December 1648. Nor were they alone of the Welsh members to lose their seats in 1648. Two Welshmen only, John Jones and Thomas Wogan, were involved in the king's trial and signed the death warrant. Very few of the old established gentry families of Wales actively co-operated with the new regime and it was not until the Restoration that they emerged again as leaders of Welsh society.

SUGGESTED READING

A. H. Dodd: *Studies in Stuart Wales.*

J. Gwynn Williams: 'Wales and the Civil War', in *Wales through the Ages.*

J. F. Rees: *Studies in Welsh History*, chapters v, vi, vii.

A. L. Leach: *The History of the Civil War (1642–1649) in Pembrokeshire.* London, 1937.

Articles on the war in different parts of Wales are to be found in *N.L.W. Jnl.* and the publications of the various county history societies.

13. Wales and the Commonwealth

WHEN the hopes of those Welshmen who had longed for an end to the fighting were at last realized there were many for whom it brought little comfort. The hard core of royalists in every county of Wales found it difficult to accept the new regime; moderate parliamentarians who had fought well during the Civil War disapproved of the events of 1648–9 and retired from active life. Some of those who had supported the king suffered the sequestration of their estates; others had to compound for theirs by the payment of fines which varied according to the degree of their royalism and the extent of their estates. Before long other sections of Welsh society had their own reasons for resenting the new regime.

But the years that separated the execution of Charles I from the restoration of his son constitute an important chapter in the history of Wales. They witnessed a positive effort to puritanize the Welsh which, though it achieved only a limited immediate sucess, laid the foundations for the later development of Nonconformity. In conjunction with this went a state-supported system of education on a scale which was not repeated until the nineteenth century. During the interregnum representatives of sections of society previously excluded from participation in government became politically involved, especially at local level. Finally, there were quite substantial changes in the ownership of land in Wales. The land which came on to the market as a result of sequestration and sales was bought by those who had supported or won the favour of the winning side in the war. Some new county families of the first rank emerged, the economic foundations of whose newly won prestige were the lands thus acquired. The territorial acquisitions of others were more modest, but sufficient to modify the pattern of landownership in Wales.

Though some of this was reversed or undone during the years that followed 1660, sufficient remained to ensure that the

O

years of the Commonwealth were no irrelevant interlude in the history of Wales.

Religion and education

On 22 February 1650 Parliament ordered the publishing of the *Act for the better propagation and preaching of the Gospel in Wales*, and so launched the grand design for the puritanizing of the Welsh people. The over-all direction and responsibility for this undertaking was given to a specially constituted commission of seventy-one members headed by Thomas Harrison. The composition of the commission is interesting. A quarter of its members were Englishmen, most of whom came from the English border counties; of the remainder the majority were drawn from the ranks of the county squires, prosperous yeomen and lawyers of those parts of Wales which had been most exposed to anglicizing influences. There were very few either from the distinctively Welsh counties or from among the older Welsh gentry families. Some of the commissioners had been deeply committed to the parliamentary cause from the outbreak of the war, and among these were a number of uncompromising Puritans. Others were later converts to the parliamentary side, and among these there were some whose conversion had, in part at least, been dictated by motives of self-interest. The Act also established a body of Approvers, twenty-five ministers of the Gospel, whose function was to recommend and approve men as ministers of religion. Of this latter body fourteen at least had already been preaching and ministering to the spiritual needs of the Welsh people. A substantial number of them were Englishmen and the majority of the Welshmen concerned were from the eastern counties of Wales. There was among them little uniformity in respect of doctrine or ideas concerning Church government—for the most part they could be termed 'independents', though there were, on the one hand, convinced Baptists and, on the other, former clergymen of the Church of England in their ranks.

The Commission was given a wide measure of authority in respect of the ejection, appointment, and maintenance of ministers of religion and school teachers. Five or more of its members could hear and determine charges of delinquency, scandal, malignancy, and non-residence which were brought against any clergyman or schoolmaster, and to eject him from his living. They could instruct a clergyman who held more than one living to decide which of his livings he wished to retain and to remove him from the others. They could grant certificates to preach the gospel or to teach to persons who were recommended and approved by the Approvers. They could make a financial allowance to the wives and children of ejected ministers. Twelve or more of the commissioners had authority to receive and dispose of the incomes of livings and the rents, issues, and profits of all impropriations and glebelands for the maintenance of the ministers—to pay their stipends and provide pensions to their widows and children.

Over and above all this, the commissioners—or any five or more of them—were given full authority to hear all complaints of misdemeanours, oppressions, or injuries in Wales. They could instruct the defendants to appear before them to answer the charges brought against them and to pass judgement. They were constituted a Committee of Indemnity with powers to hear and determine all matters which could be settled by the parliamentary Committee of Indemnity in London, subject to a right of appeal to the latter body. This, for all practical purposes, made the Commission responsible for the local administration of Wales, a fact which gained added strength from the other commitments of the members. A few were members of the Council of State, many were military commanders, while others collected assessments, were on the Committee of Compounding and Sequestration, were members of Parliament, or were high sheriffs of counties.

The main task of the Commission fell into two parts—to destroy the old, established system and replace it by a new organization. The first was, not unnaturally, easier than the second. Anglican clergymen were ejected for a variety of reasons —low moral standards, loyalty to the king and the established Church, pluralism, refusal to swear an oath of alliegiance to the new regime, and illegal inductions. Altogether, some 278 clergymen were ejected during the three years that followed the passing of the Act. Allowances were paid to the wives and children of many of them, but not all—nor were they paid regularly. A few of the ejected had private means, though these were often inadequate; others provided for themselves and their families by keeping private schools, by writing or by obtaining charity from relatives. Others were more fortunate—some had their livings restored to them on appeal; some, though officially ejected, continued to hold their livings; some were appointed schoolmasters under the Act; while others received donations or were allowed to hold sequestered premises as tenants. The ways in which they responded to their fates varied as much as did their fortunes. Some accepted their lot; a few continued to conduct Church services in private houses; while others preached more or less openly to their former parishioners. They were encouraged to do this by the sympathy which existed among the people for many of the ejected, by the unpopularity and the insufficient numbers of the preaching ministers who took their place, and by the difficulties of supervising the more remote districts effectively. Some felt the need for more strenuous action—they agitated among their former parishioners, wrote or translated expositions of the Anglican faith or pamphleteered against the new order. The most outspoken among them was Alexander Griffith who, after being ejected from his livings of Glasbury and Llanwnog, conducted a war of words with Vavasor Powell.

The Commission found its other major responsibility—that of appointing ministers to preach the gospel in Wales—a much more difficult undertaking. There were very few who possessed the necessary qualifications and fewer still for whom a ministry in the remote parts of Wales exercised any attraction. The language problem further reduced the number of possible recruits. The result was that there were few appointments to settled livings. True, a not insignificant number of the Anglican clergy had satisfied the Commission's requirements and had not been ejected. In 1652 there were 127 'old ministers' at work in South Wales and, with the exception of Denbighshire, a fair sprinkling of them in North Wales. In Flintshire, for instance, only three clergymen had been ejected and one of these had merely lost a living which he held in plurality. This was, of course, exceptionally low, but Merioneth had lost no more than eight of its clergymen. Some of the schoolmasters, too, helped by preaching the gospel in the districts to which they had been appointed.

The paucity of suitable ministers compelled the Commission

to adopt the itinerant system, whereby individual ministers were allocated to particular districts. Many of the Approvers were employed in this way—Ambrose Mostyn, for instance, ministered to congregations in Wrexham and north-east Montgomeryshire; Morgan Llwyd, from his base in the Wrexham area, travelled as far west as Llŷn to preach; Vavasor Powell travelled throughout the counties of mid Wales; Henry Walter was engaged in Glamorgan and Monmouthshire; while John Miles was organizing Baptist churches from the borders of Hereford to Carmarthen. In addition to the approvers, there is evidence of some sixty-three itinerant preachers who were active in Wales during these years. Twenty of these were engaged in one part or other of Breconshire, Radnorshire, and Monmouthshire; twenty-two whose sphere of activity was Glamorgan and Carmarthenshire; eight were at work in Pembrokeshire and Cardiganshire; there were twelve who operated in North Wales—and there was that 'Preacher amongst the Welsh people', George Edward. The majority of them had to pass through a probationary period before qualifying as itinerant preachers, although the more highly esteemed were probably excused this.

Some of the itinerants were trained theologians and preachers of ability; but learning was at a premium among most of them. There were many former soldiers, farmers, and tradesmen, the enthusiasm of whose preaching provoked much hostility. Sympathizers with the old Church could not reconcile themselves to these new ministers; they attacked some and insulted most. Nor were they alone in their dissatisfaction with the new system. Older, and more conservative, Puritans expressed their disapproval of the inexperience of some and the inadequacy of others among the itinerants. Congregations were confused and distracted by the conflicting views which they propagated. Some resented the new teachings as imported from England, especially when they were presented in the English language. But the most serious weakness, perhaps, was the utter inability of the Commissioners to recruit a sufficiency of preachers. This meant too few settled ministers and too large an area of responsibility for individual itinerants. The inevitable result of all this was that church services were infrequently and irregularly held.

Many of the itinerants were sincere and pious men who made

an impact upon their congregations and helped to improve standards of conduct among Welshmen. But the task which confronted them was an impossible one. Whatever measure of success was possible was nullified by the inherent deficiencies of the itinerant system; by weaknesses in the administration of the project; and by hostility among the people. Many of the itinerants settled down to minister to the spiritual needs of particular districts—by 1653 Walter Cradock was settled at Usk, Charles Edwards at Llanrhaiadr-ym-mochnant, and there were others who did likewise. Bitter doctrinal conflicts broke out, especially on the question of state control of religious teaching. When the Act had operated for its three years it was allowed to lapse.

The events of 1653 taught the Commonwealth leaders a sharp lesson. A new system of government was formulated and a new approach to the puritanizing of Wales inaugurated. A *Commission for the Approbation of Publicque Preachers*—the Triers— was established, composed of nine laymen and twenty-nine ministers, which operated from London. It was composed of moderate men who represented the different positions within Nonconformity. In theory it possessed wide authority concerning the appointment of any minister; its goodwill was necessary for any increase in a minister's salary; and its certificate was the equivalent of the old process of induction and institution. In fact, however, its freedom of action was limited—first by the authority exercised by the Protector who had inherited the patronage of all royal livings and seems also to have presented to livings formerly in the gift of bishops, corporate bodies, and private individuals; secondly by the powers vested in the Trustees for Maintenance who were empowered to present to livings which had previously been in the gift of the old Anglican hierarchy.

The itinerant system was abandoned. The financial provision for itinerant preachers was discontinued; many itinerants were appointed to settled livings. Four 'Receivers of Wales' were appointed to collect arrears of rents and profits and to receive the revenues from sequestered premises which had been let. From the money thus collected they were to pay to ministers the salaries which had been sanctioned by the Trustees. The intention was to pay the ministers salaries of £100 a year but, although a number of them did receive this much, very many more had to be content with considerably less. A comprehensive reorganization of the parishes was intended—small parishes were to be united, large ones to be divided and parts to be re-allocated to neighbouring parishes. This, like the task of finding suitable ministers, proved to be much more difficult than was anticipated, and was only carried out on a comparatively small scale.

The nucleus of the new ministry was the former itinerants who had been appointed to settled livings. These were added to by new appointments, but during the first three years the number of these was quite inadequate and it was not until 1657 that the number of appointments made assumed fairly respectable proportions. It was, therefore, found necessary to permit a measure of itinerant preaching, but this in no way solved the problem. Some ministers were allowed to hold more than one living, but this new pluralism created its own difficulties for it produced non-residence. Nor was it simply a matter of insufficient numbers. Many of the new appointments were moderate men who, despite their learning and sound Puritanism, were incapable of exerting a powerful impact upon the people. Scarcity of candidates led to the appointment of very young men, of men who had received little or no training and of men who were not Welsh-speaking. These last appointments may well have been the result of a deliberate policy on the part of the Commonwealth government to increase the anglicizing influences at work in Wales. What is certain is that, with the exception of limited areas in the eastern counties of Wales, their inability to minister in Welsh would impose severe limitations upon their effectiveness. A scheme was also mooted to establish a college in Wales to train ministers for the country—but this came to nothing.

In addition to the state-subsidized system which was established there were many preachers in Wales who had no connection at all with the authorities. Some of these, like the Presbyterians of English Flint, had only a local impact. In this particular group the most significant individual was Philip Henry who did much to soften the rigidity of conventional Presbyterianism. He was able to make it more attractive and also to establish better relations with the State after 1658.

Others, like the Fifth Monarchists, were more concerned with their hostility to the State than with propagating the gospel. For them the rejection of the rule of the Saints in 1653 was the occasion for a comprehensive attack upon the State—its corruption and nepotism, its high taxes and suppression of old supporters. They urged the people to withdraw their loyalty to the Protectorate, and they prepared for an armed insurrection. They did not, however, gain much support in Wales despite the incessant preaching and intriguing of their outstanding personality, Vavasor Powell. Although prominent Welsh Puritans, like Morgan Llwyd and Jenkin Jones, disapproved of the Protectorate and did show some sympathy for Powell, they refused to accept his doctrine of the second coming of Jesus Christ. There were fears in some quarters of an armed insurrection by the Fifth Monarchists, but these were correctly discounted by the Protectorate's representative in Wales, Major-General Berry. When Penruddock's rebellion occurred in 1655 Vavasor Powell and his followers supported the Protectorate.

Finally, there were the Quakers. George Fox had by 1653 won converts from almost all branches of the Nonconformists and had established his centre at Swaithmore in Yorkshire. Morgan Llwyd was attracted by the teaching of the Quakers and sent two of his Wrexham congregation to Swaithmore to discover what they could of Quaker doctrine and practice. The Quakers responded by sending two missionaries to the Wrexham district in October 1653. They created a considerable impression upon their listeners, and their impact upon Morgan Llwyd himself is clearly reflected in his poetry. Later in the same year a Quaker community was established at Malpas.

Then followed a determined attempt to win converts in Wales. Thomas Holmes's itinerary through South Wales in 1654–5, when he preached at Abergavenny, Cardiff, various places in Glamorgan, Tenby, Pembroke, and Haverfordwest, was the first major undertaking. Then followed a mission to Radnorshire in 1656, conducted by John ap John—one of the two whom Llwyd had sent to Swaithmore. In the following year George Fox himself was engaged in a preaching campaign throughout Wales. From Bristol he crossed to Monmouthshire, through Glamorgan to Swansea, then north via Brecon to

Shrewsbury. From Shrewsbury he moved west into Montgomeryshire and south into Radnorshire and Hereford. Then he turned west and campaigned through the three southwestern counties of Wales, before turning north to complete his tour at Chester. This tremendous undertaking was a marked success, and was followed in 1658 by John ap John's preaching mission in South Wales.

The Quakers won converts in many places. They established groups at Llandaff, in the south-west, in Montgomeryshire and Merioneth, and at Wrexham. They were particularly successful in the Anglo-Welsh areas and exercised quite a significant influence upon the religious life of the Wales of the time. Certainly their unconventional behaviour—the wearing of their hats at the church services and their interruptions during the services—created misunderstandings. But, equally, they infused a new spirit into the religious life of the time and provided a new dimension to the religious experience of individual Welshmen.

It is impossible to measure with any degree of accuracy the relative contributions of the state-subsidised system and of those unsupported endeavours to establish Puritanism in the Wales of the 1650s. Together they were reasonably successful in South Wales—particularly in the counties of Glamorgan and Monmouth. They also exerted a substantial impact in the eastern part of the country—in the counties of Brecon, Montgomery, and part of Denbighshire. In North Wales on the whole they were much less successful. These regional differences were the products of a number of very different factors which reflected the general response in particular areas to the Commonwealth regime: the presence or otherwise of influential Puritans; the energy of local Puritan propagandists; the accessibility of areas to Puritan pressures from England; the efficiency of the state-subsidized system in particular districts; the problems posed by language differences. In general, it may be said that the record of the Puritans was no more than modestly successful: nor is this difficult to understand when one remembers the problems with which they had to contend.

First, there was the hostility of many among the ejected clergy who exercised no inconsiderable influence in those districts which they had once served. Little reliance could be placed on the co-operation of the civil magistrates, of whom many were openly unsympathetic, while many of the others had conformed to the new dispensation for personal or selfish reasons rather than conviction. From the outset there had been a widespread reluctance to accept the rule of Parliament, a reluctance which had been transformed into hostility in many areas as a result of the heavy financial exactions often unfairly levied and collected, the unending fighting to which the Commonwealth government committed the country, and the innovations which it introduced—the institution of civil marriage and the non-observance of Christmas and holy days. It was also associated with the deeply resented efforts of the new government to compel the people to be good—by the penalties which it imposed against swearing and drunkenness. All this produced insecurity and unrest which revealed themselves in local disturbances, disorders, and riots. Finally, there were those weaknesses which reduced the effectiveness of the Puritan propagandists. The conflicts between some of the more prominent of them and the authorities in London, the quarrels which they waged among themselves—especially on the question of the acceptance or otherwise of maintenance by the State, the lack of organization which was so prominent among some of the groups—all these inevitably weakened the impact of their teachings. In addition to this was the confusion caused by the contrary doctrines which they propagated and the disgust and contempt which the unseemly conduct, the ignorance, and lack of education of many of their ministers provoked.

The progress of Puritanism during the 1650s was then, understandably, not as great as its leaders had hoped. But if their propaganda had not achieved wholesale conversion, it had succeeded in directing the attention of Welshmen to basic religious issues; it had also established pockets of Puritanism in Wales. By so doing it contributed substantially to the religious awakening that occurred in Wales during the century that followed.[1]

[1] It might, perhaps, not be unfitting to allow the last word on this question to the old campaigner, Vavasor Powell, who in his *The Birds in the Cage* (1661) defended the record of the Puritans of the 1650s and closed with the words: 'Also in the beginning of the *War*, there was but one or two gathered Congregations in all *Wales*, and in some Counties scarce one that made *Profession*; yet it hath pleased the Lord so to bless the weak means there, that there were lately (and hope still

Education

The provision of educational facilities was complementary to the policy of establishing Puritanism in Wales. The importance attached by the Commonwealth government to the establishment of an efficient system of education is shown by the care taken to ensure that funds were available for the maintenance of schools and schoolmasters. Money was set aside from impropriations and tithes to provide for schoolmasters as well as ministers; safeguards were provided to exempt from sequestration those revenues of delinquents' estates which had been devoted to colleges and schools, while the salaries of existing schoolmasters and ushers were protected. The old grammar schools were allowed to function, though certain precautions were taken to ensure that the administration of the schools conformed to the ideas of the new regime. No grammar schoolmaster was ejected by the Commissioners and there was no interference in the affairs of most of the schools. Schools established by private benefactions, such as those at Llandovery, Llanegryn (Merioneth), and Aberhafesp (Montgomeryshire), were also allowed to continue, as were a small number of private schools, some of which, however, were held in secret by ejected clergymen.

The Commissioners implemented the terms of the Propagation Act concerning education by establishing some sixty free schools throughout Wales. Most of these were set up in the towns, though there are some surprising omissions. No such schools were founded, for instance, at Beaumaris, Bangor, Bottwnog, Monmouth, and Presteign. This is probably explained by the fact that there already existed grammar or private schools in these towns. A few of the schools were sited in remote villages—possibly because of the influence of a powerful individual in the locality or because there was a flourishing pocket of Puritanism in the neighbourhood. The schools were not evenly distributed and did not in any way reflect the distribution of the population. In the county of Denbigh there were eleven schools, in Carmarthenshire not one; in the counties of Montgomery and Brecon there were eight and nine

are) above 20 gathered *Churches*, in some 2, in some 3, some 4 or 500 members, with their officers, differing little in opinion and Faith, and walking in love, and in fear of the Lord.'

○ Grammar schools ■ Propagation Act schools

MAP 6. Grammar and Propagation Act Schools

respectively, in Anglesey and Caernarvonshire one each. On the whole, the concentrations of schools reflected the measure of parliamentary control achieved in the different areas or the response of their inhabitants to Puritan preaching. The schools were free, in some cases open to girls as well as boys. In many of them the education provided was more in the nature of that of a grammar than a primary school, though some, it appears likely, prepared their pupils for grammar schools, especially in those districts where grammar schools were available.

Most of the teachers were committed Puritans who preached the gospel as well—a number of them were, in fact, later to become ministers. In some cases, however, ejected clergymen were appointed schoolmasters. Of the quality of the education provided there is very little evidence—it seems likely that it varied considerably from one school to another. Some of the schoolmasters were men of very considerable learning, whereas it appears that a number were quite inadequately qualified for their task. Their opponents went so far in some cases as to claim that places without these schools were educationally better provided for than those which possessed one. However this may be, it is certainly true that there were far too few of the schools to achieve much over the country as a whole.

After 1653 there was a marked deterioration in the provision of schools. A number of factors were responsible for this. In some cases schoolmasters lost their positions because of their religious beliefs, or because of 'scandal'—drunkenness and lack of learning, and their schools were discontinued. A number of the schoolmasters were attracted by the greater rewards of the pulpit and became ministers. As schoolmasters they could not hope for a salary of more than £40 a year, while the majority were fortunate to receive some £20 a year. The inevitable consequence was a dire shortage of suitable schoolmasters and the closure of more schools. A few of the schools, unfortunately sited, decayed or were transferred to more populous centres. Of the sixty or so schools established by 1653 there is positive evidence for the continuance to 1660 of only twenty-one of them.

There is little direct evidence to indicate the impression which the schools exerted upon the Wales of their time. There can, however, be little doubt that they contributed to the progress made by Puritanism in seventeenth-century Wales. It is equally certain that they inspired later attempts to provide education for Welsh children. They were the first state-subsidized system of primary education and as such have an important place in the history of Wales.

Administration

The machinery for local government created during the Commonwealth period was a combination of old and new. On to the established administrative system was superimposed a host of committees which had evolved out of those set up by Parliament during the Civil War. At first there had been two such committees in the counties. There was the Standing Committee whose responsibilities were two-fold, to organize the resources of the county while the fighting was taking place in the area and to enforce obedience to the directives of Parliament after the area had been won by Parliament. Then there was the Committee of Accounts which regulated the county's war finances and carried out the instructions contained in the Ordinance of March 1643 of making the royalists pay for the war. Subcommittees were also set up under the supervision of the latter to hold in trust for Parliament the estates of delinquents condemned to sequestration.

In 1649 two statutory sequestration committees were established—one for North and one for South Wales, to levy the fines imposed upon the two areas for their part in the second Civil War, and county organizations were constituted to work under the direction of these area committees. In the following year the sequestration committees were abolished and their powers were taken over by the central committee at Goldsmiths Hall. This nominated three subordinate committees for Wales—one each for the North, the South, and Monmouthshire—whose members also acted as commissioners for their own counties. This was intended to nullify the pressures exerted by influential delinquents and to increase control from the central government.

The responsibilities of these committees made their members vulnerable to a wide variety of pressures and temptations—to misappropriate moneys, to conceal the delinquency of some former royalists and exaggerate the offences of others, to buy cheaply or obtain favourable leases on lands which came under their control, to obtain lucrative positions for their friends and relatives. All this produced frequent complaints against committee members—like those featured in *The Distressed Oppressed Condition of the Inhabitants of South Wales* which appeared in 1659. The petitioners claimed that £150,000 were unaccounted for from the sequestrations of delinquents' estates and ecclesiastical revenues in South Wales and Monmouthshire. The individual against whom most complaints were aimed was Colonel Philip Jones who for the greater part of the Interregnum virtually controlled South Wales. The *Articles of Impeachment* against him presented to Parliament by Bledry Morgan in 1659, though exaggerated, contained more than a modicum of truth. In this respect, Philip Jones was different from lesser men only in that he operated on a grander scale, and the plums he was able to pick were bigger and juicier.

In addition to those committees which were mainly concerned with property and finance, there were those established under the terms of the Propagation Act to examine and eject scandalous ministers and schoolmasters, to make surveys of church livings and to administer ecclesiastical revenues. Others were established to administer relief to poor prisoners; and, of course, there were the inevitable county assessment committees.

The composition of these committees illustrates the difficulties which the new government encountered in finding local partners, and helps to explain why it had to allow them a certain latitude in respect of their conduct. Among the members of the different committees there were five distinct groups. First, there were the members of the old county families, well established at the head of county society before the Civil War. On the whole, their sympathies had lain with the king and individual members had assisted Charles during the fighting. Next, there were members of those landowning families which were improving their position in social and economic terms during the seventeenth century. Some of these had supported the king, others Parliament; but many of them had kept themselves free from an over-involvement with one side or the other. The third group were those army officers who had fought with some distinction on the parliamentary side during the war, and whose proven loyalty and ability had gained for them positions of trust and authority. Then there were those committed

Puritans whose numbers had increased during the war years. Finally, there were the Englishmen, especially from the border counties, who had been recruited by the central government to stiffen the administration in Wales.

Between 1647 and 1649 Parliament was able to call on the services of a number from the upper crust of the gentry families —either of former parliamentary supporters or of one-time royalists who were prepared to compromise with the new regime. To these were added men from lesser landed families, some of whom had been converted to Puritanism, a few English border men and some army officers. The relative strengths of these different elements varied from one part of the country to another. In the counties of Denbigh and Flint, for instance, the upper-crust gentry families were well represented, whereas in Anglesey committee members were, for the most part, drawn from the middle section of landed families, while in Montgomeryshire there was a solid phalanx from the lower gentry, many of whom had been won for Parliament and Puritanism during the war. These variations were equally apparent in the south—in the Carmarthen County Committee, for example, there was a nucleus of ex-royalist gentry, whereas its Breconshire counterpart contained a hard core of moderate Presbyterians.

The Second Civil War in 1648 and the execution of the king early in the following year led to substantial changes in the composition of the local committees. A number, suspected of involvement in the events of 1648, were removed; others who had earlier co-operated with Parliament withdrew their support. The result was that after 1649 committee members were drawn more exclusively from the staunch parliamentary supporters and the lower, newer sections of county landed society; and there was, too, an increase in the number of army officers. The establishment of the Instrument of Government, after the failure of the rule of the Saints, brought yet another change in the balance of county power. Many of the soldiers were removed from the committees other than those of their own counties, and there was a significant drop in the number of the extreme Puritans. In their places members of the old county families reappeared, though they were balanced by a substantial number of those whose loyalty to the new regime was well tried.

This was reversed again in 1659 when suspicions of involvement in plots with Charles II caused the removal from the committees of representatives of the older families and brought back extreme Puritans in their places. But this did not last for long, for when negotiations for Charles II's restoration were under way the moderates reappeared in strength again. These last were not merely former royalists who had steadfastly refused to co-operate with the Commonwealth government, for there was among them a fair sprinkling of staunch parliamentarians who had come to accept the inevitability of the restoration of monarchical government.

The other, older section of the administrative machinery continued to operate, though with significant changes and, in some parts of the country, not without difficulties. There was some reluctance on the part of members of a number of the older families to pledge their loyalty to the Commonwealth and to co-operate closely with the Puritan minority. In some areas, therefore, it was not easy to recruit suitable men to act as justices, coroners, and constables. Major-General James Berry commented to Cromwell in December 1655 on the lack of suitable justices of the peace in north-west Wales with the words 'there is hardly, if at all, one man fit for a justice of the peace in those parts', though he was not equally gloomy in respect of other parts of the country.

During the Commonwealth the responsibilities of local government officials increased enormously. In addition to the work which they were already doing—and this had become very much more burdensome as a result of the war, they were given new, onerous tasks to perform. They were to detect and punish all conspiracies and secret meetings of disaffected persons who held opinions contrary to those of the Commonwealth authorities. They were to implement the law concerning civil marriage, to publish banns and settle matrimonial disputes. In addition, and perhaps most unpopular of all, they had to enforce the Puritan moral code. Some aspects of this last, like ensuring the observance of the Sabbath, were not new. But others were—they had to punish swearing and cursing, suppress drunkenness and various sports and pastimes like revels, bowling, dancing around the maypole, and bear baiting, and ensure the observance of public fast days. How effectively they

P

carried out these responsibilities it is difficult to say, but available records do suggest that a number of the justices of the peace made serious efforts to fulfil their obligations. Over and above all this, the scarcity of suitable men made it inevitable that many of the justices served also on local committees and assessment commissions. A consequence of these heavy demands upon local government, especially when coupled with the reluctance of some among the traditional governing class to co-operate with the Commonwealth, was inevitably the involvement of many who had previously been outside the circle of government.

This was true also on the national scene. The Joneses—Philip and John—were prominent members of the Council of State and served on many of its committees. John was appointed one of the three commissioners responsible for the administration of Ireland. Both became members of Cromwell's *Other House*. At Westminster, too, new Welsh voices were heard, apart from those of the two already mentioned. John Trevor created quite an impression on the lower House with his thoughtful speeches, as did Charles Lloyd of Moel-y-Garth in Montgomeryshire with his criticisms of the events of the day and Griffith Bodwrda of Caernarvon with his loquacity.

The land

The years of the Interregnum offered opportunities for many Welshmen to acquire lands, power, and social prestige. Some were rewarded for their services to Parliament by grants of land or the receipt of leases on very favourable terms. For others, the sale of ecclesiastical lands, the sequestered estates of former royalists or the property sold by these to compound for their estates and the lands granted to soldiers in lieu of pay opened the door to a brisk market in land, of which the more resourceful were quick to avail themselves. Some had ready capital for such transactions, others acquired the money in ways which would not have stood up to close scrutiny but in which the Commonwealth government had to acquiesce in order to ensure loyal co-operation at local level.

Prominent among the estate builders were the two Joneses—Philip and John, in South and North Wales respectively. The latter did not long survive the Restoration, but the former was able to enjoy his recently established prosperity until 1674. Born the son of a freehold farmer in the parish of Llangyfelach near Swansea, he spent more than £17,750 on the purchase of lands between 1647 and 1660. From the sequestered estates of the marquis of Worcester which had been granted to Oliver Cromwell he received as gifts or bought or leased considerable lands in Gower and the Vale of Glamorgan. In 1651 he bought the Herbert interest in a number of manors in the eastern part of the Vale. The years that followed saw him acquire further properties in the county of Glamorgan, and by 1655 he owned nine manors, together with lands and tenements in the counties of Pembroke and Cardigan as well as Glamorgan. The final stage in his emergence as a man of property was the purchase of the three manors of Fonmon, Penmark, and Llancadle in the Vale of Glamorgan. This transaction, completed by the lease to him of Fonmon Castle in July 1658, was protracted and expensive—together the three manors cost him over £11,000. Philip Jones was more prudent in his purchases and operated on a larger scale than most, but he was far from being the only South Walian to take his opportunities. Among his friends and associates, Rowland Dawkins of Kilvrough, Edward Herbert, Evan Lewis, and William Watkins became landed proprietors, while by a quirk of fate Henry Herbert of Coldbrook acquired substantial portions of the Raglan estates which had once been in the possession of his family. In North Wales John Jones obtained an interest in the Crown lordship of Bromfield and Yale, in the ecclesiastical manor of Gogarth and in the manors of Llandegla, Gwytherin, Meliden, and Uwchterfyn, as well as considerable property in Ireland. Further east George Twisleton purchased ex-royalist properties in the counties of Denbigh and Flint, John Glynne acquired lands and properties formerly in the possession of the earl of Derby, as also did Sir John Trevor.

As a result of all this, new county families were established, while other families reached the first rank within their own counties much more rapidly than would otherwise have been possible. There were, in consequence, quite significant changes in the upper reaches of the social structure in a number of the Welsh counties. Nor was it only the higher ranks of society that were affected, for the more ambitious acquisitors had lesser disciples. These carved out for themselves modest estates in every county in Wales.

The reaction of the Welsh

The troubles of 1648 in North and South Wales had not augured well for the acceptance by the Welsh people of the new rulers. Former royalists had been able to exploit local grievances, chief among which was the resentment against the heavy financial demands made by the new government, the harsh treatment meted out to many of the Anglican clergymen and the misconduct of members of the local committees. The extortion of money and bribes, the plundering of the sequestered estates by the government's local agents provoked anger and disgust. Feelings ran particularly high in the districts where those responsible were outsiders to whom had been entrusted key positions in the local administration. These were important factors in shaping the continued response in the counties to the Commonwealth. Occasionally they found expression in riots and local risings, like that which occurred in Cardiganshire in June 1651; more often they were the basis of the frustration and resentment which found expression in the petitions, pamphlets, poems, and ballads of the 1650s and which offered an incentive to royalist intrigues.

The final act which heralded the new regime, the execution of Charles I, outraged the sensibilities of many Welshmen and helped to determine their response to his executioners. James Howell was not the only one among his countrymen for whom it was 'that black tragedy'. The existing order in Church and State, epitomized by the institution of monarchy, had won the approval of the politically significant in Wales. Many had risen high in the service of one or the other; many more felt themselves bound by ties of loyalty and sentiment to the person of Charles.

The religious policy of the Commonwealth aroused widespread opposition. There were violent objections, on the one hand, to the persecution of the Anglican clergy and the appropriation of Church properties and revenues, and, on the other, to the new doctrines that were propagated and the men who preached them. There were criticisms of the failure to provide a sufficiency of preaching ministers, and widespread resentment at the enforcement of the Puritan moral code. Virulent pamphlets were written by dispossessed Anglican clergymen like Alexander Griffith; petitions, like that from the six counties of North Wales in July 1652, complained of the ejection of ministers, the sequestering of tithes and of vacant parishes, and hinted at the misappropriation of clerical revenues; poems and ballads poured scorn on illiterate ministers and the contradictory doctrines they preached, as well as on the innovations, like civil marriage, of the new government.

The increasing scope of governmental control, with its corollary of growing interference in people's lives, and the local instruments who were given authority to exercise this control were productive of widespread unrest and dissatisfaction. There were objections to the advancement of the uneducated and low-born to positions of power and trust in the magistracy and local administration. The former glover who had become a justice, the erstwhile stonemason who had become a military commander were the subjects of lampoons and diatribes. Equally resented were the opportunities provided such individuals to feather their own nests. All this was complicated and made more explosive by the local animosities inherited from the war and by the doubts cast upon the integrity of these new men who exercised authority at local level.

Finally, there was the general discontent produced by the economic difficulties. Some of these were the direct outcome of the war—the disruption of trade, in cattle and wool especially, and industry, the sequestrations and fines suffered by former royalists. Others were the results of factors over which the government had no control—poor harvests and the general trends in the food market. Prolonged droughts and a fall in the prices of corn and cattle had serious repercussions for the small farmers who defaulted in their rent payments, and not infrequently suffered for it. The market in land and capital investment in landed property by the new men created difficulties for the small tenantry. All this was made more burdensome by the heavy assessments required by a government committed to maintain a security network and a large standing army.

The Commonwealth had its loyal adherents and true friends in Wales: it could also rely to varying degrees on the co-operation of those who favoured firm government and of the time servers. But, for the majority, the Welsh were hostile or at best unsympathetic to their new rulers. They conformed but with little of the enthusiasm with which they welcomed the Restoration in 1660.

SUGGESTED READING

Thomas Richards: *The Puritan Movement in Wales, 1639–1653*. London, 1920.

G. F. Nuttall: *The Welsh Saints, 1640–1660*. Cardiff, 1957.

Articles:

Thomas Shankland: '*Seren Gomer*', 1901.

A. H. Dodd: 'The Background of the Quaker Migration to Pennsylvania.' *Jnl. Mer. hist. and Rec. Soc.*, 111, 1958.

A. G. Vesey: 'Colonel Philip Jones, 1618–1674', *Trans. Cymmr.*, 1966.

J. Gwynfor Jones: 'Caernarvonshire Administration: The Activities of the Justices of the Peace, 1603–1660'. *W.H.R.*, Dec. 1970.

Conclusion

THERE is abundant evidence of the revolution which took place in almost every aspect of Welsh life during the period which has been under review. For the most part, Welshmen of the time found it thoroughly acceptable, and only rarely is a discordant note of criticism heard amid the general chorus of praise. Certainly there can be no gainsaying the material benefits which accrued to those blessed with initiative and ability. Better government and the more efficient administration of justice gave Welshmen a measure of peace and security which earlier generations had not known. The period witnessed significant developments in agriculture, a substantial expansion of trade, and the successful establishment of industrial undertakings. All this is reflected in a number of ways—by the growth of towns, the nerve centres of trade and administration, by the new houses which landowners and substantial farmers built for themselves, by the concern they showed for their comfort and the attention they paid to more gracious living.

There are, however, at least two reservations to be made. First, not all Welshmen shared in the blessings; secondly, a heavy price had to be paid for them. The first may be seen most clearly if we remember that those who prospered frequently did so at the expense of others. The acquisition or consolidation of land by some meant that others lost their customary holdings and proprietory rights. Complaints were frequent from the oppressed and dispossessed—and, more often than not, there was no redress of their grievances. Again, Welshmen were anxious to occupy positions in local administration as much for the opportunities which they offered to exploit their authority as for the prestige which they bestowed. In every rank of the hierarchy of local administration there were those who showed little scruple or integrity in the pursuit of private ends—and this of necessity meant suffering and hardship for others. There

were many who fulfilled their obligations honestly and conscientiously, but in every county of Wales there were charges
of extortion and abuse of their office by local officials, and local
administration in Wales during the period has on the whole
received a bad press. Economic trends, especially the rise in
prices, favoured the producers of basic commodities; but small
tenants and wage earners were not so fortunate. The former did
not produce on a large enough scale to exploit market trends,
while wages and earnings lagged behind prices and rents.
Among the lower orders of society living standards did not
reflect the over-all economic progress that was being made.

For the second, we must take the longer view. Outstanding
among the consequences of the period were, on the one hand,
the emergence of a landed aristocracy and the establishment
of a state church over which the former exercised a dominant
control, and, on the other, the anglicization of the socially
significant section of the Welsh population which accompanied
the submergence of Welsh identity in a political complex which
was dominated by England. These have been fundamental to
the making of modern Wales. Economic stresses have now
broken the foundations of aristocratic authority and the Non-
conformist pulpit has destroyed Anglican monopoly—but not
before both had played an important part in shaping the
destiny of Wales. The other two forces have continued to
operate down to the present with steadily increasing intensity.
Beside them other consequences of the period pale into comparative insignificance.

The cultural and religious movements which came to maturity
during the last century were themselves in part a reaction to and
a revolt against those forces which had really been set in motion
by the events of the sixteenth and seventeenth centuries. They
made it possible for the Welsh-speaking *gwerin* of Wales to
assert themselves and to break the stranglehold of squire and
vicar, but they did little to halt the progress of anglicization.
To apportion blame for this is an unprofitable exercise. It would
be as incorrect to attribute it to a malevolent English government and its selfish Welsh confederates as to deny that they, in
the pursuit of their own particular interests, made their
contribution. It may, for instance, be argued that they were
functioning within the limits of a society already in the process

of change and that change is as much the product as the chemical agent of decay, or that such was the inevitable outcome of close proximity to a materially more powerful and politically better organized neighbour. Be this as it may, it was a price which many Welshmen of the time were prepared to pay for the host of new opportunities which were offered them.

It may not be irrelevant to see an analogy here with certain current trends in Wales. Circumstances in the twentieth century, especially the developments which have taken place in education, have made it possible for young Welshmen of ability to equip themselves for opportunities which their own communities could not provide. Inevitably they looked elsewhere for the means of fulfilling themselves—some with regret, others with indifference. The individuals concerned, and there are many of them, have profited; the communities stripped of their potential leaders have suffered inestimably. While one must regret the price which the communities have had to pay, it would be facile to condemn the individuals concerned and to place the whole responsibility for the decay of the communities upon their shoulders. This, writ large, it seems, was the dilemma of Wales during the two centuries with which we have been most concerned—one which has not yet been resolved.

The social changes which have followed upon the industrial growth of the last century and a half have absorbed and transmuted the old Wales. The Sabbatarian, Nonconformist-conscience-ridden Wales is now almost as much an anachronism as the Wales of the all-powerful squire and his ally the Church. But both have left their indelible marks on society and social thinking in Wales, and both have made a substantial contribution to the history of modern Wales.

Glossary of Terms

Arddel: the practice of avouching for a person's position and property; came to be interpreted as acting as guarantor for a person.

Commortha: a free benevolence (or gift) to help the victim of misfortune and/ or impoverishment.

Galanas: the blood money paid by the murderer and his relatives (within seven degrees) to the murdered man's family; if the blood money were not paid, the murdered man's family could declare a blood feud on the murderer's family.

Gavelkind: partiple inheritance; the custom of dividing the land owned by a private individual at his death among his sons and descendants to the fourth generation.

Gwerin: has no English equivalent; can be interpreted as 'the ordinary people' of Wales, though it implies more than this.

Erastian: derived from the name of the Swiss theologian Erastus, who propounded the theory of the supremacy of the State in ecclesiastical affairs.

Escheat: the right of a lord to the inheritable estates in land of a tenant who died without lawful heirs or who had been found guilty of certain criminal offences, like treason.

Gaol delivery: one of the commissions of assize, directing the judge to deliver from gaol all persons held for trial, and deal with them according to the law.

Justices of the quorum: originally designated certain justices of the peace who possessed certain qualifications, and whose presence was necessary to constitute a bench; later applied loosely to all justices of the peace.

Oyer and Terminer: 'to hear and determine'; a commission by which a judge of assize sits—by it the judge is commanded to make diligent inquiry into all criminal offences committed in the counties concerned and 'to hear and determine' them according to the law.

Prerogative Court: a court established by the royal prerogative, i.e. by the power and privilege which can only be exercised by the Crown.

Pronotary: or Prothonotary, prenotary; the chief clerk or recorder of a Court.

Quo warranto: a writ requiring a person to state by what authority he claims or holds a particular office or privilege.

Recusant: a person who refused to attend the services of the Church of England.

Weights in the coal trade: The measures used in the coal trade were expressed in terms of volume rather than weight:

Chaldron: varied in different parts of the country; the London Chaldron was in use at Neath, Swansea, and Llanelli during the second half of the seventeenth century. Four to five chaldrons were the equivalent of one wey.

Wey (*weigh*): a measure in use in the semi-anthracite districts between Aberavon and Llanelli; it was the equivalent of 4 tons.

Last: a measure used in Glamorgan from the Middle Ages; it equalled between 12 and 14 tons.

Index